3/2000

BELOVED SISTERS

A N D

LOVING FRIENDS

BELOVED SISTERS

AND

LOVING FRIENDS

*Letters from Rebecca Primus of
Royal Oak, Maryland,
and Addie Brown of
Hartford, Connecticut,
1854–1868*

EDITED BY

Farah Jasmine Griffin

ALFRED A. KNOPF   NEW YORK   1999

THIS IS A BORZOI BOOK
PUBLISHED BY ALFRED A. KNOPF, INC.

www.randomhouse.com

Knopf, Borzoi Books, and the colophon are registered
trademarks of Random House, Inc.

Grateful acknowledgment is made to Singing Horse Press for
permission to reprint an excerpt from *Muse and Drudge* by
Harryette Mullen, copyright © 1995 by Singing Horse Press.
Reprinted by permission of Singing Horse Press.

Library of Congress Cataloging-in-Publication Data
Primus, Rebecca, 1836–1932.
Beloved sisters and loving friends: Letters from Rebecca
Primus of Royal Oak, Maryland, and Addie Brown of
Hartford, Connecticut, 1854–1868. / edited by
Farah Jasmine Griffin. — 1st ed.
p.   cm.
ISBN 0-679-45128-5
1. Primus, Rebecca, 1836–1932—Correspondence.
2. Brown, Addie—Correspondence.   3. Afro-American
women—Maryland—Royal Oak—Correspondence.
4. Afro-American women—Connecticut—Hartford—
Correspondence.   5. Afro-American women—History—
19th century.   6. Reconstruction—Maryland.   7. Royal
Oak (Md.)—Biography.   8. Hartford (Conn.)—Biography.
1. Brown, Addie.   11. Griffin, Farah Jasmine.   111. Title.
F189.R69P75   1999
975.2'32—dc21   98-52930
CIP

Manufactured in the United States of America
First Edition

For my own beloved sister-friends:

Shaun D. Biggers

Cheryl L. Dorsey

Lynelle C. Granady

Nina T. Henderson

Karen F. O'Neal

and
in memory of
Nathan Irving Huggins
and
A. Leon Higginbotham, Jr.

Contents

CONTENTS

Acknowledgments

THIS project has been supported and nurtured by many wonderful and generous people. David White of the Connecticut Historical Commission shared much of his early research on the Primus papers and was always there to answer a question, send a photograph, and offer encouragement. Through numerous conversations and an ongoing correspondence, Barbara Beeching shared my enthusiasm for Addie and Rebecca. Most important, Karen Hansen introduced me to the letters and was always willing to discuss the difficulties of editing and interpreting them.

In addition, my students Jennifer Furman, Ericka Armstrong, Asia Slowe, Nicole Childers, and Michelle Wayne proved to be invaluable research assistants and typists. Of these, Ms. Wayne was a wonderful interpreter of the letters and devoted far more time and attention to them than I can ever thank her for. Ms. Valerie Savage-Pugh of the University of Pennsylvania English Department was a tireless and enthusiastic transcriber of the lengthy epistles. Maurice Black proofread the entire manuscript. I owe them all my gratitude.

Frances Smith Foster, Drew Gilpin Faust, and Stephanie Shaw all provided invaluable criticism and suggestions for revision. Carla Peterson, Carroll Smith-Rosenberg, Barbara Savage, and Evelyn Brooks Higginbotham were extraordinary supporters of this project from the start. Barbara Sicherman and Saidiya Hartman read early drafts and offered important advice. Professor Sicherman was especially generous with her time and ideas.

In Talbot County, Maryland, Mr. Lord Scottie, owner of Scottie's Taxi, Ms. Harriet Romero, and Ms. Scottie Oliver, curator of the Maryland Room, Talbot County Public Library, offered their assistance in helping me to learn about the Eastern Shore of Maryland. Scottie's hospitality, guidance, and friendship are gifts from heaven.

I am especially grateful to research fellowships from the University of Pennsylvania and summer stipends from the Women's Studies Program and the Lindback Society of the university. The angelic staff of the Bunting Institute in Cambridge gave me the space and resources to spend the first part of my fellowship year adding the final touches. Without this assistance I would never have been able to complete this project.

Members of the staffs of the Connecticut Historical Society in Hartford, the Library Company in Philadelphia, Van Pelt Library at the University of Pennsylvania, and Widener Library at Harvard University helped to facilitate my research.

My agent, Loretta Barrett, recognized the importance of this project from the very beginning, and she always offered her advice and support with enthusiasm and kindness. Vicky Wilson, my editor at Knopf, suffered countless changed deadlines and revised versions of this manuscript. For this I am grateful.

My mother, Wilhelmena Griffin, and my cousin Irvin Carson, Sr., loved to hear stories of Addie and Rebecca and helped to convince me that these letters had to be made available to readers outside the academy. Four gifted healers, Laurene Finley, Karen Jordan, Joyce Rubin, and Zulene, cared for me, mind and body, throughout. Jim and Edjohnetta Miller and their children, Ayesha and John, offered their home to me during my frequent research trips to Hartford. They also fed me, shared information, and helped to lift my spirits on a daily basis. Edjohnetta joins women like Alice Brown, Julia Turner Lowe, Vanessa Harley, Imani Perry, and my biological sister, Myra Griffin Lindsay, all of whom provide me with the crucial space of sister friendship. None have so lovingly and patiently offered this space more than the five women to whom this volume is dedicated. Nathan Huggins first introduced me to the formal study of African American history; in so doing, he changed the direction of my life. I am forever indebted to my godfather, mentor, and friend, Judge A. Leon Higginbotham, Jr. And finally, a special thank-you to Lisa Y. Sullivan.

All of these individuals and institutions assisted in the enterprise that culminates in this volume—a testament to our love, respect, and admiration for those extraordinary ordinary women, Rebecca Primus and Addie Brown.

Preface

I DID not discover Rebecca Primus and Addie Brown. I was introduced to them by Professor Karen Hansen of Brandeis University. I came to know them through various encounters with their letters as well as through conversations with and the writings of persons like Professor Hansen, David White, director of the Hartford Historical Commission, and Barbara Beeching, a graduate student in history at Trinity College, Hartford, Connecticut, who wrote an important master's thesis on the Primus family.

I knew that women like Brown and Primus existed before I ever met them. As a young college student interested in nineteenth-century black women's history, I grew frustrated with the dearth of sources on even the most famous of the women. In the early to mid 1980s, when I was working on my college honors thesis on Frances Ellen Watkins Harper, I recognized the problems confronted by scholars of black women's history. It is not that the women weren't there, as older generations of scholars had told us. No, it was that no one had made the effort to find them. At that time, Dorothy Sterling published her tremendous volume of primary sources on nineteenth-century black women, *We Are Your Sisters*. Sterling's book was the first I encountered that confirmed what I thought I had discovered: that Frances Harper the poet and novelist was the same woman as Frances Harper the abolitionist, temperance advocate, and black freedom fighter.

Since then, thanks to the efforts of scholars such as Frances Foster, Melba Joyce Boyd, and Hazel Carby and the methodologies of black women's history, we have come to know a great deal about Frances Harper. We now have a biography, an edited volume of her letters, poems, and speeches, several editions of her novel *Iola Leroy*, her magazine novels, and numerous chapters detailing her activism and analyzing her literature.

In their writings, these pioneering scholars pushed me to look for the records of black women in attics, in storerooms, in churches. In 1982, Gloria Hull, Barbara Smith, and Patricia Bell Scott emphasized the importance of finding the lesser-known black women. Their ground-breaking anthology, *All the Women Are White, All the Blacks Are Men, But Some of Us Are Brave,* urged: "Only through explaining the experience of supposedly 'ordinary' Black women whose 'unexceptional' actions enabled us and the race to survive will we be able to begin to develop an overview and an analytical framework for understanding the lives of Afro-American women." These brilliant and brave historians—most but not all of whom were African American—at times risked their careers to discover the ordinary women. I like to think of them as visionaries who knew, without ever seeing the evidence, the contours of Rebecca Primus's and Addie Brown's persons and lives.

Almost four years after finishing the college thesis on Harper, I moved to Hartford to begin teaching at Trinity College and to finish my dissertation. I continued to keep up with recent scholarship in women's history, but I had chosen to do my dissertation on twentieth-century subject matter. Just as I was finishing the dissertation, I got a call from Karen Hansen, a historical sociologist at Brandeis. Professor Hansen came across Rebecca's and Addie's letters while she was doing research for her book *A Very Social Time.* A portion of that book was devoted to the two women, and she planned to publish an article on the romantic and erotic nature of their friendship. After studying the letters, Hansen became convinced that they ought to be transcribed, edited, and published in their own volume. She began to ask around to see who might be able to do this work. She was given my name by Professor Frances Foster, a well-known scholar of nineteenth-century black women and of Frances Harper. She was also given my name by my beloved colleague at Trinity, Ron Thomas. After meeting Professor Hansen, I immediately went down to the Connecticut Historical Society and began to read the letters.

So you see, my introduction to Rebecca and Addie came through the generosity of others, and in fact, the rest of the story is not only about Rebecca and Addie but also about the community of a small but dedicated group of scholars who have been committed to bringing Rebecca Primus and Addie Brown to the attention of a broader reading public.

In editing this volume I have tried to remain true to the integrity of each woman's voice. I attempt to provide a historical context for the letters. The introductory sections, along with the notes, help to provide necessary background information. At times I provide running commentary between individual letters.

For the most part, original spellings and capitalizations have been retained. I have supplied some punctuation in Addie's letters because she often wrote an entire page without placing a period. Many of the more repetitive sections of the correspondence have been cut. Brown's letters are especially difficult to read. My research assistant, Michelle Wayne, and I have made every effort to transcribe them faithfully. On rare occasions uncertainties remained. I indicate such cuts with ellipses inside brackets. Personal names and places are identified upon first mention, either in the introductory paragraph preceding the letter or in footnotes. Historical events, public figures, books, and periodicals are also explained in the notes.

Beloved Sisters

and

Loving Friends

Introduction

"Beyond the Silence"[1]

*S*ILENCES. *Loopholes. Interstices. Allegory. Dissemblance. Politics of respectability.*

These are but a few of the terms that black women scholars use to help make sense of the silence that surrounds black women's lives and experiences.[2] Such terms refer not only to black women's literal silence around issues of personal importance to them but also to gaps in the broader historical record of the American experience.

Given the historical and political contexts in which African American women have lived, and given their own desire to shape and influence these contexts for the benefit of all Americans, it is understandable that they often felt it necessary to present highly censored "positive" images to an often hostile public. Thus many have kept the most personal aspects of their lives as well as the full range of their thoughts secret. Furthermore, until very recently, scholars did not think it important to search for evidence of black women's lives and activities. Fortunately, since the civil rights, black power, and feminist movements, a growing number of people have devoted themselves to pursuing and revealing the complex history of black women.

For years, we have been led to believe that ordinary black women left no evidence of their historical existence. We were told that they did not keep diaries or journals and that they did not write letters. However, black women historians, committed to writing black women into American history, suggested otherwise.[3]

For over sixty years, Rebecca Primus's papers have been housed in the Connecticut Historical Society.[4] Primus, the daughter of a prominent black Hartford family, was one of many women, black and white, who traveled south after the Civil War to establish schools and teach the newly freed men and women. The Hartford Freedmen's Aid Society sent Rebecca Primus to Royal Oak, Maryland, where she helped to found a

school later named in honor of her, the Primus Institute. The sixty exist-
ing letters from Primus to her family provide a rare glimpse into the life
and thoughts of a nineteenth-century New England black woman.
Primus's letters reveal her confrontations with southern prejudice, her
struggles to educate the newly freed blacks, her descriptions of Recon-
struction-era politics, as well as her joy in being surrounded by more
African Americans than she had seen in all of Hartford. Filled with
compassion, humor, and courage, the letters also tell of Primus's growing political and racial consciousness.

In addition to Primus's letters to her family, the collection houses
approximately one hundred fifty letters from Addie Brown to Rebecca
Primus. Brown was a domestic servant who lived in the households of
her various employers in Hartford, Farmington, and Waterbury, Connecticut, and in New York. Her letters cover the period from 1859 to
1868. Because she was not formally educated, Addie writes as she
would speak. Throughout the course of the correspondence she
acquires greater literacy. Her letters tell a story of a bright, intelligent,
and personable young woman who struggles to make a living under very
precarious economic circumstances. Brown's letters paint a portrait of
the lives of northern blacks in New England and New York. Finally,
Brown's letters reveal a close romantic friendship between the two
women.

Together, the letters of Rebecca Primus and Addie Brown tell us a
great deal about nineteenth-century black Hartford, Reconstruction in
Maryland, and the personal *and* public lives of two black women.
Unfortunately, I have been unsuccessful in my attempts to locate
Rebecca Primus's letters to Addie Brown. Therefore, we are left to sur-
mise Primus's responses to Brown.

The Brown-Primus correspondence provides material needed for
moving beyond both the silence in the historical record and black
women's self-imposed silence about their inner lives. The letters differ
from the historical documentation of the public lives of well-known
black women such as Frances Ellen Watkins Harper, Sojourner Truth,
and Harriet Tubman. Also, unlike the slave narratives of women like
Harriet Jacobs or the postbellum novels and stories of writers such as
Harper or Pauline Hopkins, Addie Brown and Rebecca Primus are not
concerned with publication or with a white audience. As such, their letters provide a rare glimpse into the day-to-day activities of two ordinary
black women.

Primus and Brown take black humanity for granted; thus their letters do not censor their opinions about the diversity and complexity of black life or their feelings about white people. They openly discuss their intolerance of and resistance to racism, community scandals relating to unwed pregnancies, and, in Brown's case, her love for Rebecca and her courtship with Joseph Tines, the man she eventually married. Both women reveal their thoughts about books, politics, friendship, and family. Finally, the letters broaden our current conception of nineteenth-century black women as either southern slaves or northern abolitionists. Addie and Rebecca were neither slaves nor famous abolitionists, although they shared much with these two groups of women: they were victims of American racism and active agents in the struggle against it.

But, "In dreams begin responsibilities."[5] The Brown-Primus correspondence poses the challenge of remaining sensitive to the concerns of many black women that their private voices might be used against them in the service of sexism and racism. For years, black women have battled against stereotypes that label them as promiscuous harlots or asexual but nurturing mammies. In order to combat such images, nineteenth-century African Americans sought to offer counterimages of pristine Victorian black ladies. Brown and Primus are neither promiscuous harlots, nurturing mammies, nor one dimensional Victorian ladies. They are complex, intelligent, sensual, and multidimensional women committed to both each other and black liberation. The letters challenge us to rise to the occasion of reading them, to defy any element of the negative stereotypes about black women that we may have internalized, and to accept these women in the context of their times and their communities.

In their totality, the letters prove to be about the full extent of Brown's and Primus's ambitions, desires, frustrations, and membership in a black community committed to racial uplift. But they also chronicle more intimate lives: these women's intense friendship and even romantic partnership, as well as their lives with men. In light of this, the letters reveal the contours of relationships between black women—mothers, sisters, daughters, friends, and romantic partners.

The friendship between Brown and Primus is an example of what feminist theorist Patricia Hill Collins identifies as one of the "primary focal points where Black women's consciousness has been nurtured and where African American women have spoken freely in order to articulate a self-defined standpoint."[6] While Collins asserts the dominance of such friendships in fiction by black women as evidence of their dominance in black women's lives, the correspondence between Addie Brown and Rebecca Primus is proof of the importance of sister-friendships in life as well as in fiction. For these two women, letter writing was a means of creating community, of gathering and expressing their thoughts, of seeing themselves through each other's eyes and thereby seeing themselves as something much more than society would have either of them believe. Addie Brown's open expression of love for Rebecca does not differ from that in many other letters of nineteenth-century women. Carroll Smith-Rosenberg's pioneering article of 1975, "The Female World of Love and Ritual," first identified this aspect of women's correspondence and uncovered the "abundance of manuscript evidence" that demonstrates the emotional ties between women and the development of same-sex friendships that were accepted in nineteenth-century American society.

Historians such as Smith-Rosenberg and Lillian Faderman have shown that nineteenth-century white women often slept together and were openly affectionate with each other. Both speculate that some of these relationships may have been sexual as well.[7]

If we are to believe Addie's letters, her relationship with Rebecca was not simply an affectionate "friendship" or sisterhood. Several of Addie's letters have fairly explicit references to erotic interactions between herself and Rebecca. While there are major differences of class and education between the two women, Addie was not in any way forced into these situations. In fact, she often seems to have been the assertive and insistent one. Without Rebecca's letters, we may never know the full extent of their relationship. From Addie's responses to what appear to be Rebecca's concerns, comments, and queries, it seems clear that the passion and love were mutual. Nonetheless, it is not insignificant that though Addie frequently asks Rebecca to visit her in New York and though she requests that Rebecca send for her to come to Royal Oak, neither seems to have happened.

In order to suggest the difference between Addie's letters to Rebecca and those between other women of their peer group, I have included in the appendix two stray letters that I found in the Primus collection. The first was written to Rebecca by her friend and colleague Josephine Booth. The second was from the oft-mentioned Carrie of Rebecca's letters, written to Rebecca's younger sister Bell. While both letters share the writer's affection and admiration for the recipient, neither of them matches the intensity of Addie's letters to Rebecca. A third letter comes closest in its expressions of love and devotion. It is written to Addie. There is no date, and the last page is missing, so there is no signature. However, it appears to have been written to Addie by her husband, Joseph Tines.

During a time when our society continues to posit black women's sexuality in a negative light and when we continue to suffer from homophobia, the Primus-Brown letters are important documents because they reveal the complexity of the two women and their relationship to each other. Furthermore, they provide a historical example of women who loved each other romantically and who were no less committed (in fact, were more committed than most) to the struggle for black freedom and progress. Finally, Addie and Rebecca were the extraordinary human beings we come to know not in spite of but because of the relationship they shared with each other and with others who nurtured, supported, and loved them. We cannot underestimate the historical significance of these documents.

The Primus-Brown correspondence provides a missing link between the historical documentation of the public lives of well-known black women and their unknown private lives. In selecting the letters available to compose a coherent volume, I hope to encourage others to pursue further such research. The letters demand a rewriting of the history of black New England, the history of black women in America beyond those who were exceptional, middle-class, and famous, and a history of free urban black women whose experience differs from slave women and their rural descendants. As such, the letters add to the work of scholars such as Frances Foster and Carla Peterson[8] by encouraging us to consider the experiences of northern free black women in our construction of history. Also, this correspondence encourages us to broaden our conception of black women writers to include letter writers in addition to novelists, poets, journalists, speech writers, and diarists. But most important, they are a gift of friendship and love for all of us.

Here we have the stories of two nineteenth-century African American women, Rebecca Primus and Addie Brown: stories about their lives, ambitions, struggles, and dignity; their politics, reading, and community; their commitment to black equality and to each other. It is a story that moves us *beyond the silence.*

PART ONE

The Early Years

ON February 24, 1932, the following obituary appeared in the *Hartford Courant:*

> Mrs. Rebecca Thomas, 95, widow of Charles H. Thomas, of 115 Adelaide Street, died Sunday morning at the Municipal Hospital after a long illness. She leaves three nieces, Ms. Edna Edwards of Hartford; Mrs. Jessie H. Harris of Cambridge, Mass.; and Mrs. Nellie Singleton of Detroit, Mich. The funeral will be held Tues day afternoon at 1:30 P. M. at Johnson's funeral home, 19 Pavilion Street, and at 2 o'clock at the Talcott Street Congregational Church. Rev. James A. Wright will officiate. Burial will be in the family plot in Zion Hill Cemetery.

The paragraph gives details relating to the commemoration of Rebecca Primus Thomas's death and her relationship to others, but it relays very little about the woman herself. As with so many women, especially so many African American women, the significance of her life and deeds is lost to history in this final public document of her life. To a knowing Hartford reader, the name and address might provide a hint that she had been part of one of Hartford's oldest and most prominent black families. That she was the widow of Charles Thomas connected her to another well-known black Hartford resident.[1] More information about her life and commitments might have been evident in the name of the church. However, even these identity markers link the value of her life to the deeds and reputations of others. Most important, there is no mention of her career as a teacher of freedmen.

9

Until recently, historians did not acknowledge black women's role in Reconstruction. Even W. E. B. Du Bois, who attended to the words of black participants in his important *Black Reconstruction*, published in 1935 (only three years after Primus's death), failed to note the work of black women teachers. Du Bois applauded the efforts of the New England schoolteachers, but for him these instructors, dedicated and innovative, were for the most part white.

Forty-five years later, the white feminist historian Jacqueline Jones published the first full-length study of New England teachers who went south to found schools for and to teach the freed people. In *Soldiers of Light and Love*, Jones, like Du Bois, leaves out the efforts of black teachers. Not until the publication of Linda Perkins's 1984 article "The Black Female American Missionary Association Teacher in the South 1861–1870" and Dorothy Sterling's *We Are Your Sisters* (1984) did black teachers begin to receive scholarly attention. The absence of primary sources left by these women was one of the reasons for the inattention to them.[2]

Nevertheless, Rebecca Primus was one of many northern black women who went south to teach the freed people. As with most of her peers, Rebecca saw her teaching as a political and moral calling. She set forth on a mission that would influence her tremendously. The teachers who headed south organized schools that held day sessions for children, night sessions for adults, and Sabbath schools. In addition, they visited freedmen's homes and became respected members of the communities they inhabited. Their mission was one of education and "uplift." Rebecca Primus fit the profile of other black school-marms who were "northern born, middle class, single and childless."[3] Most were in their twenties and had above-average education. Most had taught in their hometowns before going south. Many of them suffered greatly from the stresses associated with their jobs. Others were the victims of violence and harassment.[4] Primus documents all of these circumstances.

What were the factors, the conditions, that might have led Miss Primus to take up the difficult mission of relocating to the South? The answer to this question can best be found in the community that produced and nurtured her. Rebecca was born in 1836 to Holdridge Primus and Mehitable (Jacobs) Primus. She was the eldest of four children; her siblings were Nelson, Henrietta, and Isabella (Bell).[5] Her paternal great-grandfather was an African slave who won his freedom

*Holdridge Primus, Rebecca's father, in front of the Humphrey
and Seyms grocery store in Hartford.*

by fighting in the American army during the Revolutionary War.[6] Her maternal grandfather owned a cobbler shop.

In 1860, all the Primuses but the youngest, Bell, were gainfully employed. Holdridge Primus was a clerk in a well-known Hartford grocery firm, Humphrey and Seyms. His wife, Mehitable, sometimes worked as a seamstress. Nelson was a painter; he worked for a carriage maker, George Francis, and eventually moved to Boston to pursue his career as a portraitist. Henrietta was a domestic in the home of a local white businessman, Henry Ferre. The Primus family owned their home at 20 Wadsworth Street. Rebecca would return to this home after the death of her husband in 1891, living there until 1902. As property owners who were able to maintain steady employment, the Primuses were clearly part of Hartford's black middle class. However, Henrietta's employment as a domestic suggests the fluidity of class and the precarious nature of middle-class status in the African American community.

Though they lived in a predominantly white neighborhood, the Primuses were part of a cohesive black community that centered around the activities of the city's black institutions. They were members of the Talcott Street Congregational Church, one of two black Hartford churches. Rebecca continued to teach Sunday school there until her death in 1932. James Pennington, the nationally known black abolitionist, had been minister of the Talcott Street Church, which had been a site of abolitionist meetings and organizing. Furthermore, Rebecca Primus probably attended one of Hartford's African schools, where Pennington and the essayist Ann Plato had been teachers.[7] It seems that Rebecca might have taught in one of these schools as well. In her letters she speaks of her Hartford classes; she would not have taught in the city's white schools. As early as 1861, Addie writes to her, "I see you still have your private school."[8]

All of this is to say that Rebecca Primus grew up in a city with a small black population (it numbered just over seven hundred in 1860, slightly more than two percent of the total Hartford population), but she worshiped in, was educated in, and was employed by black institutions with an explicit political focus—that of black freedom and uplift.

The Hartford black community was made up of a vibrant network of families and institutions. In the letters, one encounters members of the Talcott Street Congregational Church as well as the Zion Methodist Church. The racially integrated Hartford Freedmen's Aid Society and

James Pennington, the activist pastor of Talcott Street Church.

the Prince Hall Masonic Lodge were among the community's major social and civic organizations. The latter provided many opportunities for dancing at its frequent balls.

There are descriptions of visits to Allyn Hall to hear music, trips to New York on the ferry the *Granite State,* to New Hampshire, Boston, and Philadelphia. Both Addie and Rebecca were avid readers of both the mainstream and the black press, as well as of novels, sermons, biographies, and books on history and religion.

Among the families who populate the letters were the Platos, the Sands, the Notts, and the Saunderses. Henry Nott was a black painter. William Saunders was a black tailor as well as an agent for William Lloyd Garrison's *The Liberator.* He had two sons, Thomas and Prince, both of whom were tailors; one of them married Roxanna Saunders, for whom Addie frequently sewed.

Rebecca's maternal aunt Emily married Raphael Sands, a Portuguese baker and cook. The couple and their two children, Sarah and Thomas, lived on Wadsworth Street just down the block from the Primuses. For a while Addie lived with the Sands family, and when she worked at Miss Porter's School in Farmington, Connecticut, Mr. Sands was her supervisor. Thomas Sands married a woman who, like Rebecca's younger sister, was named Bell. His family did not approve of the marriage because they thought her beneath him. Addie agreed.

Rebecca's other maternal aunt, Bathsheba (referred to in the letters as Aunt Bashy), married Reverend John Smith and had two children, Hattie and William. She later married a porter named Henry Champion. Their daughter, Mary Champion, appears frequently in Addie's letters.

Another prominent family, the Platos, were unrelated to other Platos in the city, among them the essayist Ann Plato. Gertrude Plato was a friend and contemporary of Addie's and Rebecca's. In 1863, Gertrude inherited her family's estate, valued at approximately four thousand dollars.[9] She made frequent trips and wore expensive clothing, though was not considered physically attractive. Rebecca's sister Bell was the community's beauty and attracted a number of suitors with her charm and her flirtatious nature.

Chapter One

"I've Lost a Day"

1854–1856

THERE are no letters from Rebecca to her family prior to 1865. However, two pieces of her writing survive that period: a poem, "I've Lost a Day," written in 1854, when she was eighteen, and an essay, "History of My Poodle Dog," written in 1856. While neither are literary masterpieces, they do reveal several important traits that become more apparent in the later letters.

First, both the poem and the essay suggest that she is comfortable expressing herself through her writing and that she writes in a number of forms. That she may have had literary aspirations appears in later letters when she laments being too busy to pursue her writing. Unfortunately, these are the only pieces of writing aside from the letters that seem to have survived.

The poem reveals yet another aspect of her personality that is borne out in the letters. She is highly organized and concerned with the most effective use of her time. No doubt this concern with efficiency contributed to her success as a teacher and as a fastidious administrator of her school.

The essay expresses her love of animals. The mourned poodle is eventually replaced by other pets—the cats Jim and Jim, Jr. As we will see, Rebecca dotes on pets and children. The seriousness and formality with which she customarily carries herself give way immediately in the presence of her beloved animals and the children in her life: her niece Leila and her little adopted sister, Doll.

These are perhaps the only places where Rebecca is not writing about racial politics in America. They are the efforts of a middle-class young woman who chooses to express her ambition and her emotions through her writing.

I've Lost a Day

The day how neglected it has been,
The hours how swift they've fled.
The moments, Oh, where are they?
The seconds they too, have gone;
The sound echoes in my ear,
I've lost, I've lost a day.

Ah, have I really lost a day.
It can be but the fact.
The hours are so precious, moments too
Needless have fled away.
The sound still echoes in my ears.
I've lost, I've lost a day.

Then let me treasure the days that give
And the hours more than before
Nor moments more pass by
Without some kind reflection;
That the sound no longer may respond
I've lost, I've lost a day.

Oh then let wisdom guide my feet,
Into his pleasant ways,
And no more seek the heedless path
that leads me from it to stray;
That I never more may hear the sound
Echoing, I've lost a day.

Rebecca Primus
Hartford Feb. 15, 1854

History of My Poodle Dog

Between two and three years since my Aunt made a visit down east, she spent several months there and when she returned she brought with her the handsomest little lap dog you ever saw. It's fleece was a spotless white, very long, and curled, all over its body. We were obliged to keep it shorn from its face, if not, it would get into its eyes which were black as coals, and as bright as brass buttons. We called it Ninny, it was not a very young dog. We all became very much attached to it, so that if any of us went out Ninny was sure to be with me, and made a considerable fuss if she was at any time deprived of that privilege which did not occur very often, she always slept with me, and it was impossible to get her up before noon. Every week she went through the process of a thorough bathing to which she was not very partial; however she was a very neat dog and attracted the attention of almost every age. I don't know how many offers we've had for her but nothing could induce us to sell her. Last Summer my Aunt with my sister made another visit down east and took Ninny with them, and returned home without her, with the intention of having her come home this summer if any of us went down there. But to our great surprise and sad disappointment we received intelligence of her sudden death after a short illness. The nature of her disease we are still in ignorance of. Poor, poor Ninny how we all regretted her loss. I sometimes think if she had remained with me she would not have died.

Rebecca Primus
June 20th 1856

Chapter Two

"If you was a man . . ."

1859–1860

THE Primus family home often served as a boardinghouse and employment agency for other African Americans, particularly young black women. Primus and Brown both speak of young southern women who lived in the Primus home following the Civil War, and other letters document requests from prominent white Hartford citizens to Holdridge and Mehitable for servants. Thus the Primus home served as a precursor to social service agencies such as the White Rose Mission in New York, which emerged in the latter half of the nineteenth century.[1] Founded by Victoria Earle Matthews in 1897, the White Rose Mission was a kind of settlement house that served as a community center and employment agency. Most important, it provided shelter and guidance for young black women migrants from the South.

It is not clear how or when Rebecca Primus met Addie Brown. Brown might have been one of the many young women who boarded with the Primus family and for whom they found employment. Or perhaps she was introduced to the family as a child. Addie spent her early years in Philadelphia with an unknown aunt.[2] Jeremiah Asher, Holdridge Primus's first cousin, was the pastor of the Shiloh Baptist Church in Philadelphia. Possibly in that capacity he knew the family with whom Addie resided. Whatever the case, by 1859, when her letters to Rebecca begin, Addie was already part of the Primus family circle.

The largest gaps and silences in the Primus-Brown story relate to the early life of Addie Brown. We do know that she was born on December 21, 1841.[3] Her father died when she was young, and her mother remarried against Addie's wishes. Addie had a brother named Ally Brown, who served in the Civil War—but there is little information about him.

Her earliest letters, written from Waterbury and Hartford, are primarily concerned with her day-to-day existence. Addie is often depressed, overworked, suffering from chronic headaches; she tries desperately to learn the sewing trade so that she can find employment as a seamstress. She takes care of the sick Mrs. Games (who appears to be expecting a baby, though this is never clear), and she shuns the advances of Mr. Games. She spends most of her time longing for Rebecca. Addie's letters make little mention of the political and social upheaval of the times.

The noted historian John Hope Franklin writes: "Perhaps no decade in the history of the United States has been so filled with tense and crucial moments as the ten years leading to the Civil War; and closely connected with most of these crises was the problem of slavery." After all, this was the decade that witnessed the publication of *Uncle Tom's Cabin,* by Harriet Beecher Stowe (another Hartford resident), in 1852; the Compromise of 1850—in which Congress decided that "California should enter the Union as a free state; the other territories would be organized without mention of slavery; Texas should cede certain lands to New Mexico, and be compensated; slave holders would be better protected by a stringent fugitive slave law; and there should be no slave trade in the District of Columbia"—and the Kansas-Nebraska Act of 1854, which provided that Kansas and Nebraska "should be organized as territories and that the question of slavery should be decided by the territorial legislatures."[4] In 1857, the Supreme Court handed down the Dred Scott decision. The decade closed with John Brown's raid at Harpers Ferry, Virginia, on October 16, 1859. Brown was hanged on December 2, 1859. None of this is mentioned in the letters that follow.

Waterbury Aug. 2 1859

My Loving Friend

I realy did not know what to make of your long silence. I come to conclusion that you had just forgotten me. I was more than please to received your long look for letter and at last it arrived. Dear since you last heard from me I have been very sick but now my health is very good now my heart is just bad. O Dear Friend I am allmost tired of my life. Do not scold me My Friend for I really mean what I say I will not say much more this perhaps is not very pleasant to the ear.

Mrs Games send her respects to you and says as soon she able to sit up after she is confine she will send me on so you can look for me between this and the last of this months tell me when you school commence will you please. I will tell you all the news when I see you[. . . .]

I remain your true
Affectionate Friend
Addie

one sweet kiss
you must look for me every Saturday until I do come on
tell Henrietta to write to me if she please.

    While living in Waterbury, Addie is able to visit Rebecca. She has just returned from such a visit in the letter that follows. It is clear that the community surrounding the two young women know that they are very close and provide them with sympathy when they are apart. Here we also begin to get an outline of the vibrancy of these black New England communities as Addie tells Rebecca of upcoming events and activities. It is also clear that Addie recognizes the romantic and erotic nature of her love for Rebecca: "if you was a man what would things come to?" she asks her beloved friend.

Waterbury Aug. 30 1859

My ever Dear Friend
    I no doubt you will be surprise to received a letter so soon I think it will be received with just as much pleasure this week as you will nexe my <u>Dearest Dearest Rebecca</u> my heart is allmost broke I dont know that I ever spent such hours as I have my loving friend it goes harder with me now then it ever did I am more acquainted with you it seem to me this very moments if I only had the wings of a <u>dove</u> I would not remain long in Waterbury although we cant allway be together O it tis hard
    O Dear I am so lonesome I barelly know how to contain myself if I was only near you and having one of those <u>sweet</u> kisses. Man appoint and God disappoints. There is not much news here worthy to attention there is going to be a picnic tomorry the Childrens temperance Jubilee. The hand of hope will be celebrated to it will be a

grand affair. Mr. Pete Sinclair the well known apostle of temperance will address the Gathering I supose it tis quit gay in Hartford[. . . .]

O my <u>Dear</u> Friend how I did miss you last night I did not have any one to hug me and to kiss. Rebecca dont you think I am very foolish I dont want anyone to kiss me now I turn Mr Games away this morning no <u>kisses</u> is like yours[. . . .]

You are the first Girl that I ever <u>love</u> so it you are the <u>last</u> one Dear Rebecca do not say anything against me <u>loving</u> you so for I mean just what I say O Rebecca it seem I can see you now casting those loving eyes at me if you was a man what would things come to they would after come to something very quick what do you think the matter dont laugh at me[. . . .] I must say I dont know that I every injoyed myself any better than I did when I was at your parents house. I was treated so rich by all the Family I hope I may have the extreme pleasure returning the same pleasure to you all each will remember the visit as for your self Dear H[enrietta] there is no one like her if you was to travel all over united states[. . . .] Affectionate Friend Addie
PS give my love to all the Family and kiss also to
your Mo.   Addie
please to write soon

It is not clear if Addie consents to Mr. Games's attentions. Many young female servants were subjected to sexual harassment at the hands of their employers. Addie does not mention Games after this.

Throughout her time in Waterbury, Addie longs to move to Hartford so that she can be closer to Rebecca and to the city's black community. Addie's request of Rebecca's mother reveals a great deal about the power of the Primus family, both to act as intermediaries between black and white Hartford and to provide employment and training for young black women. All in all, Addie is clear that her situation would be better served if she could but move to Hartford.

Waterbury Feb. 16 1860

My Beloved Friend
   do not be surprise to hear from me again I am <u>heart sick</u> to see

you once more again it commence snowing this morning has done so all day the snow is two feet deep I thought I would be able to be with you to night how I did miss you last night I do not my <u>Dear love</u> know how long I have got to live. My Dearest Dearest <u>Friend</u> let it be long or short I must spend my days near with you if it tis the <u>Lord</u> will

I am afraid this is gone to end of my life for I have caught a very heavy cold I do not know where it will terminated Mrs Games says I shall not return to Hartford until Monday If I only could see you if it was only a hour every day perhaps I could content myself until you are your <u>Dear Mother</u> could find me a place as to live with Mrs Games again I could not make up my mind to do so I have a perticular reason for not doing so I shall not tell you now I wish your Mother would consent to let me finish my trade with her if I could only know how to cut for my health at present would not allow me to take whole charge of a house but I could sew. Keep this to yourself what I am about to tell you Mrs Games has been more than kind these few hours to me now she says if I would only stay with her she will pay me every week I can do the sewing and help her to take her Children for that is all she want me to do I ask your silence on this Rebecca I do not want to stay with her[. . . .] I cannot be happy if I was to stay a way from you. Rebecca my <u>Dearest love</u> could any one love a person as love you   I cannot I cannot stay here any longer with out you I must I must be near you   do not forget to see about a place for me so I wont be out of work to long I will be on there Monday afternoon   right to me first will you. your most heart broken friend   Addie
PS   do not forget to pray for me
Addie

Rebecca's prayers alone are not sufficient to soothe Addie. She opens the new decade with a declaration of her commitment to Jesus. It is evident that Rebecca has been encouraging her to find salvation. With all the enthusiasm of a new convert, she marks this as a major change in her life, though one suspects that her desire to please her beloved friend is behind her fervent protestations of faith.

. . .

Waterbury Jan. 1860

My Dearest & Beloved Friend

I do not feel very well to day it has kept me from Church so I thought I would answer your letter[. . . .]

Dear Rebecca was that a dreadful thing that factory fallen in there are many aching <u>hearts</u> weeping over their <u>deads</u> there is a warnings for us in it my <u>love</u> Dear Rebecca.

Dear Rebecca I am now going to inform you of something that you long desire that is this I have found a <u>Friend</u> this is <u>Jesus</u>. My beloved you wish me happy New year it tis one it has been happy week to me why did I put it of so long I would not have spend so many unhappy hours I have spent I had I seek for <u>salvation</u> before O Rebecca could I but see you for a hour I could tell you all I cannot pen them all on paper to you but I will we'll see each other soon again.

Dear Rebecca I will tell I was determined to have a <u>change heart</u> there is a pious young lady here she visit the house two or three times so one evening she was here to tea and she was going to prayer meeting so she ask me would I like to go so I told her yes and we went I was delighted with the meeting so I went again so she has been talking to me not thinking of you my <u>love</u> it really made me unhappy. Two weeks ago I did not what was the matter with myself I was not sick in body-but-in-mind I was then to get religion for I do not know when the Lord will come

Dear Rebecca your prayers are answered I hope I will have the strength to keep up to my duty. Dear Rebecca give my love to Henrietta and tell her not to put it off any longer for now is the exceptional time. Do not cease praying for me for remember they is many obstacle in the way if we do not meet each other here on earth again we will in heaven <u>God bless</u> you. I remain your ever Dear Loving Friend Addie

PS Give my love to your dear Mother and the rest of the Family Addie

Let worldly minds the world pursue
It has no Charms for me
Once I admired its follies too
But grace has set me free
Those follies now no longer please

No mere delighted afford
Far from my heart he joys within
For I have known the lord

excuse this
writing Addie

In entering the ranks of the saved, Addie joins a tradition of African American women who sustained strong spiritual lives. Black feminist theologian Jacquelyn Grant has written: "for Black Christian women in the past, Jesus was their central frame of reference. They identified with Jesus because they believed Jesus identified with them."[5]

Addie's prayers seem to be answered when she moves to Hartford. However, it appears that Rebecca has left the city for an extended trip. So, ironically, Addie's longing for her friend is not abated. She has found work, perhaps with the assistance of Mehitable Primus.

Hartford Aug. 16 1860

My Beloved Rebecca

I have been down hearted today I wishing I was near you my head reclining on your <u>Dear bosom</u> it tis useless to wish that my love. I suppose about this time you have heard that I have left Mrs Kellogg

I am very much please to hear that you are enjoying yourself & I also delighted that you are geting fat I hope you will not lose it all after you return home[. . . .] You spoke of my health I am very well with the exception of my head. my head trouble me great deal you know I was sun struck while I was at Mrs Kellogg I was out in the sun great deal I think I have lost some of my flesh. Mrs Hartley has to notice it I spoke of it My Dear Dear Rebecca, if you dont hurry home I am afraid that you wont find my flesh I will be nothing but skin and bones.

Hartford Nov. 17 1860

My Cherish Friend

My head is better to day last night it pain me very hard O My Dear dear Rebecca when you press me to your Dear bosom . . .

24

happy I was, last night I gave any thing if I could only layed my poor aching head on your <u>bosom</u> O Dear how soon will it be I can be able to do so I suppose you think me very foolish if you do it tis all the same to me. Dear Rebecca when I am away from you I feel so unhapy it seem me the hours and days are like weeks & month will that day ever come than I can be with you oftener it seem to me when we are together our moments are limited I do not know why tis so although one comfort I have the is day coming there will be no parting. it tis very gloomy here if I was only near you now I rather have my head on your lap then pencil the few lines to you[. . . .] I am going to be layed down now good by Untill you her from me again yours for ever untill death parts us

    Addie

PS   except a secret kiss I will imprint on here so look good you may perchance find it

    Addie

    I was even so foolish to expect you last evening but all was in vaine every footsteps I heard thinking it was my loving Rebecca few days past my <u>love</u> been towards you more then I can express. Dear Rebecca one thing I am going to say is this when ever you want me to come down and stay all night you must tell me. no more until we meet from your ever Dear and loving   Addie

one sweat kiss
from your sweat lips

PART TWO

The Civil War Years

ALTHOUGH Addie Brown spent much of her early life in New York and Philadelphia, she does not appear in the federal census records or in city directories. For the most part, women were listed in the census under their husbands', fathers', or employers' households. Propertied widows or single women were listed individually. Addie's nomadic existence might have made it difficult for her to be counted.

If we relied solely on these sources, Addie Brown would not exist. Fortunately, her correspondence to Rebecca in the years immediately preceding and during the Civil War affirm her existence and firmly situate her as a member of a colorful New York African American household. In New York, Addie lived with and worked for a black family named Jackson. She refers to John Jackson and his wife as "father" and "mother," but she is clear that they are not her biological parents. Instead, they are employers who treat her "like one of the family."

James Weldon Johnson notes: "As late as 1880 the major portion of the Negro population of the city lived in Sullivan, Bleecker, Thompson, Carmine and Grove Streets—the area commonly known as Greenwich Village."[1] It seems that the Jacksons were part of this community.

Addie's letters of 1861 refer to "father's restaurant." By 1862, she refers to his "saloon." In the New York City directory of 1861, there is a John H. Jackson, colored, who owns an eating house at 824 Broadway; his home address is 68 Sullivan. He is the only black Jackson in the directory who has a restaurant. In the directory of 1862, Jackson appears again, this time with the designation "Liquor." He also appears in the Federal Census of 1860, 5th Ward, District 3, as a forty-three-year-old black male, occupation: restaurant. No women are listed in his household, though he is married.

Addie worked for the Jacksons as a domestic and cared for their nine children. Mrs. Jackson took in sewing, and Addie and another young woman, Selina, assisted her. Though the Jacksons claimed to treat her like one of their children, Addie would have preferred that they pay her more frequently. In fact, she seems to have been "in service" with Mrs. Jackson, learning the trades of dressmaking and millinery. As indicated in these early letters, Addie struggles to make a living.

In addition to Mr. Jackson's restaurant/saloon and Mrs. Jackson's sewing, the family home was a boardinghouse. Consequently it was filled with people and the tensions that come with overly crowded households. Addie mentions frequent fights between Mrs. Jackson and various boarders, especially over issues of money.

That the Jacksons ran both an eatery and a boardinghouse places them in what Leonard Curry identifies as the entrepreneurial class of free northern blacks. As such, they should have had greater access to economic opportunity than either skilled or semiskilled laborers. However, Curry warns that "the very few practitioners of entrepreneurial occupations had, if anything, even less likelihood of achieving any significant degree of economic success" than did those of the professional class (clerks, teachers, etc.).[2] This is yet more evidence of the fluidity of class boundaries in the black community. Whatever the case, Addie Brown does not seem to have benefited from the family's status. Furthermore, she seems to have been mistreated at times. This would have made the kindness of Rebecca Primus and her family all the more attractive to her.

Nonetheless, Addie Brown lived in a vibrant community where people attended church, picnics, concerts, parties, balls, and fundraisers for fugitive slaves (sometimes called "contraband"). It was an area where the activist preacher James Pennington pastored after leaving Hartford. The great abolitionist Henry Highland Garnet was there as well. On the other hand, it was also a community where large numbers of people died from consumption. "Consumption, or tuberculosis, was a common disease among the poor living in New York. In some areas of the city it was a virtual scourge."[3] Addie writes of many inhabitants contracting smallpox.

Addie's New York household consists of Mr. and Mrs. Jackson (a socialite who spends beyond her means), Aunt Charity Jackson, Selina, who works in the house, Selina's brother Warwick, Addie's brother Ally, the Jacksons' nine children, and several boarders.

Chapter Three

"Like meat to a hungre wolfe"

NEW YORK, 1861

CANNONS fired on Fort Sumter in April 1861, yet there is very little mention of the war in Addie's letters. Notices about fundraisers for the "contraband"—slaves who escaped to Union territory—and mention of the worsening health and economic standing of her community are the only evidence of the war we see here. On a day-to-day basis, Addie demonstrates little concern over the national events that surely must have had an impact on her life.

New York Apr. 4 1861

My Dear Rebecca

this is the hour I would like to hear you played[. . . .] At this moment I would give all I poses that not much to hear some music[. . . .]

Aunt C is going to Sea[1] again she expect to go in two week time if not sooner she expect to be gone four years. Selina and I will miss her very much another point I am glad she going for she is very unhappy Mother and her has fell out Aunt C says she hate Mo as much as she use to love her I feel for her its must be hard with one to love and be deceived in them and who just love a person what you can get out them will and when they have not the means to do any more not care for them any more I scorn such people it seem I hardly want to treat them with common civility[. . . .]

You ask me if I was making any skirts No My Darling I have not made any but I have one to make and the waist of this it has four breadths in it I am making now Chemise & drawers the yoke and sleeves that you gave me if I should live until that day, shall wear the

31

night that I am married I am very much oblige to you for these stamps you sent you are more then a Sister to me nexe month this great fair is coming up the Ladies with Selina and I to keep a table I dont care about it I would like it if you was going to help me if Selina was to hear me she would not like it I cant help that. This eve Aunt C and her Mother and I are going up to the [restaurant] perhaps we may have a very nice time I dont no I dont care much about it but father is so very pleasant and always delighted to see me he says sometimes I act so strong that he dont believe that I love him. He make me smile. I am going to bring this to a close for I know it not very interesting I have not much news to relate[. . . .] Now Dear it getting dark so I must close your Ever dear Devoted
    Sister Addie

Of special interest is Addie's description of a very intelligent young girl who experiences "fits" because of her intellectual ambition and academic competition with white students. This might be part of a long-standing belief among some uneducated African Americans that children who were intellectually precocious were thought to be vulnerable to "brain fever." It is ironic, however, that Addie would believe this, given her own intellectual proclivities and her admiration for Rebecca's ambition and intelligence.

Aunt Chaty (Charity) was one of the few women who found work on ships. These women often did laundry and sewing for steamboats. Some wives also went with their husbands. Because this was wartime, Aunt Chaty may have worked on one of the steamboats between New York and Connecticut. Such employment could have brought more income into the Jackson household. In later letters, we see the intricate and creative economic networks Aunt Chaty's employment set into play.

New York Apr. 13 1861

My Darling Sister
    I'm alone all the inmates of the family gone to Church. O no Aunt Chaty is not gone she feel rather indispose to day. The reason I'm home I did not get my Shoes last night Mother gave me some

money this AM so of course that was to late then so I will have to remain in the house this lovely weather.

O Rebecca I am getting somewhat discourage with myself. Dont say anything about it I rather think Mother another one added to the family she is complaining very much I told her if she did I would not stay with her for I have had my heart full of Children I was not going to take care of any more without it my own I suppose you think my Dear I am talking rather large but I mean just what I say.

[. . .]How I have wanted to see you if I only could have rested my head on your bosom for a moments give vent to my feeling I have been sad I am so full some time that I could take a knife and cut my heart out perhaps then I feel better if I could be with you daily I know that I would be happy well that cant be O my I shant worry you.

Mr. Hicks has move his family to New Y[ork] account of his Daughter Emma dont you think she has fits last summer received the prize and she is very ambitious with her books and as she was going to a white S[chool] she did not want any of them to excel her she over her mind in order to win the prize and the Dr says any excitement will throw her into them one day last week as she was getting ready for school she had two and after she got them she had one she has been pretty gay since she been here I think she will of have to denied herself some of the pleasure of this world she is keeping company with a young girls that is . . . very much about for I think she ought to go the best society if there any it not like it use to be. Selina is finish her trade now Mrs. Thompson has hired her last week I think it very nice for she is learning all this time one thing whats spoil her she is so very careless but with her work she like to cut so much and often spoils her work.

[. . .] I am waiting for my irons to get hot Mother has been out most of the day Aunt Chaty she down to her ship I believe she leaves us nexe week I want to tell you what a foolish thing she is going to do last night she will be here she going to invite about 30 of Mother and Selinas friend and are going to have three pieces of musle she think she will spend about $10 who will thank her for it the people in this house will injoy themselves and then after she is gone talks about her one in particular O what a word my irons are hot so good by my sweet Sister.

33

New York Apr. 16 1861

My Beloved Sister

We are very busy Aunt Chat has brought the linen of the ship for us to make I must tell you something to make you smile Mother says sometime ago to me Addie if you can get a . . . sewing out I can go for it would help me on with what she gave me I never had a chance out until the other day so Aunt came home on Monday Eve and was telling Selina and I that Captain wanted her to get someone to make up the linens and she did not know who to get so I happened to think what Mother said so I offer to go. Aunt Chat says you M would let you go so I was so sure that I go or rather I could go you ought to of heard me so I went to Mo and told her she says Addie when I told you that I was not able to pay you and I am now I told her it was not so that she was paying me I made her remember so she did not know what to say then she could not say any thing else that she would not be able to pay me and I go out too I could take the work in the house and do and she would give me my board for what I do I was so pro-voke there. I said I would not go and neither would I bring the work in the house what little while I had to stay and then that would be very short and came out and shut the door Mother like have all no body any so I had but a very little to say to her yesterday

[. . .] Rebecca when I come to Hartford this summer will you go up to Springfield then I would like to see it . . . stay over one night will you my love my Dear you ask me if I had any trimmings for my underclothes no my Dear I have not as yet if you like I would like you to send me one of Kelly kittens be company for me if you wont come[. . . .]

good morning Dearest
except a kiss from your
Affec Loving Sister

Addie

Addie claims to have many suitors in New York. The most persis-tent of these is Mr. Lee, a gentleman she considers marrying. She begins to express her philosophy about the institution of marriage as a practical choice that provides economic stability.

New York May 24 1861

My Darling Rebecca

  your most Affec letter to me was like pieces of meat to hungre
wolfe I will not tell how often I pursue the contents of it this eve for
the first time since I left that I gave vent to tears O Dear Dear
Rebecca no one knows the heart of your Dear Friend I am afraid I
will become irksom to the Family they say I am a change girl in
every way I will try and be agreeable as I can how can I when you
are so far off. I'm thinking of you hourly.

  [. . .] Dear Rebecca if I had the energy of the dove how swiftly I
would fly to the arms of my love.

  Dear Rebeca Mother has a great deal of work in the house I'm
very much pleased for that I must have something to occupying my
mind Rebecca what do you think Mr. Lee has here turn to me he has
been expecate his Affec towards me but I act so indifferently that he
dont know what to make of me I like him as a Friend and nothing
more then that but Dear Rebecca if I should ever see a good chance
I will take it for I'm tired roving around this unfriendly world Dear
Rebecca in all this do not forget what I have said about marrying do
not mention what I'm about to pen to you my true Friend that is this
I do believe by Mr. Lee action that he truly <u>loves me</u> I cannot recip-
rocate his love he ask me if I thought that I ever live in Hartford
again. I told him did not know he said I thought I would.

  Rebecca what do you think my old lover come home from church
with me stay sun AM the . . . to stir a little in my breast dont laugh at
me my Darling. Mother has two gentlemen boarded and one of
them has partly fell in love with me mother told him and also Selina
that no chance for him now Dear Rebecca mother says she did not
think I was so dear to her I must say she is very Affectionately to me
but if it only be lasting dont you say so to my love as for my part I try
not to be changeable although I leave that for you to judge.

  [. . .] Rebecca where do you think Mrs. Nott will go when she
dies for I think she is not . . . live please to forgive me for saying so
but that is true she know just as well as she was a living that she did
not give me but one shirt and then she hardly wanted to then but I
would persist in having it she wanted to send it down there I know
I now have it then so I made shure of it then Rebecca I dont think I
ever shall make my home again with Mrs. Nott because I dont think

35

Mrs. Nott no kind of a woman to be with Im almost disgusted with her.

Dear Rebecca we have deep bereavement in the Family Mother only Friend is dead he has been a Father to her he has staid by in all her trouble if she wanted anything would always go to him and him only he has been a near Dear Friend to this Family Rebecca it heart rendering to see his widow I saw him for the last time on Sunday he was apparently in perfect good health and very lively indeed Monday AM Mother was sent for and thought he would choke to death but they work for over him he seem to much better mother come home at 2 o'clock PM thought he would get along mother went in the evening to see he was great deal better so she came home at 1 o'clock she sent for and he was dying before Mother got up there he was dead O Rebecca how suddenly that was we all are very much afraid that Mrs. Scott will live very long now both are old and she is so nearing . . . that was the Family I thought to live with Rebecca I must bring this long letter to a close for I dont think will be very interesting to you if I only exchange this pen and paper for a seat by my loving Rebecca it is possible and must be thus seperation how long how long <u>God</u> knows and he only my heart is breaking for you and only you good night from your sweet Affec.

Addie

PS give my love to your Dear Mother and all the rest of the Family give my love to your Aunt Em and all the rest of the Friend Addie

In the following letter, Addie relates the many complications that arise from Mr. Scott's failure to leave a will. The subsequent family drama reads like a nineteenth-century "passing" novel, in which a protagonist of mixed race "passes" for white.

New York June 7 1861

My Darling Rebecca

[. . .] I would be in such deep reverie I would really think your was by me when my attention would be call how sad I would feel Ive felt like bursting in floods of tears. Mother had to go up to see her

Aunt Selina accompany her that left me entirely alone I can assure you I gave in to my feelings wretched I did feel in fact I felt so all the evening

[. . .] Mr. Scott did not make any will so his Widow was worried about of there is some of his relations and to come in for their share and she does not want them to have any for when he was living they did not recognize him I suppose you wonder how that they past for white. O that skin that skin Mrs. . . .

[. . .] Do not mention this to any one will you this I have been entertain by a very inteligence young man Mr. Toars he says he is very much please with me he was asking me about NY I was sick of it he said he was astonish at me I told him he would be more so before he wanted to be less Dear Rebecca Mr. Lee still comes to see me he said he was coming to see me once a week he did not come last week so he sent me a letter so I ans it seeing that I not see him or reply perhaps Ive offended him my old lover call to see me Dearest Mother say I ought not to do as do Dear Rebecca the flames within my breast and head consume me for before I would summit no no no! I would take Mr. Lee fast my Darling I must bring this letter to close for Ive two dresses to finish by tomorrow night so my love good by my own sweet Friend
    yours Devotedly Addie
    [. . .] good night
    Addie

At this point in the correspondence, Addie is twenty years old and Rebecca twenty-five. Given her youth, it is not surprising that Addie, who has many suitors and ongoing flirtations, is beginning to consider marriage. Addie's willingness to share information regarding her suitors and admirers suggests that she and Rebecca did not regard these secondary flirtations as threats to their relationship. Nonetheless, one cannot help but think that there are times when Addie is trying to provoke a jealous response from Rebecca.

In the midst of her world, Addie is losing friends and neighbors to death and disease. She makes few allusions, however, to the war, although she is very critical of Mrs. Jackson for focusing so much on "worldly" things in this context.

New York May 30 1861

To my only Dear & Loving Friend

I thought I would rest myself from sewing by writing a few lines to the one that I truly love and only one Dear Rebecca I have been so very busy today that hardly know myself but the mend of it all I received a letter from the one that I idolize the letter took away the bulk of my work did not appear so irksome to me. Rebecca I want to tell you one thing that is this if I went with out eating for two or three days and then a person was to bring me something to eat and a letter from you and they say that I was only to have one or the other I would take the letter that would be enough food for me.

[. . .] Rebecca Im waiting for Mother to get up for breakfast they do not rise as early here as they do in Hartford sometimes I get so provoke at them up all night most and then lie bed all the AM Dear Rebecca I'm not going to get in that habit if can possible help it for I think it dreadful dont you my love? Dearest the people are dying here very fast I was telling Mother that they out to be thinking of something else beside the worldly affairs there was Mr. Tillman at Mr. Scott funeral last Sat and while he was giving of the story he said Mr. Scott I will be the nexe one will follow but Sunday Eve he went to church apparently in the best of health came home very . . . and set to talk with his family when all once he took on sudden change his wife ask him what was the matter he went to go upstairs just before he got up he died dont you think that was sudden, now I must go down and get my breakfast good by my loving Friend until nexe time.

New York June 24 1861
Mon 6 o'clock A.M.

My Darling & Beloved Rebecca

[. . .] You know I told you that I thought that I had offended Mr. Lee well I have not the letter has drawn him to me he has been here two or three times every week Mother told me she was going to ask Mr. Lee to come and spend the fourth and I thought she was jesting but I see she was not she ask him he said he would I have now got to dress the 9 Children so I must bring this to a close I hope you will not be disappointed with letter give my love to the Family kiss your Mother and your Aunt Emily for me and kiss yourself if you can believe me I remain your Devoted

Addie

Addie probably represents many young African American women of the period, far more of whom were in Addie's position than in Rebecca's. Being "in service" means that Addie's workday never ends; she is an all-around house servant, nursemaid, and seamstress.

New York June 25 1861

My most Beloved Friend

O Dear how tired I am of sewing my fingers is even sore I told Mother I will not sew any more to night it tis ten o'clock I will rest myself by penning a few scattering thought to the <u>Idol of my heart.</u> We have go five dresses to finish by Saturday night dont you think we have to be very expeditious my Darling I can imagine that your are saying to your Dear self it serve me right dont my love be to serious with me.

[. . .] Rebecca do not think I'm flattering myself what I'm about to inform you well it tis this I'm the favorite of this Family and also the family lives up Stairs Dear Rebecca I have come to conclusion that I'm human being O Rebecca I want to tell you while I think of it Mr. Lee made me a present of a book it tis very pretty it quite laughable to see what he has written in it to me he has got a rose in it and got the initial of my and the rose and language of the rose is true <u>Love</u> I received on Thursday so on Saturday Selina ask me to let her see my book so I got it for her she ask me if I know what it meant I told her that I had not time to look at it I wish you had of heard her how she went on about and said she would tell Mr. Lee I would not be surprise if she did tell him Mother would like very much for me to have the Gentleman she like him very much she says how is it about you my love. Dear Rebecca there was most horrible accident happen here last week cross the St. from us you ever want to witness there was two colored men got to fighting and one them cut the other face to pieces it make me feel faint to think of it the St. is dreadful to live in but very good business street we have great deal work sometimes more than we can do for the last two or three weeks we have been sewing on black the people are dying very fast here the smallpox is very bad here I am safe on that for I had a . . . touch of it.

[. . .] I will hope to

Remain your Pet

Addie Brown

We are beginning to see evidence of the war in Addie's letters, although she refrains from any sustained engagement with the political events of the day.

New York July 2 1861

My Beloved Rebecca

[. . .] I will tell you, my Aunt that I live with once in Philadelphia, her son, he here with the 7 Reg & so he heard that I was in NY so he call to see me. We had quit pleasant time. I was more than surprise to see him for I thought there was so down on me that would not take the pains to ever inquire so after me. I guess I'm human after all dont you think so Dearest. Will you not say yes. Well I will imagine you are saying so. . . .

New York July 13 1861

My Ever Dear & Darling Friend

[. . .] Mr. Lee inform you that I look great deal better now fatter nobody see but himself for some of my clothes intirely to big for me I must have lost some of my flesh you will see as you say when I come on this will I hope be soon well my Dearest I am sitting quite alone Thinking of the past and present and dreaming of the future wondering if the blank will be filled with the joys or sorrows of this checkered life oh my Darling[. . . .]

I must tell you about last Sunday Mother Uncle is Dead he was buried last Thursday A.M. the Family of course did not attend Church so Mother said to us girls that we must go up Sunday P.M. see the corpse we had some 20 min walk before we got to the cars and then tis a hour ride up there we started from the house at 6 o'clock and got there at 8 o'clock so we did not stay very long they when come to take the cars to come home it was so full we could not get in so Warwick this is Selina brother he said to us let us walk little ways up and perhaps we can get in the nexe so we kept walking it was beautiful ever cars past was just as full as the first if I spoke of you once half doz times to selina wishing you was with us I would have enjoyed much better then I did[. . . .] Good bye until the nexe time your Dearest

Addie

New York July 14 1861
Sunday A.M. 11 o'clock

My Dear & Dearest Rebecca

As tis a rainy Day and do not feel very well so I did not attend church I have been reading in the Bible first chapter first book of Samuel and I stop reading I have been in a deep revirer about you and wondering if it was raining in Hartford or not. Yesterday I was very busy I never got done sewing until eleven last night one consolation I have that I will have some rest nexe month if I live that long Mrs. Nott was telling me before I left that when I come in they had some sewing for me to do for her but my Darling I think she will not have it done by me I dont expect to take a needle in my hand after I leave to make a visit in Hartford (unless necessity compell me to so) Rebecca the Shilo Church & the St. Phill Church[2] had a picnic last Tuesday I did not go although I had several invitations they say they had beautiful time they injoyed themselves very much there going to be a private one two week from now some young ladies are getting it up I'm not going to that either I'm home from Monday untill Sunday then I manage to get to Church as a duty who as I have a love for the Church. Dear Rebecca we have a minister in the house with us he is a good man he call me his Daughter Addie he think everything of me but the . . . all he be blind he can see a very little so last Thursday I went to church to hear him I was very much delighted to hear him I had the pleasure of leading him home his church is in the same St. I live in only two St. above make it pleasant O I forgot he is a Baptist minister[. . . .]

The first explicit mention of the Civil War occurs in the following letter. Addie is probably referring to a series of small battles that occurred on June 3 and July 13, which resulted in the creation of West Virginia as a state loyal to the Union.

We also get a sense of the economic hardships faced by the black community during these years and of the function of the churches as not only spiritual and political centers but also the primary location of social interaction. In addition, Addie is an observer of, if not a participant in, black street culture. In the letters that follow, we learn something of her highly critical views of this aspect of her community.

New York July 22 1861

My Most Darling Friend

Only to think there is only 17 days when I will able to be imbrace in your loving arms I hope once more seem I can hardly have patience to wait that limited time My Dear there is going to be a picinic nexe week I would give any thing if you was only here to attend too for I know you would be delighted they have very nice picnic here some of the young ladies are getting it up every ladies that goes take something and then the Gentlemen are toss 50 cts pieces Mother want me to go and so I have partly promise her I will go she says she will not go without me she think it tis on account of Mr. Lee I told her she was sadly mistaken so rather to have any one think that I will go in spite of everything[. . . .] My Dear our work is getting stuck I'm very glad for Im very tired how is your Ma's work is she just as busy as ever?

They was a young Col girl was taken up last Tuesday for being intoxicated I dont think she hardly could be over 17 years old it was directly opposite us she laid flat on the work and she . . . there was two or three hard to get in front of her to keep her clothes down in fact the st was in excitement all day must there was four taken up & three was white do you blame me my darling not wanting to live in New York.

I see by the papers that they have commence to fighting I'm very glad of it. It make time very dull here Father restaurant is not doing anything it worry Mother very much for she has very large Family I told her the other day that I would go to Hartford to live again no indeed I should now I'm here with her again I shall stay she says I'm just the same to her as if I was her own Child all I have to say I hope she will continue to think so do not mention what I have pen here will you my love for its Family affairs.

What beautiful moonlight evenings we are having I sometimes sit by the winder and wonder what you are doing whether you are thinking of me there or not I dont think we have together injoyed many moonlight evenings have we? if we have not I hope will take time Rebecca when I think of it I will tell you when I'm coming on it be the 8 of Aug it will be on Thursday or Friday AM you will meet the boat . . . do to come for I will be looking for you with all the eyes that I got in my head they are not good for much now[. . . .]

New York July 28 1861
Monday 4 A.M.

My own Darling Friend

[. . .] I only attend Church in the A.M. Mother has went & also Father the latter has not attend church before in two or three years & Mother but once since I have been home I suppose you are wondering the reason I did not go well I will tell you the youngest of us had a boil on his forehead he was not a fit subject to attend church so I staid home Selina she did not go in the A.M. our church is close until the first Sunday in September then it will be open again it give chance all those want recreations I for one of the number I intend to take it too I will mention it again I'm coming the 8 Aug. so on Friday A.M. I will expect you down to the boat do not fail coming by all means you cant imagine how much I want to see you my loving Friend[. . . .]

I ever remain the same Affec & loving Addie except one sweat kiss from her truly <u>love</u> thee Dearly

Addie

During a time when many free blacks were somewhat cautious about their movements for fear of being taken for slaves or kidnapped and sold into slavery, Addie, Rebecca, and their peers nonetheless seemed to travel quite freely throughout the Northeast. For Rebecca and her sister Bell, travel was primarily linked to their social and familial network; they visited friends and relatives in New York, Philadelphia, and Boston. While Addie traveled socially as well, most of her travel was linked to work or a search for employment opportunity.

Addie's letters following her visits with Rebecca in Hartford relay a sense of the interactions between the two women. The two friends have been writing now for two years.

New York Aug. 16 1861

My Dearest & most Affec Friend

I thought before going to my work I would pen a few lines to my Darling Rebecca wish is Dearer to me then any thing on this earth. I arrived here safe but with a very bad headache & not much better

43

now I got here at 20 min. of 11 o'clock and went to sewing at half past 11 and sew until 12 at night I sew until I almost fainted. I was so sick that Selina had to undress me[. . . .] Mr. Lee paid the utmost attention to me he come home with me and say he going to call Tuesday to see me Dear Rebecca it was kind chilly so I wore your sack home I will send it nexe week with Mrs. Nott things will that do my love

O my Dear will you Remember my Rubbers dont you let her have them

Mother received me very lovingly more so then I wonder her for it may not last long what do you say about Selina also in fact all the family Ive got a new name they all call me sis excuse this short letter for I hardly know what I am doing my head pains me very bad I have got a dress to make by to night so do not think hard me writing this letter.

from your ever

Dear and loving Addie

PS Mother send her love to your Mo would like to see her very much I will write a letter to you soon this only a note Addie

except a sweat kiss

Hartford Aug. 31 1861

My Dear Friend

Im now going to comply to your request you would like to know my feelings toward you when I come here it seems strange that you should ask such a question did you think that I did not <u>love</u> you as much as I profess or what was it? it was not that my <u>love</u> you remember the day I come up on the P.M. I come over to your house or in the eve you come home with me you know the conversations we had I felt hurt about it I did not expected it I try to forget it as you ask me to do but ever time I come near you I thought of it and thought perhaps you did and that make me feel as I did you spoke in the manner that you could not trust me out of your site for this I would do most anything if I did not think you would hear of it my Darling that not so for I'm not ashamed to do anything that un proper in your site or out of your site Dear Rebecca the love I have you I will commit that I was rather in a hurry in everything you know my love you are better offense to young man and you know you dont care to have any one as go with me and course I dont feel that fear now to come to you I tell you how I feel towards you that is this like a Child would feel toward a Mother how has forbidden Gentlemen to go with her Daughter and she <u>loves</u> her <u>Mother</u> to that extent that you dont want to displease and still she would like to have her say in that line and sometimes when I think of it all most here for my hearts. Dear Rebecca no ones know the love I have for you I have tried to tell you but have not Rebecca there is one thing no <u>one</u> on the face of this earth that love any more than I do and you are the only that I love or ever try to love nobody will come between us in love if they do anything else the one thing that I do truly wish from the bottom of my <u>heart</u> that you could to talk free with me in everything I must close this

hoping to see you
soon from you Dearest
and Devoted Addie

Rebecca was not the only Primus daughter with whom Addie had a close friendship. Rebecca's vivacious younger sister Bell visited Addie in the fall of 1861. The New York household welcomes her into their extended family and entertains her with a whirlwind of social activity.

New York Sept. 17 1861

My Darling & most Noble Friend

My thought been upon you all this day I would like to see you very much its only one thing keep me that is money it tis 11 o'clock I supose you are sleeping while I'm pening a few lines to you Bell she ingage in looking out of the window would you like to know what she is looking at my <u>love</u> well I will tell you across the street from us a set of col people playing and dancing there is quite a mob gathered around them it no wonder that our <u>race</u> is so degraded since Ive been in NY and get to thinking and see the actions of our people I wish that I did not belongs to the race but it cant be help now so I will have to make the best of it. I with the rest of the Family was delighted to see Bell she bout got in so late that we had gave her up and much disappointed about half past 2 o'clock she made her appearance <u>O my Dear my Dear Rebecca</u> I must thank you for the loaf of B you send me it was splendid and we had it that night for

tea this eve Bell and my sister and I went to market then we return
home with our things and then went to the shoemakers and then
from there made a call and also heard mass about 11 we retire for the
night on Sunday all day attend church in the eve we made call again
and then we left there and took a long walk & we felt quite tired
when we return home Monday we went over to Jersey city and call
to Miss Kninles school she was very much please to see Bell and also
surprise she has a very nice little school she took us and made a call
on one of her Friends we expect to go again this week we left home
half past 10 and got back at 6½ today we was to go to Barnum's but
we disappointed on account of the rain and defer it untill Saturday
Bell has little romance to tell you about today we are invited to Mrs.
Peterson and think some thing of going tomorrow Thursday we are
going to the Central Park if it pleasant four of us in company we
have not got anything for Friday as yet that day look our for it self
we are gig up to Father saloon all of the Friends are very much
please with Bell think she is very fine young Lady Selina is delighted
with her as well as myself. Well my Dearest Friend it growing late
and B is sleeping finally and I must be doing the same so I must
bring this to a close my bidding you kind and gentle good night your
for Ever   Addie

Addie's attitude toward the men in her life fluctuates. At times she is
ambivalent about them and about marriage as well. Her primary emotional relationship is with Rebecca, though she does not discount the
possibility of marriage. In this way she is much like the middle-class
white women described by scholars such as Carroll Smith-Rosenberg
and Lillian Faderman.

New York Sept. 25 1861

My Darling Friend
    [. . .] All this day I allmost felt like shedding tear I will my Dear
inform you few of my <u>thoughts</u> do you ever think that we will live
together anymore or live within two or three miles of each other is it
possible that we are not able to clasp each other in our arm but once
a year O my Dear Dear Rebecca must it be so never when I think of

it make me unhappy. Rebecca within a year if thers no change I will make one perhaps it will displease you very much for I must be near you if possible I was alone all day the Children goes to school and mother went down to see Grandma how I wish that you was here Der Rebecca Mr. Lee comes here yet to see me Mother says if she was in his place and I treat her so she would never come any more to see me I dont see what it tis about me that he can give me up there is a another Gent in love with me has been here three evenings this week my old Lover when he get a chance he tis with me two out of the three what will I do? I appeal to you for advice will you not give it me love dont say no for you are the only one I look up to my Friend I sometime think strongly of getting married sometime I think and see things it make me feel unhappy if I was only near you I could embrace all to you well my Darling I will not say any about this is geting quite late and I must prepare for retiring for the night Rebecca I miss Bell very much I felt very lonesome without her excellent company I enjoyed myself very much the only fault I found rest of the Family was that she did not stay long enough we did not get around half. Did she tell you about her sleeping party we went to? When I thinks of it I have to laugh there was considerable romance in Bell visit here NY I dont thats forget well Rebecca I'm getting tired so I must close by bidding a sweet good night

    your loving Friend
    Addie

The circumstances leading to Addie's pessimistic view of men are not clear, but she is very emphatic here.

New York Scpt. 28 1861

My Loved Friend

    I have got up rather early this A.M. breakfast is not quite ready so I thought Id pen a few lines to you.

    [. . .] Mrs. Nott told me the day I left Hartford that Fred thought a great deal of me I thought she was joking but there was a Lady there at the same time she said it was so what has he done with himself H F she will not like it all will she my Friend but my part I

47

have no faith in no man what they say goes in one ear and comes out the other sometimes when I get to thinking about different things in particular the fact I almost <u>hate</u> the <u>site</u> of a <u>man</u> I wish that I could talk to you as freely I think on different subject are we still going to remain so is there never going to be any change with either one us well I'm getting hungre I tell you here comes one of my little Brother so I must go now good morning my Darling untill you hear from again[. . . .]

New York Sept. 29 1861

My Darling Friend

Ive just come from downstairs from a harghty laugh I will tell what occur this P.M. I went to church when it was out Mr. Jacobs escorted me home when I got to the door I ask him if he would could come in he said no that he would call in the eve. The folk say that he comes to see me I tell them to the contrary. Selina she did not expected her Lover so she went to her room to write to him. I came up to put the Children to bed then I went to reveling I got tired then threw myself on the bed thinking of my beloved Friend wondering what was she doing at that present moments while in that deep reverie I fell a sleep. I got up in a little while and found that I was in the dark so I went downstairs and found Mr. Jacobs there Mother call me in the parlo. Mo left. I had to entertain the Gent, while in deep conversation there came a ring at the door so I went to who should it be but Selina Lover then the four of us. I did not feel like seeing company for I did not feel very well I dreadful cold in my head. After Mr. M come in Mr. J would not talk any you know I'm no great talker so there we to set so when it got 9 o'clock that he would go Selina was provoke about it half past nine he sit and ten he still. I threw out as many hints as I could and still he never took them. I got up went out of the room and staid out quite a while. Grandma went in to bid them good night so about half past ten he start off. I was so glad so Selina come in the room and was telling Mother what I said to him. My Darling Friend have you been there so if you have then you can feel for me.

How I wish to be in Hartford this P.M. coming from Church remind me of when I was there when you and me would be return-ing from Church having you whisper in my ears sweet words or ask-

48

ing what is the matter with you my Dear girl I have no one to day
that I'm called by sweet and Affectionate words but they not you all
day yesterday and even last night I wishing that I was in your loving
arms and you would be imprinting sweat kisses[. . . .] I must bring
this to a close for it tis 11 o'clock I must soon retire for the night prepare to get up tomorrow A.M. early so good night my sweet Friend
and except one fond kiss

Believed me to be your most Dear and Near Friend   Addie

Though Addie has been very forthright about her emotional connection
to Rebecca, her dream of "other things" is one of the first hints of the
truly erotic nature of their relationship.

New York Oct. 2 1861

My Beloved Rebecca

I have just put the Children to bed and mother got company and
I dont care much about going down I thought I would pen a few
lines to you my Darling I rec those things by Mr. Lee that cake is
pleasant I cut it last night I gave all a taste of it. They was delighted
with it you thought it was little to sweet but it was just right you
know that you never could get anything to sweet for me[. . . .] I'm
very much oblige to you for the I have had the headache for the last
two or three weeks all of them here is about crazy to see you and get
aquainted with you personal O Dear Im looking forward to the time
if it should arrive well I live in hopes every A.M. I think it one day
less I dreampt of you last night I thought I was seting on your lap
with my head on your bosom other things connected with it. I will
not tell you at present. When I wake up in the night and found it was
all a dream I was so disappointed.

[. . .] My Dear Dear Friend do you think that my feelings are
change <u>God</u> knows there are not only will you think so only will you
harbor such thoughts and feelings toward me only will you not forgive and forget what I said and done when I was there last summer if
ever I done anything in my life that I deeply repent it was what I
done and said while I was with you you will ever have that against
me Oh Heavens forbid that you should my Dearest Friend will you

49

not forgive and forget do do please I have done wrong and if anything ungrateful that was My Dear Im not perfect why will you be so
hard I have read your letter several times I have shed tears and bitter
[. . .] Dear Rebecca have I not always be candid with you if not I
will for the future Dear Rebecca may I ask you to forgive and forget
your Friend Addie

New York Nov. 14 1861

My Ever Dear Friend
    [. . .] Week before last Selina came home very lively keep us a
laughing for a great while so in the mean time she said she had some
letters to write so she ask Mother to give her some money to buy
some paper so she says Addie dont you want to go with me well I
said yes so I went up stairs to get my things to put on she came up
behind me I seen she had something in hands she began to undress
her self I said what are you doing you will see well I did see she had
on Mr. Brooke clothes and was going out with them she wanted to
fool the family we went a little way then came back I went in the
house they had mentioned something of the kind for Aunt Chat had
come up stairs and found her clothes on the floor and other thing
she could not change her voice so she did not have as much fun as
she anticipated Mrs. Scott would not believe it was her.
    [. . .] Rebecca there is a very rich widower here the other night
he gave the society in the church $20 what do you think of that so
nexe week is thanksgiving Mother is going to have a dinner
party[. . . .] I'm very oblige to you for that skirt in what way can I
ever repay you for your kindness you must give my love to your
mother Aunt and the rest of the Friend[. . .] except one sweat kiss
from your loving Addie

Free black communities throughout the country established private
schools that were often funded by their wealthier members. Thus far,
records of Primus's Hartford school have not been located.

New York Dec. [n.d.] 1861

My Dear & Devoted Friend
    Its just one week to day since I rec your kind and Affec letter that

day I was very sick I think a part of it was cause of my anxiety about yours I thought you was sick in fact I had all kind of imaginary thoughts at present I feel quite well both in body and mind. I see you still have your private school have you descend down yet with your pupils I often wish that I could take a birds eye view at you especially when your are playing some of my favorites. I will tell you how I spend Thanksgiving we did expect company they disappointed us we expected father he did not come we had dinner at 4 o'clock after that Mother & Mr. B went up in the parlor Mrs. Scott went to her room the Children went out in the st Selina staid down by a good fire and I having a pleasant Chit Chat and I of course was talking of you then we was disturb by a ring at the door it was Mr. Burton called to see if B would go out with him Mother & B Selina & Mr. Burton went to the academy of music they was very much please they wish me to go but I believe I had made up my mind through the day to write to you in the evening after all[. . . .] Now my Darling you remember what you said at the closing of your as you wish to let it rest there all I will still love you tenderly and truly give my love to all believed me to remain your lovingly

    Addie Brown

PS please to excuse this letter the mistake and writing

New York Dec. 8 1861

My Dearest & Affec Friend

    I seat myself with pleasing task in writing a few lines to the object of my thoughts. I've not attend church today Mother has been sick all or part of the family has remain home to day I have bent over your written gems of thought I have sighed and wish that I could feel your warm hand clasp my own to look into the depths of your eyes and hear your voice how I long to be embrace once more in your loving arms but it will be all in vain. Selina Lover is here this eve for the first time within three week he has been very sick he ought not to be out now I suppose he could not stay away any longer love is a great thing one day last week I went to the Doctor for Mrs. Scott & on my way there I met Mr. Lee he was very polite indeed its the first time I seen him since I gave him his dismissal[. . . .] I will have to stop now my light is given out and also time that I had retire here is one or two verse of poetry I want to pen I must hurry

ALONE

Thou art not with me and the hours
All wearily go flitting by
A gloom is on my heart and brow
That seeks relief in many sigh

I dare not dwell upon the past
Those joyous hours that knew not pain
I dare not ask the coming years
If we shall ever meet again

I only know thou art not here
And life has lost its sweetness to me
And though my lips may wear a smile
My heart is sad and all alone

now my Dear Rebecca I must bid you a kind good night

One of the great strengths of these letters is the manner in which they push aside the veil that covers much of nineteenth-century black life. Here, in this instance of black family traditions that have remained undocumented, we witness a festive Christmas celebration that is probably not too different from that of white Victorian households.

New York Dec. 25 1861

My Dearest & Devoted Friend

I suppose you think its time that you had ans to you very kind and interesting letter when I rec yours I was very sick I had been so for two or three days you know that I inform you in my last of having a cold it would not leave me untill it put me in my bed I suffer very much O Dear Rebecca how I did miss you one night I felt very bad I had such excruciating pains all over me and then thinking of you I cried so that Aunt Chat gave me a scolding she thought I would make myself worse. At present I feel somewhat better I spoke of Aunt Chat she has been home one week yesterday when she came she found us in bed Selina and I are so disappointed she is not going to remain this winter to home just hear me at home she going to sea again I believed she will get $45 a month don't you think that a great deal? I sometime wish it was me I think she will do well if she only be saving with it not spend on this that dont think her much she going to be little more saving for the future O hear she is asking me who I am writing to I have told she says bless her dear heart tell her I wish her a Merry Christmas and happy New Year and hope you will live to see many more she think of you often you are in her dreams & thought she had a beautiful time in Hudson if you had of been there you would of injoyed yourself very much what she let me see I forget the last is this except a kiss she is a sweat girl. I believed that all.

Now Dear Rebecca how did you spend Christmas well I hope I will tell you how I spend mine I went to church they thought if I was to wrap myself up warm and walk slow that I could it was extremely cold. All the family went there was 10 of us quite a number dont you think so? When church was out the Sunday school had a festival they had a tree & presents for all the scholars two or three made some remark Aunt Chat left for any of us, when we got home it was 5 o'clock and she had dinner for us. Selina had her Friend Rebecca and also her Lover mother had a Christmas tree none of us was allowed to go in the parlor about five minutes before 7 we miss Mother & Mr. B of course at 7 they open the doors and the parlor did look beautiful they had the tree all lit up and all the lamps they could find you ought of seen our Children they did not know what to make of it. If it will be agreeable I will tell you about the present there was one for each one of us on the tree father had a dressing gown & smoking cap and pair of slippers Mother a net for her hair and a lamp mat Mrs. Scott a pair of stocking and handkerchief Aunt Chat a hood Ally and Warwick a pair of skates Johnny a suit of clothes Jon & Walter a suit of soldier clothes and Selina a dress I also got one. Mr. & Mrs. Alston came in to see the tree about 9 there was four young Ladies came there were fine Gentlemen they staid untill 12 we had Egg nog and cake we had very nice time Mother and the rest of the family anticipate having a very nice time New year day that a great calling day with the Gents you know what I do if I had money of course no you dont well I would come and spend that day with you for I would injoy myself much better in your society then home O Dear how do want to see you I must try & come up to Hartford this winter I often wish Aunt Chat would say Addie

53

don't you want to go to Hartford I would say I guess I would then we'd go well I may wish she often speak of you and said she would like to see you. I'm going to tell you little more news do not mention it to any one Mrs. Hector has left her Husband she is staying nexe door she come in to see me Friday Angeline going out to [. . .] Mrs. H say of her Husband do differently by her she will live with him again not untill he does both of them have made up there mind never to go on a boat again I think they will be very much indeed by the community dont you think so well my dear my head is aching so I must close this by wishing you a merry Christmas and a very happy New Year

for I am as ever your Loving

Addie

PS please to give my love to the family to your Aunt Emily and a kiss how I would like to see her

Addie

Chapter Four

"Call you my sister"

1862–1864

ADDIE'S first letter of the new year finds her still in New York, living with the Jacksons. Here, she paints a portrait of domesticity. Her brother Ally reads a book as she writes by the fire. However Addie learned to read, in this she is clearly exceptional among her peers. From now on, she will begin to write more about her reading to Rebecca.

Ally's book is probably *The Lamp and the Lantern, or Light for the Tent and Traveler,* by James Hamilton. Published in 1853, this text was about the important influence of the Bible on the lives of young men.

Although these are personal letters, they give us a sense of the way the Civil War affected New York's black community. By the fall of 1862, Addie has moved to Hartford, and there are fewer letters between herself and Rebecca.

New York Sun. Jan. 10, 1862

My Dearly & Beloved Friend

It is a very gloomy day it has been rainy all the a.m. now it is stop I have been thinking of you and wondering what you are about well I will imagine you with pupils around you and also giving them good instructions I guess by this time they all very fond of you. I sometime wish that I was a school girl again for this one reason so that I could be under you charge then I could be with the <u>object of my affections daily</u> and hourly while now I'm diprive of it to day, My <u>love</u> I have been very unhappy you say to yourself what is the cause of it. I was going to say I hardly know myself but that not so. Rebecca I want to see you very much I think of you daily & dream of you nightly sometime they are pleasant ones then again unpleasant I hinted to mother about going to Hartford on some Saturday and stay until Monday but she will not take the hint and one thing the business is very dull here [. . .] my Dear I felt very bad when I read your letter you spoking of writing me with a severe headach you know I would pity a day with headach for I know it is. My darling I want ask you one favor, I do not know weather you will grant are not I is to this do not write to me when you in any pain no matter were.

[. . .] My brother Ally he his sitting along side me reading a book called the Lamp lighty our cat laying on the rug sleeping Aunt Chat she is down stairs sewing and geting dinner at the same time I wish dinner was ready I feel somewhat hungre[. . . .]

I seem to love thee more and more now my dear I must go the fire in the front room is gone out so I must go make it up for the evening some one be coming in so good by my loving Friend I untill you here from me again yours truly

Addie

Addie refers to Barnum's American Museum, founded by P. T. Barnum in 1840 and located at the intersection of Park Row and Broadway. Throughout the 1860s, the popular venue was known for "exhibits, performances and sensational attractions." Among these were the Siamese Twins and the "Man Monkey"—William Henry Johnson, an eighteen-year-old black dwarf who was billed as the "missing link" and referred to in the press as a "cross between a nigger and a baboon."[1]

New York Jan. 12, 1862

My dear Friend

The rain is keeping me from church not only me but the rest of the family it make me feel sad for I have become a teacher in the Sunday school. I do not care about missing any Sun Although I'm confident that my class will not be there not only the rain but it dreadfull walking the walks is just like sheets of ice. I will inform you how we spend the last day of the old year & the first of the new

[. . .] in the eve a gent call to see us and about 10 oclock we had a oyster supper then after supper which about 11 one part of the family went in the parlor while the other clean up the room then we sing just is the old year was bidding farwell to us all we sing a hym and then after we wish a happy New years to each other and retire.

[. . .] New Year day mother kept a open house we had 31 calls. Among them was Mr. Lee about 2 P.M. Aunt C & Selina & I went to the church & see a marriage the bride did look beautiful her dress was white lace flower as for the bride maid I did not admired her very much there was a great many out to witness the affair. I made Selina laugh Mr. McNeil gave her his likeness so she had it in her bossom so I told her take it up to Mr. Alston and ask him to marry them he said she invited original the eve we was all very tired as for myself I was heart sick we could not we retired for there some one coming in out when there was no one there mother would take me sofa Selina & I the other Grand M the rocking chair. Aunt C [look at] the door everytime the bell rang each one would spring up as if something was after us. I do not know what the people thought as for mother she went to sleep while they was here so about 1 o'clock we all retire so the nexe day Aunt C & I took the children & went to Barnums they was delighted they never been before.

The first winter of the Civil War was a time of economic hardship and ill health for the Jackson household. Consequently, Addie found herself with an extra-heavy workload and little money. Her discussion of the social events organized by her community—events that will raise money and collect clothing for the "contraband"—offer a glimpse of the community's war efforts.

Significantly, Addie mentions a committee to raise funds for an orphan asylum. By 1863, New York's Colored Orphan Asylum had been burned down in the Civil War draft riot, when economic competition between white immigrants fearful of job competition from free blacks exploded in fits of violence in which one hundred people were killed. Addie left New York prior to the riot.

New York Sun. [Jan.] 14, 1862

My Dearest Friend

I suppose you looking forward to you letter you will see that I have commence it. Sickness has prevail Aunt C is very sick the Dr tends her I have just come from upstairs giving her medicine. Father is also home sick. He his been home for two or three days the Dr. think he his getting a tumor in his breast he think his has been hurt some way. I feel very sorry although he is no relation but I feel near to him he his very kind to me and I know he love me as the same as his own and sometime he reprimand me not loving him as not being his child. I can not as I would like I stood alone in this family. He is a fine noble man he has many fine quality. He has few that his wife knows not of perhaps do not want to know them now I must a few moments to go and give A.C. her medicine she take it every hour.

Here I'm again I have got two fulltime. Walter is crying or was with earache I have got them both quiet. For the last week its been regular hospital. I bid the headache I will not promise that I will write long as I feel somewhat tired I have been runing all day. Selina is home for a day or two now she is writing to her particular friend that remind me of something. Mr. Lee called this week. Mr. Burns-well and his friend Mr. Furnace are getting a surprise party going to have it tomorrow eve also mother and few of her friends going to get up Calico Ball for she benefit of the [?] assylum. Many of the sol-diers that use to be ingage in the assylum are withdrawn some body must keep it up or try to I hope they will. Well my love I must close it getting late you must give my love to Aunt and tell her I think of her often & kiss her quit often and often wish that it was her herself[. . . .]

New York Jan. 30, 1862

My Dearly Beloved Rebecca

Just eight days to day since I rec your kind interesting Epistle you must excuse me for keeping you waiting so long for a ans I have been very busy indeed Aunt Chaty has been very sick we was little wor-ried about her you remember her room she was sick in there I attend her every hour in the day I had to give her the medicine one or two night I was a wake with her. Mother says she was not able to go up and down stairs I was completely wore out for I had to take the bulk of the work I'm almost sick I do not mean bodily sickness Mother has not any work and father business is very dull M is sometime so disagreeable there is no living with her I often wish that I never come to NY.

[. . .] Aunt Chaty she is much better so much so that she is down and very livly she is just left me she wish to know what is the matter with me and I only gave her was a kiss[. . . .] I will inform of the news the first thing mother feel so deep by interested in the contraband that she propose giving a calico ball. They going to have it the [?] of Feb. There is ladies engage in it after the ball they or going to give the dresses to them and the money is left is to go towards purchasing books and slates there is a great many is going those that never attend ball are going perhaps I will go I would like to see how they will look was one night befor last Mrs. Lisa Williams was there. Her dress was white silk and white lace of over it and look up. They was young lady went that her mother was again it so she had her sister to lay her things out the day her bedroom is up stairs so she her mother good night and her mother of course thing she had retire for the night instead of that she went to dress she had a white dress double skirt and the slop one had 8 rows of velvet and the stop one was in print and every part had a velvet bow. Selina saw her said look beautiful. Rebecca I was surprise to here that she would do such a thing or to deceived her own dear mother. I could not do so if I wanted to go I would have told that I was going and went out before her every body not like you. The ladies also making arangement for a fair for the orphan assylum. They think they will have it in May. Mother also in committee she will now live in the St. She will have something to called her out daily.

O my Darling I read a book called Women Friendship. It was a book I wish that I could send it to you for to read it dos not belong to me or even to the family the author of it is Grace Aguilar I will give you little of it.

[Addie quotes extensively, without quotation marks, from the novel.]

Friendship demands quality of station true affections devoid of selfisness beware dear Florence I fear this warm attachment must end in disappointment fully as I can sympathize in its present happiness was the warning address of Mrs. Leslie to animated girl who on the receipt of a note and its rapid perusal had bounded towards her mother with an exclamation of irrepressible joy. disappointment dearest mother how can that be? was the eager reply because friendship even more than love demands equality of station friends cannot be to each other what they ought to be if the rank of one party be among the noble of the land that of the other lowly as your own[. . . .]

Now my fond friend, I must close for the fire is about out and Selina want to go to bed so good night.

Grace Aguilar's *Women's Friendships,* published in 1850, tells the story of Lady Ida, an aristocrat, and the middle-class Florence. The friendship suffers a blow when Lady Ida marries and Florence meets with misfortune. The two reestablish their friendship when Florence learns of her noble birth. Surely Addie was reminded of the differences in class and education between herself and Rebecca. Perhaps this accounts for the change in the letters of 1862. Addie begins to write much more of what she is reading as well as of neighborhood events and the news.

In the letter that follows, Addie also gives her reasons for wanting to marry. Neither romance nor love comes before the desire for economic and emotional security.

Henry Highland Garnet was a famous African American minister and abolitionist.

The Golden Legacy: A Story of Life's Phases was written by Mrs. H. J. Moore and published in 1856.

New York Feb. 23, 1862

Darling my own Dear Friend

I have again perruse you sweat and affec loving e[pistle] it seem to me it made every nerve vibrate in me I could not express the feeling. You spoke of my unexpected visit last Friday my Darling I dont that purposely I must say I was highly paid for doing so.

[. . .] You spoke of injoying my society any length of time all gone I dont agree with you there for if I live long enough I expect many many hour with you and alone.

[. . .] Loved one I want to ask you one question—that is will you not look at my marrying in a different light then you do love me my Darlin? I'm here with mother perhaps I see you about three time in a year happy more time unhappy I will get my money regular for two or three week and then iregular. What would you rather see me do have one that truly <u>love</u> me that would give me and or give him up and remain in this home? O could live with you or even be with you parts of the day. I would never Rebecca do not feel thus perhaps it may all for the best now think it over it and tell me weather you agree with me or not now my Dearest I will bring this subject to a close[. . . .]

Last eve I went to a concert it was given in our church it was this first annual one it was given by SS they done well they was a little girl I dont think that she was much larger then Walter and she sing beautiful [?] My Dear the Church was full some of the people had to stand up it seems to me that our people are very neglegance attending church but when ever any thing going they manage to get out on Sunday the nexe can get out nexe week there is going to be one at Mr. Garnet church had a surprise party to his house a $100 in provision and $42 in money dont you think that doing well? Mr. G has a great many friends both white and Col [. . . .]

My Dear Rebecca did you ever read a book called the <u>Golden Legacy</u>? O that was a beautiful book I have nothing to read just yet but I will soon find something tell Bell that the young ladies are get-ing up they surprise party Selina was speaking of extending invita-tion to her the are getting up sooner then they expect for one of the young ladies is going away her family are going to move to Phila. they feel very bad about leaving NY now my Dear I must tell you what Aunt Chat says and bring my epistle to a close. She was very glad to hear that you was well and the rest of the family she would like to see you very much as for her health its miserable she says that sometime she think that she not long for this world I cant remember the rest so you wont care will you my love give my love to your mother and the rest of the family except a sweet kiss from you Ever Dear and Devoted

Addie
PS my Dearest I feel this moment if I could throw my arm around you neck and lay until my soul was in heaven

Addie

The following reference by Addie to "coloured people time" refers to a humorous colloquialism for habitual lateness that is used to explain black people's relationship to industrialized notions of time.

New York Mar. 5, 1862

My Ever Dear & Darling Friend

I have a few moments to spare so I thought I would pen a few thoughts to the <u>object of my affections</u> I rec your sweet and interesting epistle this P.M. I have already perruse it contents three times I will not promise if three times be all we have been very busy to day the washing was not on Monday.

The Undine Club had there party Mon Eve the Club consist of five young ladies Miss Buce & Parker & Bowers Duplaycy & Selina all the ladies bought something and the gentleman was taxed 50cts they had three pieces of music. I guess they was about fifty here it was a very stormy night the rain just poured down I made Selina very angre I told her I would not be home to the party I did not care about it the inmates of the house on Selina side thought I was not treating her right so keep peace I remain at home the ladies was looking destine Gay.

[. . .] Rebecca I have taken a sever[e] cold the doors was all open and I had on a low neck dress it seem lately I take cold very easy. My Dear my old Lover was here that eve after the company had dispuse [disperse] father was teasing me and said he was going to tell Mr. Lee about him and I my Darling can I help if the gentleman will pay me attention.

Now my Dearest I must make an apology for Selina she intended to send a note to Bell for the party she had so much to do and not thinking they would have it so soon thought she would have plenty of time just like coloured people time[. . . .] is Buce and her mother family going to move to Phila. nexe week the girls all feel very bad she is one of the gayest of the gay my Dear if you have told Bell about it please to Bell how she came not to receive her invitation my Darling I suppose you think that enough of that now my Love I must rest my pen for the night I have cough so much that my headache me very bad so I will bid you a sweet and gentle good night O that I could a sweet kiss and fond imbrace

The following letter is from Charity A. Jackson, the Aunt Chaty of Addie's letters. It reveals an alternative description of Addie's attraction and desire for her suitor, Mr. Lee.

New York Mar. 1862

Dear Rebecca

I take this opportunity write these few lines to you hoping you are well which leave me at present give my love to your mother and father and sisters and brother I do not know them but I take the liberty of doing so Dear Rebecca I wish that you were here to see Addie she look so sad and melencahly she look as if she lost all her friends she make me feel very sad I often take you footstep and Mr. Lee to comfort her I dont know what he would do without Addie has been very sich I to take the best of care for your sake and Mr. Lee she rec two letters from Mr. Lee and I never seen anyone so overjoyed as she was I wish you had of been a witch and been at the window you say you do not know what love is Addie does I can assure I would have written to you before but I did not know weather it would be except it everytime. Addie rec you letter she said you send your love to me so I take that pleasure of writing a few lines to you no more at present I remain your affectionate friend

Charity A Jackson

Please to ans this when you write to my Dear Addie.

[n.d.]

I'm like a bad penny my time has not come yet O Rebecca its a beautiful day I would like to go to church they I had better remain home. I rec two letters from Mr Lee they both came at once he is very well he think he will remain in Key West two or three months and then they going to Mobile, He inquired very particular for your health and what do you think he wants to know what do you think of me tramp over his <u>heart</u>? Weather you approve of it are not. He write very nice letter he said it will not be long before he will return and make me his wife. He said that he his met with great many ladies since he is begone but none compare with his sweet Addie he says his love is stronger then ever. Dear Rebecca I never shall love any person as I do you[. . . .]

Dear Rebecca do not say anything about mother was angre because I was sick she expect to go to the Old Fellow Ball and she afraid she would not get her dress in time. Mother say she hardly can get along time is so hard but is alway find money when she want to go ball and party. She went out last eve brought a white dress she is going to have double skirt and loop up rises and gay to wear a black lace cape and her head to be dress [by] hairdressers. But I must tell you what Grandma said that mother was going head long to the dead while she was going she go looking right for him that was a great expression to make about a child I do not know what the world is coming to. Aunt Chat was going so she has made up her mind to remain in home with her sweet Addie so she says[. . . .]

I remain your Ever Dear and
Devoted   Addie
Please to excuse this letter.

The sentiments of the following letters are Addie's, but the language clearly is not. Perhaps in her efforts toward self-improvement she has either had someone write them for her or copied them from one of the many books she was reading. The book Addie mentions is *Practical Christianity: A Treatise Specially Designed for Young Men* by John S. C. Abbott (1862).

New York Mar. 16, 1862
My Ever Darling Rebecca
[. . .] <u>Dear Friend</u> how perfectly still how hushed is all around but for the heavy breathing of those sunk in deep slumber there is no object in all creation accessible to human eyes half so calculated to life the soul from earth as the moon and sky at night well my Darling I suppose you think enough of escputiate [expatiate] about the moon. I am not sleepy so I thought pen a few thought while I think of it last Sunday P.M. I was reading a book called the <u>Practical Christianity</u> it is a beautiful book Mrs. Scott is reading it now if you have no objection I will give you little idea of it.
"What is it to be Christian several young men were one evening sitting around the fire in a college room when the conversation

turned upon the subject of religion one of the young men said perhaps with unintentional exaggeration but with sincerity 'if I could by
having my right arm cut off be sure that I was a Christian I would
submit to the operation unhesitatingly I have often tried to be a
Christian but in vain I shall not try any more.' "

    My Dear dont you know there are semilar remarks are made
every day there are thousands who think that they really desire to
become Christians but that there is some inseperable obstacle in the
way they have inward misgivings that it is no true that they wish to
become reconciled to <u>God</u> but that he is not willing to become reconciled to them [. . .] except a sweet kiss from your whence little
friend and loving and Devoted.

Addie

The end of the following letter, in which Addie tells Rebecca about
Aunt Chat's ill-fitting false teeth, is one of the most amusing in the collection. Clearly the two women's relationship allowed them to let down
their hair and share a hearty laugh. One senses Addie's great pleasure
in her solitude at writing to her beloved friend. Throughout many letters
such as this, one can share in the laughter her stories must have
invoked in Rebecca.

New York Mar. 30, 1862

My Dearest Sister
    [. . .] Think my <u>Dearest Sister</u> I am near the breathing the same
air with your arm gently drawn around me my head reclining on
your noble breast in perfect confidence and love. But alas the dream
is over the charm is broken I alook to the stern realities of my position but to find myself alone of what would I not give at this
moment to be with or near you my soul longs for it ask for it[. . . .]
    Rebecca I want to tell you Aunt Chat along side of me fixing her
teeth in her mouth you will say to yourself what teeth? She has a set.
Those stumpet she had they all out. I dont think she look well with
them for they are one sided the Dentist will have to file her gums I
wish you could see her she went out yesterday to spend the P.M. the
friends told her they add to her beauty. Dear Rebecca with out joke-
ing Aunt C think she is pretty she say every body has told her now

65

since she had got her teeth she [. . .] those are in the house I could not help last night as sick as I was looking in the glass for a half hour at herself I laugh at her for she look so funy now my Dear I dont think I write any more good night my loving Sister.

[Oh] Rebecca I forgot to tell you that Mrs. Thompson has move she left very meanly she was not to move untill the first of May that was the bargain when she moved in when the children had they party she got very angry to think they had a violin she said that she was living amongst heathen people she made a remark to Mrs. Scott as soon as she could she going to move so when Selina and the rest of the girls had their party it was a death blow to her so the last of that week Mrs. T was moving out and left mother pay her rent. Don't you think that was mean in her to do so such as life. Aunt Chaty is looking out of the window at the people going to church so she just put her head in asking me who am I writing to she say give my love to Dear Rebecca and tell her I rec her letter and was very sick at the time but now she is quite well she want to know if you cant find her a service place for her a cook place she think she feel better if you will she will go on and take you for a mother and a sister and a husband and companion something else I forgot so my Dear I wont write any more I must go toward the fire and prepare for bed I dont know what Aunt C see in the St at night I ask her I told you as before at the people going to church once again good night sweet Sister.

[. . .] Aunt Chaty my brother Ally and I spent a very pleasant evening together not with standing my <u>heart</u> was with you. Last Sunday morn there was a large fire down town it was a cane store Ally said they was thrown the case out by the had full every fireman got one he tried to get one but being so very large or rather tall he could not get one he something like me about 9 oclock that same morn there was a den were Col people lives was on fire he said it was amusing to see them some had clothes in some did not and the firemens give them all good dunking Nexe wed Eve confremations to our church going to be fourteen confirm Miss Hatie Bowers is one of the number she want Selina to be not this year[. . . .]

The letter that follows reveals three interesting aspects of Addie's life. First, once again she complains of not being paid for her work. Having claimed her as part of the family provides "Mother" with an excuse for failing to pay regular wages. Second, note her response to Rebecca's request that Addie call her sister. The relationship exists on a complex continuum. Finally, observe her explanation for Aunt Chat's claim that she is in love with Mr. Lee.

New York Mar. [?] 1862

My Own Darling & Beloved Rebecca

It is now half past ten and all alone a hour ago you could not hear you ears for there was about 40 here I suppose you ask yourself what they was all doing here as usuall a surprise party this evening the gents are getting it up for Miss Bruce her last farwell party the family except to go Thursday P.M. again you ask why I was not one of the number my Darling I think that too much of a good thing good for nothing. This winter is been intirely to gay although I have not attend to everything has been given. Mother and Selina they have been trying to get me to go. Mr. Bodie is the head one geting it up and he seemed to be quite displeased because I would not go I cant help that wish I could. When billows roll and waves around me rise one thought of <u>thee</u> will clear the darkest skies.

My Dearest to day I rec you very kind & Affectionate Epistle to night I feel in good spirit one things in your letter it gave me a great deal of pleasure you spoke of Aunt Chat writing to you I was much surprise as you was she think everything of you she speaks in the highest terms. Dear Rebecca dont you think its a great pity she neather read or write so she got me to pen those lines to you she spoke of me looking sad. Dear Rebecca I did not know my feeling was such that they would be observed in my continince [countenance] I do feel very sad sometime. Mother sometimes get very disagreeable it on account of father business and the family being so very large I want to leave here I tell her if I was to go I would make one less she will not hear of it then she think I dont love her she think right I like her very well I treat her according to my feelings but I cannot help it is the saying is I never forget what I remember my Dear. Do not say anything about it mother has not paid me for a month now and I want a great many things. As for work we have none aint likly to get any I dont think my <u>sweet</u> Rebecca you say let you share my sorrows I do not want to make you

67

miserable[. . .] if it your wish you shall share both now my Dearest
here is nexe question you ask a favor and that is this <u>to call</u> you my
sister and then you ask me if it will be agreeable O my Darling Darling you know it would it has been my wish for sometime I dare not
ask my Dear I cannot find words to express my feeling towards you is
all I can say I will address you as such. Do not wish Mrs. Nott send
for me if she was different I would not mind living with her she beg
me to come back to her in the spring my <u>heart</u> almost melted to her
pleading and complaints they are right about our <u>love</u> for each other.

[. . .] Rebecca Mr. Lee letters I was very much please to rec his
letter but not in the way that Aunt Chaty spoke I told her that was
not what I done and neather was they my feelings she beg me to pen
them to you I done so I do not wish to make any thing to appear
Aunt Chat is a person like to magnify anything even Selina think I
was very cold and indifferent with him my Darling you would be the
last one that I would want to deceive in anything I dont think I have
and I am I will not do it now if I have tell me. I want to tell you what
he ask me if I love you better then I did him I told him yes I did
[. . . .]

Addie

Six months have passed since Addie's last letter. It is not clear how
long she has been in Hartford, but that may explain the absence of correspondence.

The Hartford letters of this period are notes between visits. They
give us a sense of the interaction between Rebecca and Addie when
they are together. Addie mentions a picture that Rebecca has given her.
Although the two friends exchanged their likenesses, I have been
unable to locate any. The friends have been corresponding for three
years now.

Hartford Sept. 11, 1862

My Darling & Beloved Sister

How are you this beautiful morning? Well and in good spirit I
hope. O Dear me it seem to me it has been a week since Ive seen
you. I wonder if you have miss my society as much as I have miss
yours? Sweet Sister I have perused your note again it make the six

time I cannot [?] why you thought that I was indifferent towards you that A.M. My Darling I did not feel so. Although I felt sad that morning I awake before you I impress several kisses upon your lips and gave you a fond embrace. While I was in that position a shade of sadness stole over me and it has not been remove yet since I have been here I have tried to make myself agreeable but I daunt know wheather I have succeed are not[. . . .] Dearest Sister I dont know how to express my thanks to you for those picture. My feelings are even now are indiscriable it shall be as pricious to me as the other thing you gave me. I am very much oblige to you for them. O Dear here come Gertrude well I must leave you breakfast is ready so good morning. My Darling for a while.

9 oclock

Here I am sweet one looking at you but not a smile on your face. I have kiss you and you wont even return one. Never mind I will untill the original come out here tomorrow morning. You must come my Dear for my sake and also come and disappoint Gertrude and her mother for they think you will not come. G play for me all the eve we spent a very pleasant one. Well my Dear I will hefter [have to] bring this to a close they will not like me being so long absence from them do come for you Little and Loving Sister.

Addie

Hartford Sept. 18, 1862

My Own Truly Loved Sister

I have been pening a few lines to Mr. Lee I just feel like doing the same to you so I made his letter very brief. Dear Sister you have been just an hour a way from me when I think how soon it will be when we will be seperated for weeks instead of hours its makes me realy sick. Dear Rebecca I dont know how it is I feel nearer to you now then ever before although you always been very very Dear to me. Since I have been here, I have injoyed your society very much so much so I hate to have you away from me one moment. Rebecca my Darling you cant imagine what pleasure I take in perrusing those notes it send such a thrilling sensation through me particular were you say I do indeed love you with my whole heart. My Dear you say I am intirely ignorant of the depth of your love not quite my per-cious Darling I am little wise of it I cant help being so to see how much you do for me daily also the little token of love leaving out the large one Dearest Sister I hope you feeling will never again change towards me to think I was on edge of losing your <u>purest love</u> O how my heart leap for joy when I think I have regain it as strong as it was before perhaps stronger. Dear Sister I will not pen you a long note because I must wash my dress I am comeing their to see you last it offerd you so much pleasure you gave me such a affectionate look I cant resist coming. Good morning my Dear & Dearest Sister.

Addie

[. . .] From your Darling Little Sister it tis good by

Addie

One sweet kiss

From the letter that follows, one can surmise that Addie had been flirting with Rebecca's brother, Nelson. Neither Rebecca nor her family approve. Primus scholar Barbara Beeching suggests that the family—unlike Rebecca—was concerned by the class differences between the two.

Hartford Sept. 21, 1862

My Dearest Sister

I feel sad tonight for I dont think that you have got over the feeling you had towards me when you bid me good night it seem cold and would not even kiss me that something you have never done yet. My Beloved Sister why is it you will intertain those feelings towards me. This Eve I ask your forgiveness you say if I desire it I then ask to forget you say yes but how cold it was said and then I ask you to kiss me I thought your kiss indecate all. My Darling in the manner you left me I dont think you have thrust it from your mind. Dear Sister I wish that my feelings would become calous I should never feel as I do sometime I dont suppose I would if I did not <u>love</u> you as I do you know I often told you ther is no one I <u>love</u> as I do you not even the man I expect in the future to call husband why will you feel so towards me it is growing late I hate to retire without you. Dear Rebecca I would like to tell you one think please dont get angre at me for it is this, I shall not be as friendly with your brother as I have

been I know you dont like it and I also understand another member
of the family dont like it. You know I like your family very much and
sometime like to in there society very much but for the future I will
treat him as I would any other young man acquaintace I hope you
will forgive what I have pen here I did not do it to hurt your feelings
in no way I will have to close my light is giving out so I will have to
return I hope you will feel better tomorrow you have a very bad cold
I think you aught to take something for it good night it a sad night to
me your Affectionate Sister.

Addie

Addie's next letter does not tell us why she has had to destroy Rebecca's
note, but perhaps this is one reason that Rebecca's letters to Addie are
no longer available.

Hartford Oct. 20, 1862

My Dear Sister
    No doubt you have giving up all hope if rec a note or answers to
some of yours its better late than never. I am not going to attend
church today its also very unpleasant. I hope I will have the pleasure
of being in your society this P.M. and Eve. My Darling will you
inform me what had came over the spirits of your dream last night
you always make me feel sad when ever I see you so you know with
me its second nature and I have many thing to accur to make me feel
so. Last night I was dreaming of you its was neither pleasant [nor]
unpleasant I awake with a my old companion by my I feel better now.
My Beloved Sister I have again perruse the note I rec on 15th I am
sorry that I have got to destroy it. Well is it must be. In it you ask me
what did I think that morning I awake nothing of [?] you know my
feelings on that point. One thing my fondest Sister you say you are
bent and bond to leave your home dont my Dear Dear friend do anything that you will repent you have never had to go out in the world
do for yourself Rebecca just think of <u>her</u> that you <u>live</u> see how she
had been through. <u>God forbid</u> that ever you go through as much that
your poor mother that growing old you ought not to leave she has no
one to sooth her to supply her feeble heart to look up to her with a
smile but her first born even her youngest how she treat her mother

they know not the worth of a mother untill after they are gone perhaps they have many fault but my Dear you must over look all.
    [. . .] Good Morning.
                            Your Darling Sister Addie

Throughout the letters, Addie occasionally compares her love for her
male suitors to that for Rebecca.

                                        Hartford Oct. 28, 1862
My Darling Sister
    It hard to have you leave me. I could not help sheding a tear after
you had left It is so lonesome here when night comes.
    Rebecca you dont know what to make of me never mind the day
will come someday you will know me entirely. I hope you seen Mr.
Lee. Dear Sister I like him much better then I did he has truly been
kind to me <u>but he never</u> be to me as you are [?] its been by you and
you alone since I have been wondering how I could get another
[job] I was counting the money I would rec. O my Darling Darling
Sister I thank you kindly for it. I never can and never be able to
express my gratitude to you[. . . .]My Darling why did you say that I
ought to chose a better person then you for a friend and Sister? I
could never find any one would be able to walk in your old shoes.
Look at that one that I called <u>mother</u> has she been a true friend to
me <u>No</u> took a stranger to her bossom and even love him more then
she did her own husband that lie in under the souls for her I hope I
never be the means of killing anyone. <u>My Dear Sister</u> for my sake
never pen those words again for you make me feel quite sad[. . . .] so
adviere [adieu] for a while you loving little Sister.
    I am just preparing to retire for the night 10 o'clock. Mr. Lee has
been here I was rather surprise to see him. I was very sorry to think I
was not able to go to the Allyn Hall. I hope it wont always be so
good night my Sister.
    I hope it wont be long before I be able to lay in your arms.

Addie

                            .   .   .

It seems Addie's early efforts to be a Christian and to impress Rebecca with her religious devotion have failed. Here she questions her faith, for she is no longer as devoted to her religious practices as she used to be. She also reports an important confession to Mr. Lee. In this and occasional letters that follow, Addie refers to herself as Aerthena and Rebecca as Stella. I have not been able to ascertain if they have any meaning beyond being pet names. Perhaps they were characters in a book the two had read.

Hartford Dec. 9, 1862

9 p.m.

My Darling Sister

Just feeling like pening a few lines to <u>thee</u> I thought I would do it on the umpulse of the moment. I was very much please to see you this P.M. you seem to be in such a hurry I hardly had time to look at you I have finish facing my bonnet if I have time I will call to see you tomorrow I hope Thursday will soon come then I will have the extrem pleasure of seeing you again. Dear Sister I dont know what you think about what going to pen it tis this—we are in each other society a very little what is the course of it perhaps it is your school that monopolizes you time? I sometime things aint like it use to be what do you think about it My Darling.

My Dear I dreampt of you last night I dont sleep good I am so cold I miss you very much and also you feather bed. I took a hot iron up to bed and warm the bed all over jump right into. I kept little warm by that means I wish that we could sleep together this winter I would like it very much would you not Stella. I injoy those doughnut very much I was little hungre when Bell brought them.

Dear Rebecca I dont know what Mr. Lee will think I would not let him kiss me for nearly two weeks so tonight I have ans the long note he sent me this P.M. he inform me he wrote it in your Schoolroom. So he said in his note that I owed him great many kisses so I thought I would let him know I told him I did not like his kisses. I dont know how he will feel about it I thought I might as well tell him as to think it dont you think so my only and Dearest Sister.

I could not stand it any longer. Dear Rebecca in the note he says he will meet me at the Church I dont understand him did he tell you anything about when he call today. He is a funny man. I have not care about seeing him this week I dont care I love you that dearly now My Darling I will try and ans you so long desire letter. I am afraid that you will be some disappointed on religion I dont feel as I use to and I have tried do as you[. . . .] my mind is far from it.

Sometime I feel very very unhappy I have also neglect reading the Bible regular and I think that has been the main point. My Dearest Dearest Sister I think sometime when I am in your society that you dont seem [?] as much pleasure as you once did is that so & my Dear you must tell me if so[. . . .]

Mrs. Nott is getting [ready] for bed so I will bring my missive to aclose. Mr. Lee says he want to get religion I hope he will get it I dont think he is very happy I ask him sometime ago the ans he made it was me that worried him I hope he will worry in the right way.

[. . .] I must come to a brief close by biding you a sweet good night and pleasant dreams I remain your Affec and Loving Sister Aerthena

         except a sweet kiss

The following letters were written during the height of the Civil War, during which there was much activity in Connecticut. Regiments from the area were fighting. Harriet Beecher Stowe was a resident in the city. Still, Addie makes very little mention of the war or any related political events. Given that Rebecca's family seems to have been deeply involved in civic activities, it is significant that the two friends do not find it necessary to discuss such issues in their correspondence.

A year has passed since the last recorded letter from Addie to Rebecca. Again, perhaps this is because the women are living in the same city. In fact, Addie is now living in Rebecca's neighborhood. The following letter contains one of the most explicit passages concerning the nature of the physical relationship between the two women. Addie tries to convince a resistant Rebecca to acknowledge what is happening between them.

Hartford Jan. 8, 1864

My Truly Loved Sister

Although its but a few moments since I have left you I thought while you are discharging your duty I will pencil a few thoughts to thee. No doubt you would like to know how I got home nicely that loving imbrace kept my spirits up untill I reach home. I spent a very very pleasant day.

Dear Stella you dont know how bad I felt to see you in so much pain and to think I could not do anything to help O my Darling dont eat any more sweet affec for they do not agree with you. I know that I love you [?] I never could feel as I did my sympathize was so great that I had straight pain [?] I often heard [?] but I would not believe them I know by experience.

Dear Stella do you ever think of our visit last summer? I do very often. Sometime I think its all of dreams what happy days those was will they ever come again. O dont say no. I live in hopes that will be together nothing will separate us but death. While sitting on your lap I had a very thrilling sensation pass through me today. Did the same occur to you [?] I ask you would not tell me. Sister why will you perfer darkness sometime instead of light I suppose you wonder what I mean, well I will tell you. All day I have trying to have you tell me something you would not untill you sleep with me. Why cant you make up that [?] with me dont you think we can love and [?] each other just the same you know my dear just what I mean come let us try. O Dear here <u>come</u> somebody to disturb me[. . . .]

I am sorry that I cant have you to sleep with me tonight perhaps its all for the best now my Darling Sister I must leave you a little while it 9 am I guess you are thinking about leting you school out I hope you will not [?] I hope you will have pleasant night rest except a kiss good night.

Your [?] Sister
Aerthena

To Stella

I will never forget thee darling
Though thou art far from me I'm
ever of thee thinking my heart
belongs to thee of thee by day
I ponder of thee by night I dream
This world without thee darling
A lonely place would seem.

PART THREE

The Reconstruction Years

APRIL 1865 brought the end of the Civil War and the assassination of President Lincoln. Not long thereafter, in November, Rebecca Primus left Hartford to teach the freedmen of Maryland. She was twenty-nine years old.[1] Primus was one of two black teachers sponsored by the Hartford Freedmen's Aid Society.[2] After an initial stay in Baltimore, she was assigned to Royal Oak, in Talbot County, on the Eastern Shore of Maryland.

The Eastern Shore was familiar to Primus through the pages of Frederick Douglass's *Narrative of the Life of Frederick Douglass—An American Slave* (1845). While in Royal Oak, she boarded with Mr. and Mrs. Charles Thomas. Thomas, a free black landowner and one of the most committed trustees of the Royal Oak School, purchased his freedom and at one time worked as a horse trainer on the Lloyd plantation, where Douglass once lived.[3]

Rebecca stayed in Royal Oak until the Hartford Freedmen's Aid Society dissolved. She returned to Hartford in 1869. Within three years, Charles Thomas joined her, and they were married.

Rebecca's letters are public documents, written primarily to her parents and sisters but with the full understanding that they are sometimes shared with other members of the community. Thus, with the exception of discussions about her health, Rebecca rarely writes about her private life. She speaks often of her love and concern for relatives, friends, and pets. On occasion she refers to her best friend, Addie. In Rebecca's letters, Addie appears as a loving sister-friend, often mentioned in the same way she speaks of her own sisters, Henrietta and Bell.

In Hartford, Addie Brown established a network of friends and extended family. Her Connecticut letters provide a vibrant portrait of nineteenth-century black Hartford. Addie shares her frustration over the precarious nature of her employment, negotiations with her employers, and the poor state of her health (she suffered from chronic headaches). She also discusses the family and extended family who help sustain her.

Throughout her correspondence, three things are consistent: the strength of the bond between herself and Rebecca; the precarious nature of her economic well-being (Addie's letters document the relative instability of her employment options, her day-to-day struggles to make enough money to survive, and the displacement she experiences as she moves from household to household as a live-in servant); and her never-ending sense of humor in relaying gossip to Rebecca. It is impossible to read Addie's letters without laughing at her vivid descriptions and tale-telling.

During the nine years of her correspondence with Rebecca Primus, Addie Brown wrote from almost as many addresses. From Hartford on December 1, 1865, she wrote: "You wonder my dear Sister of my being out I am not at work at present we was discharged last eve no more work the business is dull with them I could cried when he told me though I was sure of work all winter. Rebecca don't you think my words are true that is this either a feast or a famine." Again, in February 1866: "Rebecca I have been working for nothing comparatively speaking. Now I have come to a decided stand that people shall pay me for my work."

When this phase of the correspondence begins, Addie is twenty-four years old. She works at George Smith's Dye House on Weld Street in Hartford; the establishment mended, cleaned, and dyed garments. Addie worked there as a seamstress, a rare form of employment for black women, most of whom were relegated to domestic service. Even as domestics, black women found themselves in stiff competition with Irish immigrants. Addie now lives with the Sands family at 12 Wadsworth Street, just down the street from the Primus home. Emily Sands is Rebecca's maternal aunt. The letters also introduce us to Joseph Tines, Addie's most persistent suitor—the man she later marries.

Throughout the years of Reconstruction, both young women come into their own. Rebecca Primus becomes more politicized; she also comes to identify more with southern blacks, for whom she at first has a distanced curiosity. Addie Brown is as fiercely determined and dignified as Rebecca. Her letters defy the stereotypes of black domestics. First of all, she is literate. Though filled with misspellings and poor grammar, her letters reveal the lively, individual voice of a woman who keeps up with current events and seems to read more books than does her more educated friend. As time passes, Addie's voice grows more confident and self-assured. Her writing improves, and she takes advantage of every opportunity to improve herself and her station in life.

Chapter Five

"There is great excitement about putting money in the bank"

1865

UPON her arrival in Baltimore, Rebecca is immediately struck by the large number of black people: "I guess I have already seen about as many colored people as there are in the whole of Hartford." In 1860, there were ninety thousand slaves in the state of Maryland; the black community of Baltimore made up approximately thirteen percent of the city's population. This is in stark contrast to Hartford, where blacks were approximately two percent of the total population. Historian Barbara Fields notes: "Throughout the nineteenth century, the ratio of free to slave among black people rose steadily [in Maryland]. By the eve of the Civil War, free black people were nearly as numerous as slaves."[1] Consequently, the state had a strong and historic black presence. Because the Emancipation Proclamation of 1863 freed slaves only in the Confederate States, slavery wasn't abolished in Maryland (which remained loyal to the Union) until 1864. Not long after abolition, the state enacted Black Codes, which forbade blacks to testify in court and apprenticed 2,500 children to former slave owners. During the short window of opportunity provided by the Civil War, Maryland's blacks tried to exercise their citizenship rights before they were taken away by such oppressive laws.

By the time of Rebecca's arrival in Baltimore, approximately twenty-five percent of Maryland's blacks had migrated to the cities of Baltimore and Cambridge.

During her stay in Maryland, Rebecca would return to Baltimore. It was a stopover when she returned from holidays with her family, the site of an occasional visit to get away from her day-to-day tasks, and a place to touch base with other northern teachers throughout the state. Because these black teachers would not have been welcomed in boardinghouses and inns frequented by whites, black Baltimoreans established a network of residences where blacks were welcome.

Baltimore, Nov. 8, 1865

My Dear Parents & Sister

It is now ½ past two o'ck, it was my intention to have devoted this forenoon to writing, but I went away at 9 o'ck to see Mr. Graham & he sent me to assist a white gentleman in one of the schools of freed children here, on account of his being ill, and I only returned a few moments since, though I did not come direct from school, as Mrs. Hall had left word with Mr. Graham to have me call upon her. I did so and had a colored gentleman who is stopping at Mrs. Coopers to conduct me to her boarding house. She wished me to tell you that she had been quite anxious about me for fear I had got lost or met with some difficulty enroute. If I remain here in the city she wants me to call & see her often and she will look out for me. I think I shall like her much.

I am going to remain here until next week and in the meantime I shall be employed in this school I attended this A.M. They have two sessions a day, the first from 9½ A.M. to ½ past 12 o'ck P.M. The second from 7½ eve'g to 9½ for adults. The school is in a four story building upon the third floor it is fitted up for the purpose, with desks, blackboards etc. Similar to those home, there are four departments and this gentleman is the principal. The others are taught by ladies one of whom is a colored lady—almost white—from Canada. I shall probably be sent to my station some time next week. Mr. Graham says he will secure a good and comfortable place for me. A white gentleman brought in a commission from some other society while I was there and he is to be sent tomorrow A.M. to Cambridge, a hundred miles distant.

The gentleman I have alluded to above is from Philadelphia, and leaves for a place called Centerville some fifty miles off somewhere near to Miss Howards station. He is a young man and apparently quite smart, he will accompany me around to school this eve'g. I have a pleasant boarding place with a very agreeable family and on a delightful street—it is the rendezvous for the colored teachers under this society.

I arrived here about ten o'clock in company with a gentleman from Boston whom I spoke with in the cars and asked him to get a carriage for me, he spent the night here and this A.M. continued on his journey to a country place west of this to see his sick mother whom he thought to be dying. The train was delayed, both between N.Y. & Phil. and between Phil. & Bal. It was very near twelve yesterday noon when we left Jersey City, and then between Trenton & one other place, the name of which I do not recollect now we got upon the wrong track & came up face to face with a train loaded with coal, so we went back several miles so as to switch off upon the right track, which delayed us from twenty minutes to half an hour, we arrived at Kensington the upper part of Philadelphia at about four o'ck then all the passengers for Baltimore and Wash'g took the horse cars and was conveyed to the opposite side of the city to the southern depot time—one hour—at five or fifteen minutes after again started on the Southern train & such flying over the ground I never before experienced, the train was obliged to make up for lost time. There are seventeen stopping places between Phil. & Baltimore we stopped at two thirds of them. I had the company of a gentleman friend of Mr. Tines as far as Phil. who was very kind to me & with whom I shared my lunch as he had none. We reached Baltimore at nine or a little after. We took a carriage & we had another time flying over the paved streets for two or three miles, I was so frightened I could think of nothing for I expected we should be dashed to pieces every moment. Oh I hope I shall never experience another such a ride. Our baggage came by express the A.M. the conductor takes you check in the cars with the place you are to stop at, & gives you the express man's card with the number of your checks upon it, otherwise you can not obtain you baggage so soon—sometimes for two or three days. I feel very thankful to know & think I have arrived here safely & with all that belongs to me. It is 96 miles from N.Y. to Phil. & from Phil. to Baltimore the distance is 100 miles.

It is beautiful here today & quite mild. I have been a long distance from my boarding place & returned alone & I guess I have already seen about as many colored people as there are in the whole of Hartford.

My expenses from N.Y. have been as follows—on the cars $6.65 carriage 30¢ & for baggage 50¢ on the boat $2.00 & from the boat to Jersey City 15 for baggage. Please write upon the receipt of this that I may receive it ere I leave for other ports. Give my love to all—I find I've brought away one of the keys to the Front door so if I should return unexpectedly & it should come at night or when you were all out I should have no trouble in getting in. I am sorry I've got it for I know you'll need it.

I retired at twelve last night and got up at eight this A.M. I shall not be up so late tonight I'll assure you. I must get some rest if possible though I do not feel so very fatigued after all. Accept my love to your selves and direct your letters to 184 Park St. near Richmond.

> From your affectionate
> daughter & sister
> Rebecca

This is Addie's first letter after her extended separation from Rebecca. It is also the first to mention Mr. Tines—the gentleman Addie will eventually marry. She seems to have known him since her childhood in Philadelphia. In Rebecca's absence, she also seems to have the space to consider a serious relationship with Tines, although it is clear that her affection for him in no way competes with her love for Rebecca. Rebecca's family and friends recognize the closeness of the relationship between the two women and seem to treat Addie's emotional response to Rebecca's departure as a girlhood crush.[2]

> Hartford Nov. 8, 1865
> 8 oclock P.M.

My Dearest & Absent Sister

What a surprise I rec when I return home from my work this eve its impossible for me to express my feelings to you. I am delighted that you got as far as NY safe and I trust to <u>God</u> that you will get to your place of destination safe and quite well. How I have miss you I have lost all no more pleasure for me now Aunt Emily ask me last eve if I was going to carry that sober face until you return she also said if Mr. T[ines] was to see me think that I care more for you then I did for him I told I did love you more then I ever would him she said I better not tell him so it would be the truth and [?] else. Monday night when we came pass the house it look like someone was dead. Belle was not home she went up to Ms Davis after she came from the boat her <u>beau</u> accompany her I went in the house tonight for the first you mother said she did know but that I had [?] she said I must come in and not feel that all was gone because you had[. . . .]

Addie

Addie expresses a desire to visit Rebecca. While she writes of trips to New Haven, New York, and Philadelphia, it does not seem Addie ever receives an invitation or the gift of a trip that she constantly requests from Rebecca. Also, in this letter Addie mentions her brother and his request that she return to New York for Thanksgiving. After this she appears to be estranged from her extended family in New York. Selina is the only one with whom she seems to stay in contact.

Addie shares information about the Hartford black community's preparation for the return of the Twenty-ninth Regiment. The Twenty-ninth was one of two black regiments from Connecticut, the source of much pride for Hartford's black residents.

Nov. 10, 7 P.M.

My Own Darling Sister

I was delighted when I rec your affectionate letter I hardly [expected] until tomorrow my heart feel quite light now I am please to know that you have arrived safe.

Rebecca I am very lonely ever will be untill you return or I come to you. Dear Sister when ever you sent for me I shall come nothing will prevent but sickness.

I suppose you would like to know how I get along. Very Well. Yesterday they set me to put numbers on the things it took a hour. I done it so well I had to do it again today. Mr. Smith gave some of them a shame face the case that they keep the vent in was a inch thick with dust he ask me if I would clean it for him he called me Miss Brown he seem to be quite please with my work. This P.M. I have been working on blankets I had quite a little rest. I have not been out since you have <u>left me</u> Aunt Emily ask me if I was going to meeting last Eve my headache I did not feel like it.

I dread Sunday to come. I got a letter from Mr. Tines this P.M. he said I must be sure and come down to the boat Sunday. I have not seen him since Monday when he vowed to me. He says I must not worry to much best of friends must part how can I help it[?] No one feel as I about you and never will.

I have heard today that Mr. Green is under arrest they think that he will recover his poor daughter must feel bad seem to me I never would want to see him. Henrietta was telling me today that the colored ladies & gent had a ball at Talcott Hall night before last they are going to have them ever once in awhile[. . . .]

I red'd a letter from Ally Brown last eve he has been very sick again he wanted me to come down to NY Thanksgiving. He wants to have us all together once more Selina expect to get married in the Spring. I do not know who to ans the letter you know what way I don't expect to see NY untill you say come. Thomas Sands is in NY sick. He got his discharge as soon as he gets able he will return home here to his parents.

The 29 Regiment expected home tomorrow in the city of Hartford. They will be a many rejoice hearts. Aunt Em is [going to] go and receive them[. . . .] They had a vacation to Mrs. Bruce house today sold everything they could even to old shoes and old bonnets. Mrs. Primus and Sands attend it the latter pay [. . .] got some preserves dishes and something else I forgot[. . . .] Dear Sister I want you to get this as soon as you can I am going to mail it myself so I must close for it will bee too late for me to go do my love write soon again at the sme place they have all my love & affection accept as many kiss as you can get if I could get near you I would give you a good hug. I remain your loving

Sister Addie

The following experience at the dye house is a rare and cherished one for Addie. Few black women worked outside of domestic service and even fewer were addressed as "Miss" by their white employers. This is one of the only job situations that seems to have boosted her sense of self.

Addie and Rebecca's friendship permitted the two women to see themselves in each other's eyes. This assured them of their strengths of character, of their gifts and talents, and of the quality of their love for each other.

In the following letter, Addie encourages Rebecca to stay in Maryland because it would be very difficult for her to return home, given her exposure to different people and places. Addie does this in spite of her concern that should Rebecca follow her advice, their own relationship would suffer. Her admiration for her friend is also quite apparent here.

Hartford Nov. 16, 1865

My True & only Dear Sister

What a pleasure it would be to me to address you <u>My Husband</u> and if so do you think for one moment you would be where you are with out me? No, never. To my surprise you send me a ans sooner then I expected how delighted I was even those around me could see that I was. It come to hand 3 oclock P.M. I work with much lighted heart then I have all this week.

This morn. I told Aunt Emily I would accompany her to meeting this eve if she went I soon change my mind this P.M. I ask H this A.M. if she would let me send two or three lines to you in her letter she said no of course she did not mean it. Now I will have the pleasure of sending a letter instead H.

Let me perruse her letter from you I have been thinking if you did return home again I dont think you would be contented you are rec what you soul have been thursting for you never could get it here that is to be in a society of intelligence & interlectual people I know that you injoy it I only wish that I was their to see you what is the use to be amongst the ignorance all the time now my Darling Sister I will ans yur letter I must stop and purruse it again.

Dear Sister you say you hope I will do well in your absence I will try to do so for your sake you say absence strengthens friendship and our love will not grow cold mine will never I will always love you and you only if you were to remain there how pleasant it would be for me to come there too I would like to very much or were ever else you are station. Mr. Tines was speaking of you yesterday saying when you return home that I must meet you in Phila. I suppose he will see that I will get there by that.

That lady you speak of Miss Williams give her my love in return and say to her if you please that if she was to see me she might fall out in love with the picture I feel sorry about her and her friend. I know it will not be so with us we have loved each other to long. I see you like Baltimore very much you speaking of the St. door steps & walk being so clean it remind me of Phila for they are just so. <u>Sister</u> I hope Miss W will not walk you to much if she does I will have to send her a few lines so you found someone that you was acquainted. Eliza will be delighted is she married lady

Dear Rebecca your retiring at 8 change to 12 oclock what make you do so you will wear yourself out in so doing. We are having beautiful weather today[. . . .] H was saying you will be sending word that you intend to Mary having so many <u>gent</u> calling I shall have to think so myself[. . . .] Miss Eliza & Mr. Hall Brook accompany Mr. Tines & myself to the Methodist church. Mr. Tines was not feeling well he had told me twice to give his kindest regards to you and please to hear that you have or did arrive there safe he also said he spent a very pleasant time in your society.

I get along very nicely to the Dye House I was sewing nearly all day yesterday and all this morn we was paid last night I rec $19.00 you dont know how please I felt Dear Sister just look back $4.00 per month what a jump up I did not walk up Aunt Em only take $2.00 a week from me she said if provision was not so high she would not take anything H $2.50 dont mention it for Aunt Em dont want her to know it dont you think she is kind Miss E Saunders gave me some blue veils to make me a bonnet. Mrs. S want to make it for me she is also going to give me some flowers for it they are very kind Mrs. S think you wont write to her I told her you would when you get setled do write to her my Dear Rebecca and disappointed.

I took dinner with Eliza Sunday Sarah accompany me there of [. . .] I must tell you what foolishness John Rodney wants when the 29 reg return of cause they reception will be at the City Hall while they are eating to have Colt Band to play for them he is allmost a fool if not quite he also wants 36 gallons of oysters for them he says that they wants this Reg rec better than any has been rec yet now

Dearest & Darling Sister I believe I have pen you all the news if I could only see you and have one kiss would I be happy H has not return home and almost eleven she is with John Francis Aunt Emily and rest of the send there love even to mayor Mr. Tines is going to spend one week in Hartford then he is going to see his parents I hope they will be something on to the Allyn Hall then he is going to bring the strings nexe week he came down yesterday and got the [?] so to get thee more for it he would like to see you about somethings he says him Aunt Emily having great time with me and you are not her to take my parts do write to Aunt Em for she would like to have you she says she would like to have you.

I had Jim in my lap this week Mrs. Primus says he miss you very much he keep following her around the house.

[. . .] I must bid you good night I only wish that I could sleep with you tonight I have miss you very much how long am I going to be without you. Aunt Emily sends her love to you and will write to some of the day good night my Dearest love one more kiss.

Your ever dear Sister

Addie

This next letter is one of the occasions where Addie implies a comparison between Mr. Tines and Rebecca. Instead of claiming that the relationships are fundamentally different, as she will do later on, here she suggests competition between the two. At this time she prefers her relationship with Rebecca. The two young women have been corresponding for over five years.

Hartford Nov. 19, 1865

My Dear & Only Sister

It is a rainy Sunday and not one of the family is out I feel very lonely this day all this A.M. I have been reading but never the less my thoughts is been with you if I could see you a few moment how happy I would be. O why have you left me alone no one to love me an give me a fond imbrace how I long for yours.

I dont suppose I will see Mr Tines for I am little incline to think that he is afraid of the rain. If you could come I would not care. Friday Eve I spend quite pleasantly two of the girls from the shops came down to the house I took the liberty of taking them in No 20 [the Primus home]. Several was in their while I was injoying the sweet notes there came a knock at the door who should it be but Eliza. I was about to ask her in when she told me she brought a lady to see me I look and it was Miss Ward from NH I was very much please to see her. They spent a hour with me she also wants me to come down and make her a visit this winter.

Mr. Hayes is coming down here Tuesday. As soon as I get my guitar fix he is going to give me some lessons. O my I must tell you Miss Ward inform me that Mr. Muse is going to NH to preach he has [expected] their call they going to give him $800.00 they are per-fectly delighted with him[. . . .] I do feel realy high spirited it is most night I have not made my tollet so I must bid you adviere until you hear from me again.

Addie

This letter is most interesting for its description of the return of the Twenty-ninth Regiment to Hartford. The unit, formed late in 1863, "was one of the first regiments to enter the Confederate capital before returning to Connecticut to be discharged."[3] Although Hartford was a northern city, with a long-standing free black community, it was not free of racism, either institutional (blacks were denied the vote until 1876) or social—a fact made all the clearer when the city's black citi-zens turned out to celebrate the return of the Twenty-ninth.

[n.d.]

My Darling Sister

It has been some days since I have call I was delighted to hear from you yesterday you have no idea what pleasure you give me every week.[4] Dear Sister I do feel very lonely they all gone out but Sarah & myself. Aunt Emily has gone up to the church a festival there the proceed to aid the sick.

[. . .] Been nothing but excitement nexe to colored people for once can say they have had the city. The 29 & 31 regiments arrived here this A.M. one at 8 and the other at 11 o'clock they did look hard enough they have been coming from New Orleans two months who do you think has come to life [?] Robison he look very thin and to get home to his family they was telling they had nothing to eat for two days. Last eve they was expected here Mr. Rodney has made a perfect fool of himself he would not let just sick ones into the Hall last night.

Henrietta very angre. I could not help but to laugh to hear her go on. I went up to meeting with Aunt Em every other person we met had niggar in his or her mouth they was so mad to think the white was compel to make a fuss over them. On our return home some of them said niggar to us Aunt Em ask them if that what they had for there supper. If they did could not of relish it.

The Buckingham riffle factory and the light gards receive them the colored people [came] from all direction one of them walk along hugging his lady in the st. Henrietta ask Mr. Smith[5] if we could go out to see them he said of course. We was gone from 9 to 12. I heard this P.M. that it was the fullest regiment has come home yet[. . . .] I expect they will have a lively meeting nexe Sunday A.M. to the Methodist I think I shall go if nothing happens.

Madam Rumor[6] says that Henrietta is married to John Francis that good for nothing man. Mr. Green his recoverer is rather doubtfull he aught to linger a long while to reflect. Aunt Emily has return home the festival is postpone untill nexe week. Mr. Ridney is going to have a ball nexe week the ticket will be $5.00 I guess will not many attend it Mr. Seth Terry is dead Mrs. Julia Willson is here looking after Mr. H Jones I hope she will get some of the money[. . . .]

Henrietta wish me to give her love to you what did she write to you about me do tell me will[. . . .] Dear Sister I have you letter open before me I carry each letter in my pocket untill I rec another and perruse between 12 & 1 every day.

I dont thank Miss C hugging you lip so closely I would tell her so if I was there too. I expect you are having fine time I would like to be there injoying it with you my Dear Sister. I am glad to hear that you are please with Mr. Graham I wish you would contribute to that paper you must tell me about that Emancipation meeting. Dear Sister when you get settle you will send for me to come down.

[. . .] Mr. Tines came last Sunday and we went over to Levina and found Charly very sick and Mrs. Fuller is up here she has a son in the 29th [Regiment] she is not so loving to me as use to be things has changes. Dear Rebecca you ask how I am going to have my bonnet made with a cap crown and plain front and white roses in side and a strip of red velit. I am going after it tomorrow night. The Sag Harbor boat is done runing made her last strip Monday[. . . .]

Dear Sister the week that Mr. Tines stop back that I will become more attached to him & time will tell. I am little angre at him now last Sunday he told me that he would be down here Wednesday that A.M. I got a note that instead coming at noon him and Mr. Carter would come in the Eve at 7 oclock they was going to lay over both boat was here then of course I look for them no one came. I thought of every thing I had a note ans to the one he gave me Sunday think-ing he would come down the nexe day he did not both of the boat went to get the regiment and the Granit left here this A.M. at $\frac{1}{2}$ 10 oclock I heard they want to make her regular trips so they will be up tomorrow he might of staid back this Eve I have not seen him since Sunday. I dont care wheather I see him.

I shall certainly care for Jim for your sake only I feel very sorry for Miss Williams and her friend I hope nothing will ever separate us. Dearest Friend and only true one give my love to Miss Williams and tell her I should be very much please to have her write to me I should like to know what going on in Baltimore after my dear Sister leave the city I would like to see her also if she should write give her my address my love if you will not care about it. I forgot it impossi-ble to keep the bonnet Mrs. S made for me [for your] return but I will try and keep the one that Bell untill you return if you think you ever will you must excuse all mistake from you loving sister.

Addie

Hartford Dec. 1, 1865

My Dearest Sister

I am greatly disappointed not hearing from you today. You have been so kind to write me every week since your absence until this week I went to the Post office this eve hoping to rec a letter I cannot express my feelings when told there was none for me.

I was up streets today I stop in to see Eliza she inform me that she had rec a letter from you Wednesday she seem to be perfectly delighted. You wonder my dear Sister of my being out I am not at work at present we was discharged last eve no more work the busi-ness is dull with them I could cried when he told me I thought I was sure of work all winter. Rebecca dont you think my words are true that is this either a feast or a famine.

Monday I expect to go to Mrs. S to sew. Mrs. Couch wants me one or two days also Mrs. Doughlass wants some sewing Mrs. Swans is going to interceed for me also I hope I will get along this winter.

[. . .] I do not know what to think of H she has been acting so disagreeable ever since Monday night. It make it so unpleasant for me we have to sleep together but I am through working with her she is going to service soon as she get a place[.] She is quite angre about leaving the Dye House she could of been in a place only there in the family and had her $3.00 per week.

Rebecca I must tell you Mrs. S made my bonnet I wish you could of taken a peep at it I did not wear it last Sunday I remain at home all day I have taken it all to peices and Bell is going to make to tomorrow for me Mrs. S ask me how I like it I told how I did like it. She made several excuses about the frame I guess Miss S dont quite like that I let her make it. Its the first I can assure you the last.

Mrs. Buclah is going to break up and go to her husband he has got well again I dont think if I was in her place if I could trust my life with him. She says she feel little afraid too she expect to leave latter part of new week. My beloved Sister I have dreampt of you two nights if I could only see you once more and one fond imbrace how long will it be thus. I have made number of calls my friends appear to be please to see me some of them thinks I am looking very well.

[. . .] O Rebecca what do you think Madam Rumour say that Mr. Tines and I are ingage what do you think of that. Mr. H Jones came up this in rather last night in the Granit I have not seen my friend since last Saturday eve the boat got in about 6:P.M. and he came down to see me he accompany me to Mrs. Saunders he intend to go down on the boat and he got left. On our way home we same across the Park and he heard the boat whistles he bid me good night I look around and could not see anything but his coattail but his running was all in vain. I am getting sleepy so I must close hoping to hear from you tomorrow good night.

Dearest Sister I shall call soon

Addie

This undated letter from Rebecca directs her family to send letters to Mr. Thomas's address, thereby suggesting that she is in Royal Oak. The letter is probably from November or December of 1865.

Dear Parent and Sister

I expect you will think I'm writing a very lengthy epistle, and I think so myself. However, I'm about to stop now for I have nearly exhausted my train of thought. I shall then begin a letter to Jane and perhaps another.

Have you been for my picture yet and how does it look and what do you think of having others taken and disposed of as I proposed? I will forward the money when I find it is safe to do so. I should like one given to Addie on her birthday of the 21st of this month, and also to Henrietta on hers, the 28th. However, I do not want them to know of it until they rec. them. If you can get one for Aunt Em and Aunt Bashy[7] by Christmas or New Years do so.

If you desire to send anything to me at any time while I'm here, send it in the care of Mr. Jno. T. Graham and he will forward it to me. I am to hold a weekly correspondence with him Have any of my old school bills been settled yet?

I hope the school is getting along well, look out for your bills, Bell.[8] Remember me to all kind and inquiring friends. Tell them where I am and my future prospects. Give my love to all the family connexions, and accept the largest and best to yourselves.

I remain your affectionate Daughter & Sister, Rebecca.

Direct in the care of Mr. Chas. Thomas, Royal Oak, Talbot County, Md.

P.S. 6 P.M. I rec'd. your long interesting letter & one from Addie this P.M. I'm delighted to rec. them.

Addie reveals an aspect of Rebecca's relationship with her sister Henrietta. When Henrietta expresses a desire for education, Addie interprets it as sibling rivalry.

Dec. 3, 1865

My Dear & Dearest Sister

At present no one at home but Sarah & I. Mr. Sand has not return Aunt Em and Tommy has gone to Church.

[. . .] Yesterday for the first I went in to your home by the request of your mother and spent a few hours how lonely I was in spite of all efforts my eyes would fill with tears. Jim was laying off at his ease he look fin[e]ly. Doubltless he would like to see his mistress.

Bell gave these letter they rec from you that morning and also one from Nelson.[9] Dear Sister I must tell you about the style I accompany H to church this A.M. for the purpose of hearing Mr. Daughlass which we had that pleasure some of the ladies are looking very gay Eliza has come out I have never seen her look so well her bonnet is drub and trim with blue velit and also a loose sack coat I hardly knew her when she came in only by her walk you did not send her your address.

Troff Johnson is here in fact he has been here over a week exhibiting a magicalistic to the Methodist and also a festival the Methodist want to liquidable a debt so they are having festival for that purpose it will be again tomorrow night I have not attended any of them. Mr. Conerver festival prove a failure.

[. . .] Some of the people Col and White are making there for-tune of the soldiers. Mrs. Haris had made $300.00 and also have eight of them to board she sent word to me by her sister this P.M. to come and take supper with them they was going to have turkey. I escept of the invitation when I got there I was inform I was to eat after the boarders was through I wish to be excuse and came home to the first table I injoyed very much I did not tell Aunt Emily my reason for coming home.

Rebecca the course of the lectures has commence last Tuesday Eve Mr. Chappin I have anticapate so much pleasure this winter thinking of attending the lecture with you Levina & Mr. & Mrs. Saunders went to the first one L has her coat done and look very nice. Miss Cross & Johnson also came out with light coat and bon-net both alike ther are rushing things I am behind the age and will in every things. Mrs. Haris is coming in fine style nexe Sunday she also going to have a set of furs I expect she will make the money fly. The Church this P.M. was quite full great many soldiers Mr. Phillap is looking very well indeed I guess the [?] agreed with them and also Mr. E Jackson he look very wishful at Bell.

[. . .] I will try and ans your very loving and interesting missive. Dear Rebecca I do try and take the best of care of myself you must not mind Henrietta to much. I do not envy your injoyment but I would like to be there and be a silent preticipant how much knowledge one can obtain by that way. Dear Sister I am please to know that you are some where you can be drawn out for there is no one her was capable of so doing. Your interlectual powers like a deep well. Mr. Johnson inform one of the members of your family a very highly compliment of you from Springfield I feel proud of it.

Give my love to Miss Williams I would be very much please to come on to Baltimore and will if my life is spared. Henrietta is wish she could have the mind some folks have I was quite surprise to hear her talk as she did last night after we retire which was not untill 12 oclock she feels of the need of a good <u>education</u> so this morning we was talking about you and also of writing Baltimore I told why dont she go said no never while you are ther I will tell you the rest of the remark you was so much then she was that she would not let the people know that you was her sister. My <u>Dear</u> I will have to come to a brief close I have a pain in my side have had it all day please to direct my letter to N. 12 Wadsworth St the family send there love to.

Hartford Dec. 10, 1865

My Dear & Absent Sister

I would like to know what you are doing this morning perhaps preparing for church I am not going to attend today for this reason I have no thick shoes I did not feel very well yesterday I did not get out all day. Dear Rebecca I am very lonely her now Aunt Emily and Thommy took there departure for down East last Tuesday I have not heard from them as yet. Your mother brought a letter in here Thursday Morn from you to perruse. I suppose by this time you have got to your place of destination I sincerly hope you will get along doubtless you will I am sorry you did not get my letter before you started. How did you spend your thankgiven I will tell you how I spent mine. Sarah & I got the work done by 9 oclock I then dress myself and went to sewing on my dress like yours. About ½ ten A.M. Mr. Tines & Mr. Carter came in the gent that use to go with M Robison. They staid until 12 I had music most of the time Mr. E is a very fine player Mr. Tine has fix my guitar and sound very nicely.

Mr. T has been quite attentive to me this week he has been or rather down here three times this week will be his last he think the boat will not run any longer he has promise me that he will come up quite often from NH this winter to see me. Dear Sister I flatter myself that he think a great deal of me I tried him yesterday something I said to him. O Rebecca how do you suppose that told me that he loved me and also ask me for my company. I know you cant guess so I will tell you no one but your friend <u>Gabriel Moore</u> he came in most every night he wish me to give his best regards to Miss Rebecca he also said if he could write I he would write to you Rebecca I feel worried I suppose you will say I am always borrowing trouble I will tell you what it is I dont think Mr. Sands is long for this world he has got a horrid cough yesterday I send Sarah up to him for something for to eat today she found her father quite sick pray dont mentions it I dont think Aunt E take very good care of her husban[. . . .]

Jim came in to see me last night he ask Aunty Primes where she was going if to see Addie he said he want to come too I was washing up my tea things he staid down with me untill your mother put a mustard part on Mr. Sands side then when your mother was ready to go he bid me adviere and wish me to come in and see him[. . . .] My Brother dont write any more to me I suppose he dont like it I did not come I wish I had of gone as I was not to work. I sent Sarah to Ms Crowell[10] with the lace she ask if I was at home being inform that I was sorry they did not know like to had me come their I am sorry too I told Mr. T he thought I would get along not to worried how can I help it. I hope dear Sister I will hear from you this week.

Please to direct you letter No 12 Wadsworth St.

Except all my best love for yourself

I remain you loving Sister

Addie

Dec. 13, 1865

My Darling Sister

I have at last rec your long look for letter your mother just brought in to me[. . . .] Mr. Smith brought it down and said it been there almost a week I would like to know the meaning of that I thought you would not keep me waiting so long if you was well. Dearest Sister I am glad you arrive to your place of <u>destination.</u> No doubt you will get along very nicely if not the least doubt that you will gain the esteem and affections all around you. I hope it will agree with you think little of yourself as well of others[. . . .] Mr. Sands home sick I am doing all I can for him the proper person is his wife. He mean so I cant bear to hear him Bell staid with me last night and Mr. Sand wake me a little after three wish me to take the key up to Mr. John Randle. You know where he lives, so Bell said I should not go without her so we got ready and after we got out in the street it was raining very hard and it was so dark I was realy afraid and so was Bell so we went after Mr. Asher. He went with us willingly. I got quite wet I have not seen[. . .]

Dear Sister you mother has gave me six pairs of draws to make for a lady. I want to get money enough together to pay for a coat I got. On Monday your mother got it for me it was $17.00 the prices was $22.00 the reason I got it at that price Bell went to Mr. Stars to get nine she like except the light one she thought she would have a black so Mr. Stars said if she would take one that he would take five dollars off so they said they let him know. Bell got one into Griswell only $45.00 it is a beautiful coat so they thought I better take the $17.00 one and pay Mrs. Primus when I get the money I dont know when that will be I only got $6.00 towards its new I wish you could get something for me to do down there how quickly I would come.

Mr. Tines call yesterday he was quite affectionate to me yes my love we have got good friends again I am the same little Addie judging other wrongly I will not be able to write very lengthy missive I have got to geet some of these draws done this week I am sorry that I did not get your letter before. O Mr. Tines wish me to give his best regard to you and he would like to see you very much. All send there love to you except my best love from your affectionate Sister

Addie

PS Mr. Tines is in Phila I rec a letter last Friday he is not well.
Addie

Chapter Six

"Justice, impartial justice . . ."

WINTER/SPRING 1866

R EBECCA'S letters in the spring of 1866 introduce the major
themes of her correspondence with her family. She keeps them up
to date on the customs, weather, and politics of the Eastern Shore. The
customs interest her because they differ a great deal from those of her
own region. Rebecca's observations suggest that there are definite dis-
tinctions between black southerners and black Yankees, between free
blacks and freed blacks. The weather is of profound importance
because it determines her activities, where she will go, whether she will
be able to hold school. Most important, the letters present both the
larger political struggles in which the freed people are engaged and the
day-to-day struggles of all blacks to be treated as free citizens of this
fragile democracy.

Primus's weekly letters to her parents serve as documents that nar-
rate one of the most important dimensions of African American history—the very first steps from slavery to freedom. This period, which
historians have named Presidential Reconstruction, witnessed the passage of the Fourteenth, Fifteenth, and Sixteenth Amendments to the
Constitution. In Primus's letters we hear the story of black people who
for the first time engaged in congressional politics and attempted to
exercise newly won rights that continued to be denied them. She
sketches a portrait of black citizens utilizing the courts to protect their
rights, eagerly seeking work, and educating themselves and their children. Fully aware of herself as an active participant in the emancipation process, she is a liaison between the free blacks of New England
and the newly freed ones of Maryland.

As such, she recognizes her responsibilities as threefold: first, she
must educate black children and adults alike; second, she must act as a

role model for them; and third and just as important, she has to keep her family and community in Hartford informed about the process of emancipation. Although her letters clearly illustrate the class and regional biases of her uplift ideology, her dedication and commitment to the cause of freedmen are unfaltering.[1] In Rebecca's eyes, her future is directly linked to the future of the race.

Rebecca, the politically informed correspondent, announces her support of the Civil Rights Bill of 1866, which "defined all persons born in the United States (except Indians) as national citizens and spelled out rights they were to enjoy equally without regard to race—making contracts, bringing lawsuits, and enjoying the benefit of 'all laws and proceedings for the security of person and property.' "[2] However, the bill did not seek to guarantee black political rights, nor did it attempt to protect freedmen from the acts of violence to which they were subjected. President Andrew Johnson eventually vetoed the Civil Rights Bill.

Even Rebecca and other teachers are not immune to intimidation and violence. She has confrontations with the postmaster, Mr. Charles Lane, who refuses to deliver her mail and tampers with her abolitionist newspapers.

At every turn, blacks were met with resistance to their efforts to exercise their newly earned rights. Nevertheless, as John W. Alvord reported, freed people of the Eastern Shore, "as usual, are alive to the importance of the work and feel that it is a vital point in their future welfare. They are doing all they can to help along plans for their education."[3]

Rebecca's letters, we learn, are not written simply for her family but also provide reports and analyses for a larger community with whom they are shared. Although she protests against having her letters read by others, she uses her epistles to rally support for the efforts of the freed people, particularly as they attempt to build schools.

Although there is only one surviving letter from Rebecca during the winter of 1866, Addie continues to write weekly. Her letters imply Rebecca's responses and keep us informed of the Hartford circle. During most of 1866 she works as a domestic—taking care of children and cleaning—as well as taking in sewing from various black and white Hartford women. Rebecca writes of the herbal remedies she takes for stomach trouble. Senna, wormwood, and balsam of fir are all herbal laxatives.[4]

[n.d.]⁵

[. . .] I rec'd. a letter from Gertrude on Tuesday. She also sent me a couple of papers, the Courant & a Republican. She informs me that they were moving to 153 Market St. How come they to sell their house and purchase down in that part of the city? I am quite surprised. She says the will of the late Mrs. Bunce is to be contested. Is it correct?

I have written but one letter this week & that was to Mr. Israel to send him my Bill for salary. I made it out & thought I sent it with my report. Did I send it to you instead? With yours & Addie's I've rec'd. five this week.

[. . .] I'm very much pleased with the 2 books. Some one also sent me a copy of the "National Anti-Slavery Standard," a weekly paper published by the Am. A–S Soc. N.Y. I've not read it yet. The Independent that I rec'd. last Saturday was exceedingly interesting and I've read about everything there is in it. It contains a great deal about Johnson,⁶ and much important news from all sources. I sent Miss Usher the first one also the Freedmen's Record. Of late I have been highly favored with reading matter. I can digest it all easily I find.

Your letter, full of interest and news, gave me great pleasure as usual. I do not remember writing to you that I was not feeling well. I had taken a dose of Senna that week & my stomach felt badly all the following week. I drink my worm wood to give me an appetite for I seldom relish my food unless I do. As for that Balsam of Fir, I had entirely forgotten it and it's purpose. I will try it as you prescribed[. . . .]

What has induced Henry Jones to move to Boston? I read in the Republican that the colored population at Boston is estimated at about 3,000, some of whom are worth $50,000 a piece. I think that speaks well for the industrious ones there.

I'm glad to hear from Jim once more, also to know that he is well and as independent as ever. He did not mean <u>harm</u> in looking at your birds mother, and I think you must have a witness to prove the deed of his attempt to possess one of them, that time to which you allude. Give my love to him & tell him to be a good boy till I come then we'll make it all <u>right</u>. I never forget him though I do not think to mention him always when I'm writing. Still I always look for something about him when you write. Little Jim is well & as lively as a cricket. He slept in my bed last night, but I opened the window and let him out before day. He's a very neat cat & is very particular to <u>ask</u> when he desires to go out. He sends his love to all.

Freemasonry, the first secret order for black Americans in the New World, was organized in 1775 by a black Bostonian, Prince Hall. Though black Masons were barred from white lodges, Hall and his fellow Masons were initiated by British military men. Less than a decade later, in 1784, these black Masons received their charter as African Lodge No. 459 by the Mother Grand Lodge of England. From then on, all black lodges were known as Prince Hall Masons. Rebecca's father was a member of Hartford's black lodge. The black Masons of Hartford were central to the institution- and community-building efforts of the city's black population.[7] In 1868, James Ralston, grand master of the Prince Hall Masons, petitioned the Connecticut state legislature to desegregate Connecticut's schools.[8] As Addie's letters demonstrate, the Masons also hosted black Hartford's major social activities.

With this letter, Addie introduces Bell Sands, Rebecca's new cousin-in-law. Mrs. Sands represents a different kind of woman from Addie or Rebecca. She is the fodder for a great deal of gossip in Addie's letters as well as in the community as a whole. Although she is a flirtatious, sensual extrovert who incites the wrath of the women of the community, she seems to be well liked by the men and loved by her very devoted husband, Thomas Sands.

Jan. 1, 1866

Dear Sister

I wish you a happy New Year. It has been very dull New Years to me I have been sewing all day and this eve Mr. Thomas [Sands] & Wife and I are invited to a Candy pull to Mrs. Mcguire. Guess we are not going untill 9 P.M. it is rather disagreeable night and its has been so all day. We went to the Methodist last eve and we got there it was crow[d]ed we hardly got a seat it was 10clock when we got home Mr. Ross spoke very plainly to his members since he had been there not one of them offer him a piece of bread a glass of water he ask them if they called that Christianity some of them must of taken little of it. Henrietta inform me last night that you had not rec any

letters from home last week I wrote to you on the 24th of Dec I hope
you have got it. The Masons Banquet came up very nicely quite a
number attend and several strangers was there Mrs. L Nott was
there and was dancing all the time. I saw her that afternoon and told
me that she was not going to dance. Bell fainted she dance to much.
Rebecca I wish you could take a view at Thomas wife every body is
surprise at his taste as well as myself. I dont think she is educated she
does not show it I realy hafter look myself[. . . .]

Your mother send you several paper and would like to know
wheather you had rec them or not. Mrs. Bell Sands wish me to
inform you that you had another cousin she is very lovly indeed I
just got thoughs draws done you mother charges 75cts a pair[. . . .]

Addie describes a visit to a prison and to Colt Arms, a state-of-the-art
gun factory founded by Samuel Colt. The company provided housing for
its employees and sponsored many events for the city of Hartford. Colt's
palatial estate drew admiration from many Hartford citizens.

Hartford Jan. 7 1866

My Dearly Adopted Sister

I will bid you good morning I thought I would call to see you and
spend a few hours with you. It is a snowing and it will prevent me
attending Church today. The two Mrs. Sands has a note book and I
presume we are going to have some singing. Mr. Thomas is reading
over his lecture. Mr. Sands has not return yet. Last Wednesday A.M.
I rec your loving interesting letter I peruse it in the cars on my way
to the State prison in company with Thomas & his wife.

I felt very sorry for the prisoners there was 184 out of that number was 7 colored. I was very anxious to see them go to dinner so we
waited untill the hour they out and all march for the pails as they
went to their cells had a pan in their hands. I thought it was a basin
of water to wash in they had quite a laugh at me I suppose they had
a table and all could sit around it. On our way home we visited Colts
Willow factory. I was very much please with the works one of the
rooms we was insulted. I did not take any pleasure the Man that
took us around had to speak to them. We enjoyed it little better they
imployed 150 hands quite a number. We went to visit Mrs. Colts

grounds and the hot houses. Father Kemp and his troupe is coming tomorrow night. I would like to hear them again.

Mr. & Mrs. Jones is here and staying with your Mother she is just the same she runs in when ever she get a chance to do so day before yesterday she came in was in hardly five min. before her husband wish her to return home and afterwards rec a severe scolding for going out that eve. We expect Mr. Philips and his brother and Mr. A you know who I mean[. . . .]

Dear Rebecca Thomas has just handed me his gold pen to write with I like it very much it writes very easy I would like to own one. you speaking about your injunctions being carried out I have notice that I have been kind care for by your Mother & Sister I did not know that it had been you own. Miss Elizabeth Sanders rec your letter and was quite please I hear I think of going there this week. you ask what is the matter with Bell & Julia on account of <u>Moses</u> she <u>loves</u> him when Bell was in Boston she had a good time and she hardly see him now Mrs. Ives sets him out nicely and said that no daughter of hers would go with him Mr. Ives knows but wont says I suppose he is to much like himself. I was told yesterday that Mr. Aldridge told your Mother that he had not seen any young lady he loved as he did Bell by all appearances that his love is return for they are together every night even to Saturday night I would get very tired of that is it was me and my <u>friend</u>. I rec a letter from him Thursday he was quite well he inquired very particular after your health.

[. . .] Rebecca you say that you lie awake in bed it is the same with myself I even wake up in the night and keep awake for an hour at a time my whole thought dwell upon you sometime once in a while Mr. Tines. I am sleeping on a feather bed too and together with Sarah I keep pretty warm this winter.

[. . .] I give Thomas you message and felt quite disappointed for he would like have one letter from you wish me to give you a description of his wife I like her very well she is very lively I dont think she is fit to be a wife[. . . .] she think every thing of her husband she is a half a head taller and she is the color of Harriet Rime and the look of it in part that her hair may be as long as Mrs. Aiker she wears a net all the time Aunt Emily tell me that Thomas is going to have her study I am afraid it will be quite a task for she dont care about <u>books</u> she has been here nearly two weeks it will be Monday and I only seen a book in her hand but once I ask her if she did not like to read her ans was sometime. I think I have said enough[. . . .]

The week Mr. Tines was here we spent the eve with Bell so Thomas came in and we was setting together I like to hear him talk he is very interesting we was talking considerable and I caught Mr. T looking at me twice so Bell inform me that he was looking at me all the time. He did not [know] that Thomas was married at that time so he write and wanted to know if any other Gentleman stood nearer to me then he did I had to smile when I read it.

Thomas call me his Sister he would look upon as such. The Methodist had a festival last week two night got to fighting and four was taken to the watch house. I suppose you have reopen your school how are you getting along and by the time you have a full school. will you tell me in your nexe the age of youngest and oldest dont put your self to much trouble[. . . .]

Aunt Emily I think loves Thomas better than she does Sarah for she show it I think she likes <u>males</u> better then <u>female</u> I think he think good deal of her.

My Beloved Sister I have wrote all that would be of interest Bell Sands to me tell you again that you have a cousin she speaks of you often I wonder what make her? I hope to hear from you soon the family their love to you

except my best love from your
Affectionate Sister
Addie
except a kiss

Hartford Jan. 16 1866

My Dearly Beloved Sister

[. . .] You ask me what I wore that the Mason Banquet I wore my new dress and white flowers in my head Bell also wore the same I dance a little I find my <u>head</u> will not allow me to indulge too freely before long I will have to cease altogether. In reference to Henrietta I am afraid she will not be able to inform you My Dear Sister we see each other very little she know nothing about my health but My Darling I will inform you all.

You dont seem to understand about Thomas wife I think you can judge better for yourself when you see her you ask if he seem to manifest much affection at times I rec as much from him as she does and his Mother more then any of us. She is very agreeable indeed she has been very kind to me. She inform me that she spend $26.70 in twenty months and did not have to pay any bread out of it she says what ever she wanted she got cake or candy & ice cream she has not much clothes she dont wear any night dress. I could not sleep in bed with my husband if I had any I know you would not my fastidious Sister[. . . .]

You ask me how I come to repeat my visit to Eliza I will tell you how you wish me to give the Album on Christmas day I done so on the 26 I rec your letter with a note inclose in it to her I was going up then so I stop in and gave it to her. You ask who do I mean by Mrs. Bell Sands [?] Thomas wife she send the message to you she likes you hearing your family speaking so frequently of you. When Bell Primus is in here we have to say No 20 Bell. We have great deal of fun in here sometime. Bell brought me in a very nice little cake Saturday I eat it yesterday it was very nice I have not had my piece of turkey yet.

Dear Sister I am not greiving after for Mr. Tines my <u>love</u> is not so much for him for that is his last letter inform me that he will be in NY this week I heard the Granite is going to run to NH soon he told Bell that he was going to try to come to Hartford before the winter over[. . . .]

Dear Rebecca dont say anything I would not be at all surprise if Mr. Tines want me to marry him nexe fall and what have I got nothing if I had been dealt rightly might of had money now so it is[. . . .]

The following letter is especially interesting because Addie acknowledges that she loves and wants to be with Rebecca, then announces that she is glad Rebecca approves of her relationship with Mr. Tines. She has decided that each relationship meets different needs.

Addie's refusal to attend a concert at Hartford's Allyn Hall because of a minstrel show is also relevant.

Hartford Jan. 21 1866

My Dearest and Loving Sister
I wish that I could exchange pen & paper for a seat by your side

& reclining in your <u>arm</u> as I have in days gone by. Dear Rebecca for the first since you have been gone I attended SS Mr. Cross seem to be much please to see me he said he was glad to see so many out. The lesson was chap 13 of St. John first to the 15 verses nexe Sunday Mat 5 first to the 13 and wish all the classes commit to memory. Aunt Emily just inform me that it would SS concert[. . . .]

Tomorrow eve there will be a debating at Talcott Church Mr. Fred Cross & Mr. G Robison. Miss A Cross read. Mrs. Mary Randle has composition if nothing happens I must attend. Yesterday A.M. Mr. Asher ask me if I would go to Allyn Hall I did not go for they has the minstrils[. . . .]

Dear Rebecca I have been in little trouble this week I broke Aunt Emily butter dish and I know felt very sorry about it. She did not say much or I either. Went on so for two days so this A.M. she say if I did not want to speak to her I need not for she did not want any one to speak if they did not wish to. She also say she judge people by that way. She made feel very bad for she ought to know by this time that I think a great of her we are good <u>friends</u> now I shall try and keep so for the future.

Last Thursday A.M. I went to see Bell I was speaking of you so Bell says come up stairs I will give you Becca letter so when got up there I did not notice how B ask for the letter I know your Mother was not incline to let her have it so she went in the bedroom I told Bell I would not read if she got it. I thought it was very funny for she always wanted me to read her letters and even took the pains to bring them in to me for to peruse. Your Mother brought it I would not take it at first the reason she would not give it to Bell she spoke imprudent to her. She had to insist upon me taking it. At the mean time Mr. Jones came up and wanted to [see] if it was a gentleman letter I hesitate to peruse she said or no. She said I thought as much of you if you was a gentleman she also said if cither one of us was a gent we would marry. I was quite surprise at the remark Mr. James & I had quite a little argument. He says when I found some one to <u>love</u> I will throw you over my shoulder. I told I [him] I have unshaken confidence in your love. I do sincerely believe him never. You Mother also agreed with me. What do you think of that? He has no Idea that someone is now paying there <u>distress</u> to me I have not heard them for a week.[9]

[. . .] Madam Rumor says that Emma and her husband is

parted we dont know how true it is she goes home once in a while I believe she is still at Mrs. Carters I dont know what to think of your dream I have thought of it quite often

Dearest friend & only Sister I will never doubt your <u>love</u> for me again you say you put my picture under your pillow I wish I had the pleasure laying along side of you. I am delighted to think you are still pleas. with your boarding place. Dear Sister I am very much delighted to hear you say that you like Mr. Tines if I should marry him I hope to have some please and comfort for he likes you very much. I thank you kindly for informing me about your school I hope you will speak of your school quite often I would like to hear. Will you tell me who is Emily?

When we was going to SS we stoped in No 20 I had a nice time with Jim he grows finely he is so fat. My Darling Sister I must tell you my dream I had last Wedn I thought I had to marry Mrs. Jackson she was determine that I did not know what I should do I did not wanted to get to Mr. Tines ears I was dress in black I had my back hair curl and front as I always wear it we went Church I forgot pure white coif frings in it finger deep that was tied around my head Mrs. J and I in one carriage and my step father in the other and when we got in Church it was crowded when we came out I got in the carriage I did not know anything until home I found myself on the lounge with my dress unfasten then I commence cry continued until I awoke I was very glad it was all a dream I also dreampt of you two night one night I was standing and seeing you caress another lady and not me how bad I did feel[page missing]

Hartford Feb. 1 1866

My Darling & Adopted Sister

[. . .] You say dear Sister that your brains are so full of thoughts no wonder you forget I do wish that I had some of your <u>thoughts</u> I could get along better in this world then I do My loving Sister those beautiful lines you pen <u>does respond to them and ever will</u> I am glad you have such bright hopes of meeting us again It seem to me that you have been gone six months I heard that the society has Adopted you as their Child[. . . .] I do my dear occupy your seat and H attend occasional I also use your Hymn Book you say you hold me responsible for it I will take the best of care of it I do not care about going out in the eve I rather spend it with you. I did not attend the debating meeting when the time came I did not want to go out Bell Pretended to be provoke at my not going with them. Dear Sister I do not like to intrude on <u>lovers</u> they are very much devoted to each other you ought to see them.

[. . .] I dreampt of you last night It was a singular dream I dont rest very good at night Sarah is my bed fellow and awful one at that she is not satisfied at kicking me she grate her teeth it makes me very nervous to hear her. I would like to have had the pleasure of dining with you last Sunday I have not had any Chicken pie this year. I hope dear Sister it will be pleasant for your sake. last Monday P.M. Bell & I spen with your Mother & Bell I also staid to tea second time since you have been gone Jim go in my lap as soon as I went in remain there almost tea time and then did not want to get down then he is a fine cat. Our cat is around grow finely you wont know him. Henrietta is quite well I have not seen her this week I go to see her once in a while [. . .] I wish that I was going to be with you tonight I would like to pillow my head on your bosom good night
Addie

Friday 5 P.M.

Dear Sister I have a few moments to spare I thought I would devote them to you I have been ironing all this P.M. not been done long this A.M. I accompany Bell Sands up the street something for Thomas. On our way up there a murder was commited in the barber shop under the City Hotel you remember the concert [. . .] in Mulberry street the man that keep it short another in the temple. I think it is dreadful to think of it he tried to get away they caught him after a little search.

[. . .] I will be glad when Mrs. Crowell will want me for I think Mr. Sands is getting tired of something too Bell Sands notice. Aunt Emily has change she says she wants to go home this week on Friday but her Husband does not want her to go untill he goes no one know when that will be perhaps not this winter that my thoughts I will not belong out of my bed this night its rather dull good night
Aertheana

Feb. 12 Monday

Dear Sister

[. . .] There was a funeral at Talcott St. Church this P.M. A

Talcott Street Church, where the Primus family worshiped.

Plato died Saturday A.M. 5 o'clock leaving a babe two weeks old I heard that she died for want of good care leaves a large family of children only seven I should think Mr. Plato would feel bad. Mr. Cirben and Gerry Smith are married gone to Boston on a wedding tour she must been in want of a husband. When I came home this eve I found a letter from Mr. Tines he wish me to give his kindest regard

Dear Sister direct your letters to him No 97 Grand St.[10] in the care of Mrs. Hannie Histring. Bell Sands is sick; they say she has been out of head they lay it to me. Aunt Emily laugh I dont think she is very sick you know though smile of hers nothing like having a kind Husband My darling Sister I cant write you a very lengthy missive for I got to get back to make Miss M bed. [. . .] I have not read your report yet Miss Wells has it yet I believe now I must go I will

again soon you must not punish me for this letter they all send their
to you

> except my best
> love from your
> loving Affectionate Adopted Sister
> Addie

After the Civil War, black women had less competition from Irish
women for domestic work. Working-class white women were moving
into factory work. Addie begins to work for the Reverend John T. Huntington, a professor of Greek at Trinity College.

Hartford Feb. 18 1866

My Dear Sister

Here I am in a new home I feel realy low spirited I sew all the
week to Mrs. Saunders. Last Thursday when I return home I rec a
message left by Mrs. C Jefferson. I came here to see her. A Miss
Williams that was here is going to leave and would like to have me
come here. They say the work is not hard and Mr. Huntington gives
$2.50 a week. I thought of it and something told me try it. The girl at
Mrs. Crowell is not a going to leave until the boat commence to run.
I am afraid I will not get along Mrs. H is rather a hard person to get
along with[. . . .]

I heard to day that Mrs. Wright promise her Sister Mrs. Plato
that she would take her baby and now Mr. W will not let his wife
take it aint that mean poor Hatie has her hands full[. . . .]

What do you think Levina is in the family way again nearly five
months Mrs. Saunders told me they are going to break up and go to
Boston to live this spring I go very seldom to see them I got so I dont
want to see any of them Mrs. S and Levina went to the flora festival
last Wednesday eve Mrs. S did try so hard to have me all night last
week F too. I love my home too well to stay from it when you not
here last Friday eve Bell & her beau spent the eve with us we played
domino until ten and after they was gone I ans Mr. Tines letter I did
not write a very long letter for they all retire and you know Mr.
Sands is very choice of his gas. Tom Saunders is in NY went down
to meet his lady love Miss Brown from Phila. They say she is very

pretty E show me set of studs made out of hair that she them a
present to T there a beautiful I dont think they cost less then $16.00
Mr. P made his wife a handsome present of a pair of earings they
talk of going to NY when Mr. T return and take Minnie with them.
She is very rough child nothing refine about her—in fact no refinement in any of them[. . . .] A grand fancy dress ball coming off nexe
week on the 21 have not heard whether Bell is going or not Henrietta
expect to go I went in there after I put the children to bed and found
Mr. John Francis in there. Now dear Sister I shall ans your kind and
very interesting missive Miss Usher must be a very congial correspond then tenor of her letters are very much like yours I suppose
you will become the very best of friends in time. I am please to here
she is geting along so well now in her school. I think they making
preparations for a picnic I am glad to hear that you school in
improving I would dearly love to hear them sing. You say I never
spoke in any my of letters about you rules I have never have seen
them I have ask twice and I am done asking My Dear I have not
seen a Anglo but ever since you have been gone your Mother dont
take them and I am to <u>poor</u>[. . . .][11]

Bell Sands wants to go home now because I have come here to
live and her Husband dont want her too until he is ready to go I
think she is very fond of the Gents society they all make nothing in
kissing her. I dont think Aunt Em has much opinion of her daughter
in law.

[. . .] Henrietta is in little trouble again the people she is living
with there house is going to be sold at public auction on Tuesday
they do not know what they are going to do she the Lady I mean did
not know until she read it in the paper H says she is crying all the
time he has lived intirely too fast now he see the fruits of it even now
he has every thing that the market can afford[. . . .]

Rebecca, questioning the nature of Addie's relationship with Bell
Sands, seems to suggest she is beneath Addie and therefore not worthy
of her friendship. Given the difference in status between Addie and
Rebecca, it seems in Rebecca's eyes that class does not prohibit friendships from forming but questions of morality do. Rebecca recognizes
that though Addie is not economically middle class, she has middle-
class aspirations. Addie's response also implies Rebecca's expression

of jealousy over the growing relationship between Addie and Bell Sands.

Addie comes to a very important decision in this letter. She decides to demand pay for her work from all her employers, "colored" or "white."

Hartford Feb. 25 1866

My Dear Sister

[. . .] I am please to hear you speak so well of you school and also give you such satisfactions I am very much oblige to you for the five dolls now my cloak will be all paid for it. I have paid twelve already now I will enjoy wearing it. I suppose I had no business telling Bell she need not tell you for the future I will attend to my own business.

Dear Rebecca you ask how is Thomas wife and I are such good friends. She has always trusted me well I have never told you that I loved her for I dont and neither do I think she is my equal for there is no refinement about her and as for intelligence she has none and dont mention intellectual powers. If others treat her well and she has the impression that she like and so far is live by her Husband family and relatives I dont think an outsider has got any right show any sign of superiors or dislike. My Darling I have ans your question as well as I can this way when we meet it will be understood better.

[. . .] I spoke to your mother about your rubber boots she will see the society about it. Doubtless you would like to know how I get along here so far very well I must tell you something when Mrs. Jeff came for me she left word that Mr. H pays $2.50 when I came around to see them she told me the same last Sunday eve she began to talk about Mrs. Williams that was here in the conversation she says they never paid but two dolls and perhaps they would be willing to pay two & quarter I give her to understand that I would not stay for that so Monday P.M. Mrs. W went up to get her money and came down with out for Mr. H would not pay her prices that was two & half. I told Mrs. W and J I was going to have a talk with Mr. H if he was not willing to give me that I should leave that night when I went to him he never hesitate to give it to me. Rebecca I have been working for nothing comparitively speaking now I have come to a decision stand that people shall pay me for my work I dont care

<u>colored</u> or White. To speak plainly Mrs. J does not like it that she only get 50 cts more then the second girls. Mrs. William's think that through her they got displeased with her if she had of staid until the 16 of nexe month she would of been here one year. They say the children did not like Mrs. W they seem to like me very well the youngest make me kiss him every night when I put him to bed we see how thing will end when I have been here a month.

[. . .] Dear Sister I have told you all. Please to direct your letters No 15 Cor of Elm & Clinton Hartford
except my best kiss
your Adopted Sister
Addie

Hartford Mar. 4 1866

My Dear Sister

The bells are ringing for church how many are answering it[. . . .] I have not been out all day or rather to church. Mrs. Huntington was confine Thursday she has a daughter they seem to be very proud and delighted about it. Dont you think there was no one with her but Mrs. Jefferson I went after Dr. Taft I did not find at his office or at home. She knew that she would be sick the first of the month and was to mean to send for the nurse and did not get here until 10 A.M. nexe day they send me after Aunt Emily to come and stay that night or your Mother. I could not get either. Your Ma said that she had been out of that line of business for sometime so Mr. H sit up with her he felt mortified.

Mrs. H is very mean in somethings. Last eve she ask me if it was pleasant she would like me to take Harry to church this A.M. It was very damp and I was delighted to hear Mr. H say that he could not go out. It cleared up quite pleasant and this P.M. Mrs. J took him with her she is welcome to do it.

[. . .] The Methodist put end to the protracted meeting last Friday night Mr. Buehards one of those comments again. Some of them make it a parties getting religion every year only one female all Males.

[. . .] I had the pleasure of perusing the Rules of your School last eve that your Mother so kindly sent me by Sarah I like them very much these particular to the pupils. I suppose in time I will see your report (patience is a virtue).

[. . .] I guess your school will ahead of all of them there is but very few take such a interest as you do except your friend Mrs. Asher. I told Bell about sending you Battle Cry of Freedom[. . . .] These picture of you are excellent they do so look like you.

Addie relates two scandalous stories. The first is about Bell Sands. The second is about Rebecca's younger sister, Bell Primus. Bell's family and friends are especially concerned about her involvement with the mysterious Mr. Aldridge.

Hartford Mar. 11 1866
8 o'clock P.M.

My Dear Sister

[. . .] Bell has acted very mean toward me she know that I told her that I was not going to get it up one thing I could not get out to invite any one. I told her and her Dear friend Mr. A to tend and they said they would and Bell was to let me know whether they would have it or not and never came near me. I have not seen her until today at church[. . . .] That mean contemptable of a Aldridge has made a change girl of Bell for I am opinion she has got some of his ways[. . . .]

A Mrs. Thurston send Bell Sands a letter stating that she had peruse a letter that she sent to her Husband William Thurston asking what kind a woman was she and was going to have the penalties of the law put upon her she send it up. Thomas with one from her saying she was not guilty of such a thing Thomas then wrote to Mrs. T demanding explanations, and did not see any ans so went to NH Thursday and no better satisfied after all he might as well staid at home. One thing Bell Sands done went in to see Bell when WT was up here on a visit and was no one home but him and remain all the P.M. and the mean time kissing[. . . .] Aunt Emily has no confidence in at all.

Today I have heard some thing else two weeks ago today Aunt Emily and myself was return from Church and met Bell Primus going back I ask the cause and said she had lost something. Sarah was with her at first S went along with us and Aunt Em ask her what Bell had lost she said a letter and was out of the envelope. I said that

was smart almost week after that Mrs. Johnson told me that she
speak it of and read and then gave it to Ellen Haris she done the
same and some parts was very improper and said also that Bell
thought herself in the family way and sigh[. . . .]

This day Addie shares with Rebecca is especially interesting in showing the physical demand her work places on her, such as the number of
times she is required to go up and down the stairs during the course of
her day, not to mention her strenuous chores.

Hartford Mar. 25 1866
4 P.M.

My Dear Sister
    [. . .] I went to the Biccum last Monday night I was very much
please with the meeting the debate was if the Black Man will have
any rights that the white man bound to respect Mr. Cros Mr. Freeman & Haldin and Clogget. Mrs. Robison was to read a composition and Mrs. Mary Randle was to read they did not have time I
think something of going to morrow night if I have time or if it not
to cold. They was great many out some of the young ladies carried
on[. . . .]

Half past 7 P.M.

Dear Sister
    I have just come from up stairs I have put the children to bed I
believe I am done for the night. Do you know that I have five pairs of
stairs to go up 20 times and sometime more yesterday I counted how
many times I went up and down before breakfast six time you can
judge for yourself there is a hundred & seven steps when it time for
me to go to bed my limbs ache like the tooth ache I think I shall
leave the second week April Mr. & Mrs. Huntington dont want me
to leave and neither do the children.
    [. . .] I bought Aunt Emily a butter dish I could not get any like
the one I broke I have told you all that will be of any interest I have
to go of errands for Mrs. H most every day besides do my work,
your Adopted Sister

Hartford Apr. 1, 1866

My Dear Sister

What a beautiful day it has been this morn how I wish for you so that we could enjoy a little walk together. I suppose many has enjoyed and made happy and other has been made to mourn. Lucy Wells was buried today between the hours of 12 & 1 she had the inflammatory rheumation she was sick six or seven weeks she was 22 years old. Mr. Ross attended the funeral he spoke very well indeed Lucy died happy very large funeral.

[. . .] Mrs. H wanted me to take Harry to church I refuse doing so I am no advocate to take White Children out or to Church either in the P.M. C & I had words and all about the house leaving the bread uncovered C has been scolding every since I told her I would not do the baby washing I dont speak to her now I dont think very soon.

[. . .] I thank you very much for the perusal of the pieces about the freedman aid society It speak very well of the Royal Oak teacher.

[. . .] My Dear you asking the last time about the Jackson girls I dont know any thing about them they beaus. I did hear that Frank been out on the hills to the Green I heard that the masquerade ball they had on Wednesday was for G Daniels they had not enough to make up two sets John Francis fell over the banisters pick him up for dead. Chas Jackson was so high that they had to carry home

Nexe Sunday I will be writing to you at home please direct your letters to No 12 Wadsworth St. except my best love

your Adopted Sister Addie

In this extraordinary letter, Rebecca provides a sense of the urgency, danger, excitement, and enthusiasm that blacks and their white allies experienced during the early years of Reconstruction.

Royal Oak, Talbot Co., Md.
Sat. 8 ¼ A.M.
Apr. 7 1866

My Dear Parents & Sister

Your letter was not rec'd until yesterday. I sent to the office on

Thurs. as was told there was no mail for me, I was somewhat disappointed, however I thought I should get it on Saturday so I endeavored to quiet my mind & make myself contented, when to my surprise yours and Addie's letters were sent to me about 6 P.M. I was delighted. I'm pleased to hear that you are all well and also that the box has finally started, for I had begun to feel quite uneasy about it. There have been enquiries made at the Easton P.O. every mail day since I rec'd your letter & Mr. Thomas went himself on Wed. he is going to send for it again today. I am in hopes to receive it.

[. . .] A great many of the people are planting, plowing up their grounds etc. vegetation too, is springing forth & soon I expect everything will be looking very thrifty about here. Mr. Thomas says people begin to plant before the frost is out of the ground. They raise wheat here. He had his land sown with wheat last year. I don't know what he intends to plant this season, he owns an acre of land on this road and this upon which he lives he rents. It belongs to an old maid and Mr. Thomas wants to buy it of her but she declines to sell. The house is small but comfortable and pleasant, he says he would raise it & enlarge it by adding one more room on the lower floor for a bedroom.

There is a plenty of work here now for men & I think none have occasion to complain for want of it. All have some kind of employment; at the saw-mill where Mr. Thomas works, from four to six men are constantly employed, all colored too. A number of men follow hewing, sawing, others are at work in the fields. Although the whites are mostly Secesh[12] here they all give colored men & women employment, the greatest difficulty is they do not pay sufficient wages & if the people will not accept their terms they send off and get "contrabands," as they are here denominated, to work for them so that it takes the labor right out of these people's hands & they are obliged to submit.

I hope there will be justice, impartial justice, given to the colored people one of these days. I was reading the "Civil Rights Bill" for colored & all people, in the "Communicator" & I will send it to you that you may read it if you've not already done so. As it had passed both houses of Congress with amendments I am very anxious to know whether Prest. Johnson has signed it or not. The Bill is excellent I think, only I hope the col'd. people will not take the advantage of the privileges it prescribes.

I have had real benefit all this week in perusing the "Independent" it goes down on Johnson pretty hard, & gives him his just dues. The paper is full of able & very interesting articles, all advocating the rights of the colored man. There is a good deal in it about Conn. & the Democracy. Rev. A.G. Beman has recd. a call to Mount Zion Cong'l. ch, Cleveland Ohio. I wonder if that's the Society Mrs. Green was in Hartf'd. begging for that time?

[. . .] I thought about the meeting house's Fast Day, I'm glad there is so much sympathy manifested in behalf of the Col'd. man's Rights, and I hope the subject will continue to be agitated throughout the country by our smart intelligent col'd. men as well as white, until these rights which are so unjustly withheld from us now, have been obtained.

I would have liked one of those question books much, but you can tell me the subject of each lesson as they occur, as you've previously done, and it will answer every purpose. I'm pleased to know they've chosen Mr. Osborn to superintend the school, the choice of Miss M. Fellows to fill Miss Welch's place is a good one too. I shall be delighted with all of those books that's been sent also the papers, and all the other articles the box contains. Please tender my heartfelt thanks to the Donors.

[. . .] I cannot conceive how it is others aside from my own folks, are so desirous to peruse my letters. I cannot think they are so <u>very</u> interesting. I never expected or even thought of any others perusing them. Why don't you read them to Miss Wells yourself, for I do not think they <u>always</u> bear inspection.

[. . .] I tell Mr. Thomas I shall be obliged to enter complaints at the office about my letters for I think they must forget to send them sometimes and so they lie over.

[. . .] The children are all getting better of the measles, some have returned to school, there are several cases yet in this neighborhood, new ones.

[. . .] I'm quite surprised to hear of Miss Hamilton's boarding with colored people, Mr. Thos. says if it was here the house would be stoned. I'm glad she enjoys her labor, the freed men, women etc. in Washington are different class of people from those in this state I am told.

I rec'd. a letter from Miss Dickson at Trappe, Tues. she has 74 schol's. & until the last month every thing has gone on quietly & well

& now she's stoned by white children & repeatedly subjected to insults from white men, in passing they have brushed by her so rudely she says "as to almost dislocated her shoulders," she says she tries to bear it patiently. I feel real sorry for her, her position is truly an unenviable one. The whites are very mean there I'm told. White children take col'd. children's books from them, and otherwise misuse and ill treat them.

I've rec'd. no intelligence from any of the other teachers very lately. Now I must bid you good morning. I have been unable to write to Mrs. Cheney this week as I entered, so I must do so this P.M.

Remember me to all my friends & accept my best love to yourselves.

Your affect daughter & Sister R.P.

Apr. 8, 1866
Sun. P.M.

My dear parents & sister

I think I will add a few more lines to your letter[. . . .]

The box has not arrived yet unless it came to Easton last night. I guess the Postmaster must think its of some consequence. He is on the watch for it too. I shall get it as soon as it comes, we shall send again tomorrow & Tuesday also. The Independent & Record with a letter from Mr. Israel[13] constituted my mail yesterday. Mr. I says [he] hopes I had a pleasant vacation. I think he must be a jovial & pleasant man. Mr. Graham was at Easton last Sunday & delivered a lecture to the colored people, they are going to build their school house now[. . . .]

Rebecca

There are no letters from Rebecca to her family until June. Addie's letters suggest that Rebecca spent part of this time in Hartford.

Hartford Apr. 10 1866

My Beloved & Cherish Sister

What a unpleasant day I am very much disappointed I was in hopes that I would be able to see you this P.M. No sign of it now[. . . .] What are you doing reading or sleeping? Perhaps you have been indulging in both. Such days is this I like to be near you time passes of no small pleasanter[. . . .]

I finish that skirt and also mend one to put on to morrow Mrs. Nott use to make it a practice to sew on Sundays. Dear Sister Mr. Nott is reading the Anglo something he was reading cause me to lend listening ear it was this the marriage of Mr. H J. I hope he has done well I was quite surprise to hear it excuse me for pening this. My Beloved Sister your last note gave pleasure and also cause me pain. My One & only Sister I know that I have done wrong. It will always be a tinge of remorse.

My Darling Sister you say trust you until I have even to mistrust you <u>never</u> will <u>I have cause</u> to do so. You have been to me more than any living soul has been or ever will be you have been more to me then a <u>friend</u> or <u>Sister.</u> My Idol Sister God being the judge I do not and never did doubt your constancy or your affections. I had a little fears about something but they all have vanish never will I allow such thought again.

Sister you say if I can not trust you can you trust me. I will let my actions speak for me about you trusting me have I ever ain't trust you if I have forgive my true Sister

I wish that I could express my feelings to you excuse me for this note I am your loving
Sister Addie

Hartford Apr. 15 1866
8 A.M.

My Dearly Beloved Sister
[. . .] Monday eve I went to see Mrs. Crowell they was very glad to see me Mrs. M wanted to know when I was coming that I had been engage to come them for some time and they was very glad that I had left Mrs. Hungtington. I am going the first of May. Poor Mr. C was delighted to see me. He wanted to know if he could rely upon my word I told him I thought he could. Tuesday A.M. I help Aunt Em about the house and we dress ourselves to ree Mr. Times in the P.M. he came and was very much please to see him. He inquired very particular after your health. I was going up to Mrs. Saunders so he accompany me as far Asylum Street[. . . .] I got home about nine oclock and what do you think I came across the Park alone[. . . .] Dont you think I am getting brave now-days? Wednesday I iron all

day just before tea time I call in to see your Mother and Bell was down stairs she came up before I left and was like herself Miss Booth came in I have not seen her for sometime while she was their Sarah came in After me for Harriet was here wanted to see me she invited me to spend Thursday and also the night of this week

Thursday I dress and went [?] beautiful day it was the opening of the Milliners and Main sts was crowded with Ladies I saw few colored Ladies[. . . .]

Friday I felt realy bad I suppose I walk so much I was in all the morn siting in the same spot I am now writing to you I then went in to your Mother she invited me to take tea Bell played for me and then in the I went up to Mrs. Saunders and Bell accompany me Elizabeth lend me her Guitar it look almost as bad is the one you lent me. Aunt Emily laugh enough at it.

Saturday Sarah and I kept her house Aunt Em was out to work I busy until one I then dress to rec my <u>friend</u> Mr. T. Sarah ask me if I would comb her hair which I did and she said she wish that she had a afternoon dress to put on when I came down she a clean apron and then sit down and took her knitting to wait the coming of Mr. T. He came at last I rather think he was little provoke since he ask me for my company he has never saw me alone. I dont care about it all time but once a year I would like it Bell would like to have us call in there we contemplate doing so on Tuesday then I wont see him until the first of May.

[. . .] I have been writing a hour and half so I must leave you until this eve so adieu

Addie

5 P.M.

[. . .] Talcott St Choir give a festival on Wednesday eve here Music both sacred and secular reading and dialogue I think I shall go as you know I am very fond of music only wish you was here. Saturday I was perusing over your letters and notes one I rec Jan 29th 1861 it is a pleasure to read them if you would like to read it I will send it providing that you will send it back to me. I would like to have you peruse it.

[. . .] Except my best and also a kiss. from your loving & adopted Sister—Addie

Hartford Apr. 29 1866

My Dear & Adopted Sister

[. . .] I have been out sewing for two weeks I guess siting so steady is the cause of my pain yesterday I was sewing for Mrs. Mary Goodwin in High St and I expect to go tomorrow and Friday and Saturday and the rest of the days to Mrs. Saunders. I dont think I could stand going out everyday.

[. . .] Henrietta is living with Mr. Wilson on Asylum Hill she dont like very much she want to go to Mrs. Bedfield. I dont think I shall go to the boat while Mr. Tines is on it. He expect to go to Saratoga last of June. Mr. Tines told he rec a letter from you I rec a letter from him last night he is rather low spirited I am coming home to see him Tuesday Aunt Emily is to Farmington she went Wednesday 3 P.M. expect her back tomorrow I wish Mr. Tines was here Sundays now when I did not want him the boat was here.

[. . .] O I must tell you Thomas Saunders gave his sister a present of a silk dress Saturday. It cost $9.00 per yard. He is the best of brother she tell me. Dont mention it he expect to be married I think it will be nexe fall.

[. . .] adieu my Sister

3 P.M.

Hartford May 6 1866

My Dearest & Adopted Sister

[. . .] Aunt Emily and I are going to remain in the house this beautiful springlike day on account of our unfortunate bonnet. The place she told her to be pressed has been careless and cant find it So I dont know what she will do. I dont expect to have mine until nexe week then I shall have Bell trimmed it for me with the same ribbon I had on it last summer I am not going to get any thing new for the only I want is cotton cloth. I cam out of draws I want a pair of shoes that will cut me a great deal I have a calico dress to wear in return with one I had last summer.

Dear Sister I must tell you the news Peter Nott and his family move to Boston Levina went Wedns P.M. Peter I understand went yesterday I went there so they requested me on Monday night from my work L wish me to go up stairs with her. then she ask which of those dresses I wanted of Mrs. Nott so of course I chose the best one and if you remember that striped calico that Mr. Nott bought they had not the rest of things to pick up so I was to call for them nexe evening Peter gave me those hoops earings that Mrs. Nott use to wear. the Charter oak pair to Mrs. Fuller that done so much for Mrs. Nott while on the boat so Tuesday I call and it rain very hard that I could not return home I had to remain the rest of the night. Jennie Strims was also there helping[. . . .]

My Dear & Adopted Sister

I truly wish that I could exchange pen and paper for a seat by your side and my head reclining on your soft bosom and having a pleasured chit chat with thee. It has been a lovely day most every one looking as blooming as a June rose. I attend S.S. and Mr. Cross seem to be very much please to see me I told him your message he was delighted and wish me to give his <u>love</u> to you and think its most time that you was coming home to your Dear friends that you have left[. . . .]

We had a colored minister to preach today he is from NY. I understand Mr. Cross I do not know his name he spoke very well his text was the first chapter of Romans and 14 ver. I do not know whether He will preach tonight or not.

[. . .] A Mr. Henry E Rovins was accidentally killed Friday P.M. from New Haven to the city he was passing from one car to the other and caught his foot in the door sill falling forward rolled of the car on to the track between the cars his right arm was crushed his head had a slight wound he died when he got to Berlin he leave a wife and two children he was buried today at 1 oclock from St John Church. I do think men ought to be careful some of his friends think he had been drinking for he indulge very freely when he was at home Mr. Saunders says he was one of his best friends He showed me his picture he was a fine looking man[. . . .]

Dear Sister I shall ans your very interesting and welcome missive I received on Friday evening that same eve I spent with Bell as she invited me to do so. She had four Gents to call on her and Julia was there I heard some very sweet music. My Dear Rebecca you will not be delighted to get home then we are to welcome you home I dare not think of it I do not want to be disappointed I will tell you what I mean when you are home a few days you ask me if Levina paid me for what I done for when she was sick no she did not and never will now[. . . .]

I dreampt of you last week I thought you was at home but much change though O do not Dear Sister and <u>friend</u> change towards me again for I am lonely enough as it is[. . . .]
your loving sister
Addie

Addie is in New York for a brief visit before returning to Hartford. In both cities she enjoys a range of entertainment, amusement, and activity: from the popular venue of Barnum's to a concert featuring a piano prodigy, the young African American Blind Tom. Unfortunately, because a black classical pianist was seen as an oddity, the broader culture probably made little distinction between the young man and Barnum's "freaks." For one of the first times, Addie speaks of reading a book by a black author, and the familiarity with which she mentions it suggests that it was well known at the time.

New York May 29 1866
My Dear & Adopted Sister
You see where I am I expect to return tomorrow It has been raining all day this A.M. I went to Jersey City after my Album I found them all very sick.
[. . .] They are playing Uncle Jim at Barnum they have a [. . .] there she is only ten year old and a Gin Grunt 50 years not much laugh then. I not get out too Central Park[. . . .] My Brother and Warwick will bring me something to the boat for tomorrow he says Selina gave me a pair of cuffs. I have told you all the New York news that I know of at present.
[. . .] Miss Saunders took me to hear Blind Tom. He plays quaintly on the piano in Hartford last week two evening I have got to be very good friends with the Saunders. My Dear Sister I cannot write a long letter of late my head trouble a great deal.
your caring Sister
Addie

[. . .] the Farmington murder some time ago they arrested some men great many in Farmington know these are the guilty ones and they have had they trial and Lawyer Chapman was for them they have got clear I realy think it is a shame. I dont think they ought to be allow to remain in F. The Methodist is holding a Fair at Talcott & Post Hall it for Ben. Mr. Roes Miss Fuller wanted me to go with her I think I shall decline for I dont care anything about it I have pen you all that I can for the present so I am coming to a brief close.

Oh I am reading the <u>Life of Frederick Douglass</u>[14] I never had the pleasure before.

Chapter Seven

"I am pleased to hear of the success of those freedmen"

Summer/Fall 1866

I N his *Semi-Annual Report on Schools for Freedmen* for January 1866, John W. Alvord, inspector of Freedmen's Bureau Schools, wrote: "The educational work in Maryland has had much opposition, such as stoning children and teachers at Easton, rough-handling and blackening the teacher at Cambridge, indignation meeting in Dorchester County with resolution passed to drive out the teacher and the burning of churches and schools." Though Rebecca does not experience any of this kind of harassment, she writes about the violence visited upon Miss Dickson, a teacher in Trapp. She makes no mention of Cambridge, Maryland, where her friend Josephine is stationed.

> Royal Oak, June 2, 1866
> Sat. A.M.

Dear Parents & Sister
    [. . .] I shall not write to Mrs. F. W. Cheney till Monday, though I've the Report ready. I would like to send you one even were it not such a task—the attendance has been very good this month, the average attend. being 25. I have the same number of pupils though, one a boy, is kept at home so much to work that I think he's as good as none.
    [. . .] I've read your letters over and over, also Jim's. I am real sorry for him and I think he's been treated shamefully, for I do not think he would have ever been guilty of touching the little chicks. I

wish I had been there to have afforded him some protection. Poor fellow! His Auntie certainly did not treat him right.

I rec'd. a letter this w'k from Miss Dickson who was at Trappe, she has been very ill for five weeks, brought on by the assaults, etc. that she receives from her enemies there, she writes that she lay totally unconscious for two days and received no nourishment for nearly a week—poor thing! She had a serious time! When she had sufficiently recovered the Dr. advised a change of scenery on account of her nervousness. She went to Balt. I had only just had her health sufficiently restored to enter upon her studies again, the actuary has sent her to Chestertown to teach the rest of the term.

[. . .] I forgot to tell you in my last of a murder that occurred at Easton last Sunday night one week. It seems a very respectable colored man who resided with his family there was on his way to church and en-route he was shot by a white rascal so that he fell a dead man immediately. The villain made his escape and has not yet been caught, he is said to be skulking about in the woods sustained by his Secesh sympathizers. He is well known and detectives are after him.

Now a law been passed there fining any person the sum of five dolls. who is known to fire off a pistol or any thing else in the place. There are some very lawless fellows in these towns and there is nothing too bad for them to do to a colored person. I trust something like justice will be given to the black man one of these days, for some are persecuted almost as badly now as in the days of slavery. Miss Cummings writes me that two of the colored teachers—Miss Anderson and Mrs. Jackson, are having a law suit in Balto. with a fellow who put them out of the Ladies Room at the Depot where they were sitting waiting for the train. It was going in their favor when the fellow plead a jury trail and she says there's no telling now which way it will go. I hope however he may get the worst of it at any rate.

[. . .] I am quite surprised to hear Miss Snells shows my letters. I did not even suspect it. I shall be glad to have those Books reserved for me & these people. I guess you would think Emily was a prodigy or something else if you could see or be in the house with her. Bell is partly right about my having such hearty laughs, when we were all in Balt. together I used frequently to indulge in a good laugh in fact we all did. I think Starkweather[1] ought to be hung; if any one ever was deserving of that death he is. I am quite surprised to hear about Emma Daniels, she will never make any thing in my opinion. Her mother ought now to prosecute those who had her shut up so long just on suspicion. I suppose that Miss Butler will have a grand wedding. Bell you should by all means attend to get the fashions, you are very fashionable.

We are going to have a lecture here Sunday night by a Mr. Taylor—agent of the Us. Court. Now I must close give my love to all and accept the best to yourselves.

Your daughter & Sister Rebecca

[. . .] Mr. & Mrs. Thomas wish to be remembered to you all.

In this letter to Rebecca, Addie is obviously upset with her friend's decision not to come home to Hartford until July; furthermore, she suggests that Rebecca does not want to get together in New York, though she anticipates their meeting daily. She speaks more openly about her relationship with Mr. Tines.

Again, she talks about her economic situation, paints a grim portrait of a black laundress, and then notes that she hopes she will never have to take in laundry. This gives evidence of the small range of work available to black women in the North. Later, in the South, black laundry women would be among the most independent and organized of black laborers.[2]

The letter marks a more mature and thoughtful Addie.

Hartford June 5 1866

My Dear Adopted Sister

[. . .] I have great deal to relate to you but I am going to retain it until you come home. Now I shall peruse your letter I receive when I return. If I had of been home I would of had it Tuesday same time your mother received hers. Where do you keep your better paper? It has a beautiful ordour to it this week in particular. Doubtless you will be glad when you receive your orders to close school. Yes I intend to meet you in New York but I thought perhaps your mother was going to meet you in Baltimore then you would not care about my company from New York here although it is in my thoughts daily.

So Mr. Tines told you that I was not going to remain in Hartford any longer. I guess I will have to for a while[. . . .]

O Rebecca only to think he is only 24 years old[. . . .] I marry a man younger than myself that is against my principle. You know this. I am positive that he love me perhaps he will not care about marrying me if he should know my age it always something. Addie if not one thing it is another.

You was speaking about Bell fixing you bonnet when you return I guess she will have to if it the same style when you left they are having some very gray bonnets.

Look here Rebecca do you want to tell me that you only going to stay nine weeks? The longest been gone seven months it will be almost eight before you return. I think it is really mean.

I should like to been at that Pancake toss. So you did not participate in any of their amusement. I wonder what they think of you. O I had the pleasure of reading a little piece about Royal Oak School and their teacher Miss Rebecca Primus. I hope you will make her acquaintance before you return home My Dear[. . . .] I have had a nap and then I get up had a nice wash and all nice and sweet for you to give a sweet kiss and a embrace[. . . .] It is so very gloomy ever baby in this house is so still even the cat. Any body want quiet just come here they will find it to it full extent. I am glad that I am not in New York[. . . .] Don't you think I left my album in New York. I guess by this time it is on the boat. Mr. Tines had promise to write in it[. . . .][3]

Addie

"Well dear Sister since you have been gone you have slept with a *fellow* who would of thought of that." This surprising tidbit goes unexplained in Addie's next letter, but it certainly suggests that Rebecca shared the most intimate details of her life with Addie and that the suggested relationship was not viewed as a threat to their own.

Hartford June 17, 1866

My Dear Adopted Sister

[. . .] I also went to the festival with Bell first time since you have been absent, I enjoyed myself very well[. . . .] The minister took different ladies and promenade around the Hall ad sing[. . . .] It was quite amusing to see them even got your mother and Aunt Emily out but a very few moments[. . . .] It was at Gilman Hall[. . . .]

Well dear Sister since you have been gone you have slept with a <u>fellow</u> who would of thought of that.

Mrs. Lloyd and her family is up here. They stop to Jennie Strimes you ought to of heard her brothering and sistering folks. I have to smile sometime. All is not gold that glitters[. . . .]

Can you do something for the pain in your side? I had a little of it today I guess I am sympathizing with you. I have got to wash for Mrs. Terry she is stopping with us. Mrs. Crowell says if she don't give me anything they will make it all up to me[. . . .]

I like the new songbooks very much. They sung two this P.M. Mr. Osher told them he would like to have them meet next Saturday evening to prepare for SS.

I hear that Peter Nott is working for a firm called Streets or Walker. Don't you think they will get along. I think he will get rich[. . . .]

I cut some cloth to make some dresses for those two you gave me are about gone. Kind friends are around me. They bid me to be gay. What merriment now to chase away sadness. Yet still I am lonely for the are not here. They bid me to join in the laugh[ter] and glad[ness] I try[. . .] but I am feeling most sad and strange[. . . .]

I wrote you such a long letter last week I will not worry you this week so I will come to a close by bidding you a good night.

> Your loving Sister,
> Addie

> Hartford June 20 1866

My Dear Adopted Sister

[. . .] Miss E. Saunders and her friend from Boston Miss L was speaking of Miss Addie Howard saying that schools would close the 16th of July I said then that was encouraging little did I think if your was acquainted with this Lady you would be very much please with her she is very much of a Lady very much accomplished. She went out last year as a book keeper in a store. When she was about to return to her mother and Sister the Mississippi River was frozen and she had to cross it she thought she never could do it then she said how grand it would be to hand it down from generation to generation that she had to walk on the ice and also thought of Eliza in

Uncle Tom's Cabin.[4] It is beautiful to hear her relate it[. . . .] I often think when people has a chance to have a Education why will they throw it away. They have lost golden opportunity[. . . .]

I saw Mr. Tines yesterday and he wish me to say he leave the last of this month for Saratoga and would like to here from you again before he leave[. . . .]

Addie

The following is the only letter from Rebecca during the summer of 1866. She seems to have been in Hartford while her school was on break. In this letter, she writes of a visit to Boston, where her brother, Nelson, and his family live. This is the first time we hear of the much-adored Leila, Nelson's baby daughter.

The portraitist Nelson Primus (1843–1916) learned the painting trade at the Hartford Carriage Works. In 1858, he won a medal for his work from the Connecticut State Agricultural Society. Nelson moved to Boston in 1864 and painted prominent Bostonians. Unable to survive as a portraitist, he continued to paint carriages and even worked as a bookseller. In 1895, after the death of his wife, he moved to San Francisco's Chinatown, where he continued to paint portraits and religious studies until his death.

During her visit to Boston, Rebecca takes in the sights, visiting the Bunker Hill Monument.

Boston July 18, 1866
Wed. Eve.

Dear Mother

[. . .] We are all well, the baby is teething we think, and for that reason she has not been feeling as well as usual a few day past, but today she's been very lively and good natured. She goes out with us whenever we go and seems to enjoy it very much.

We all visited Bunker Hill Monument Saturday P.M. & while there Gen'l. Sherman came with some friends.

We attended ch. all day Sunday took tea with Henry & his wife & then she accompanied us to church at night.

Monday P.M. about sundown we were invited to take a ride which of course we accepted, & rode as far as Jamaica Plains, across Charles River.

Yesterday P.M. we all went to the museum & Bell, Amerett & I remained to the play in the eve'g. but Nelson was obliged to return home with Leila because she couldn't be kept quiet, as soon as the music commenced she to make a noise too, therefore he had to take her out. This P.M. we went down on the Commons to hear Band play but a thunder storm was coming up & we only stopped to listen to two pieces, we reached home without getting much wet & just in time too, to escape a hard shower[. . . .]

Our love to father and yourself.

Ever your affectionate Daughter Rebecca

P.S. Please excuse whatever mistakes may have occurred.

Here we have the most comprehensive portrait of the eccentric Josephine Booth, Rebecca's fellow teacher in Hartford. There is also evidence of Rebecca's rather wry, sarcastic sense of humor. In Baltimore, Rebecca enjoys a full social life centered around the other teachers and their visits to Baltimore's churches and attendance at several lectures throughout the city. Baltimore nourishes her socially, spiritually, and intellectually.

184 Park Street, Baltimore, Md.
Sept. 22, 1866
Sat. 9 A.M.

My Dear Parents & Sister

We have just breakfasted, it is a cool but very pleasant morning. My colleague had gone out (alone) for a walk she has on that elegant black sack or bague I don't know which is the most appropriate term to apply. All look at her I don't know what they think. I tell them she is rather peculiar.

[. . .] Josephine seemed to enjoy the travel, as soon as the train moved off conversation began & I suppose would have continued had I encouraged it, but finding I only ans'd. in monosyllables it lacked interest & finally ceased to my entire satisfaction.

We shared jointly the contents of my basket, and our food was appreciated with gusto, especially on her part. We had no difficulty in obtaining good seats in the cars & in retaining them throughout the route. We reached Phila. at two or a little after, changed cars, and started again about 3½ o'ck.

Hartford Sept. 26, 1866

My Dear Sister

[. . .] I received your welcome missive Monday 1 P.M. My pen cannot portray the feelings in perusing its contents. I am thankful you arrived safe in Baltimore. I hope it will be the same when you reach your place of destinations. I sincerely hope you will enjoy good health. You must take the best care of yourself. I called to see your mother yesterday I found her quite well Bell was up to Mrs. Saunders sewing. I took my album to show them. Your ma think it a very nice one. She also put her picture in it which I was very much pleased I have five of the family now. Aunt Emily is in Farmington she went Monday P.M. Miss Porter father is dead he was quite a old Man. He was in his eighty fifth year. Cedar Hill Cemetery was to be consecrated today. I rather think they would have to postpone it. I don't think anyone would dare to venture out there[. . . .]

[Addie]

184 Park Street, Balto.
Sept. 27 1866
Thurs. P.M.

My dear Parents & Sister

By today I expected to have been on my way to Eastern Shore, but instead, I am still in this large city. I have been detained here waiting for a letter respecting my pay for traveling expenses & my advance salary from New York, this has been rec'd. today, together with my new Commission, and now I can not continue my journey till Saturday, we shall leave her in the 7 o'ck. A.M. Boat[. . . .]

Nearly all of the teachers have arrived in the city, I met Miss Howard at the Rooms this morning, her sister has procured a situation to teach in N.Y. & has been there three weeks.

Miss Dickson is also here and has called upon me, she says that the ladies at the Studio Building regretted very much my transfer. She does not yet know whether she'd to be returned to her old school or not, she's assisting in one of the city schools at present.

Two of the white teachers in this city have resigned, and instead of putting competent col'd. teachers in their places, they have got some new white ones.

We called on Mr. Cook at his office this A.M. he was pleased to see us, and informed Josephine of a good place for her to go & open a school—a place called Oxford on Eastern Shore he was there last Monday & they asked him to send them a teacher, and he advised her to go there & say that he sent her. She seems quite pleased.

She gets along nicely here, and appears well, they all see there's <u>something</u> to her although she's so odd. She brought a new bonnet with her which she wore Sunday it is a dark straw and of the same shape & size of my own, the milliner also trimmed it, & you've no idea how becoming it is. I've expressed much admiration therefor. She also wore a new dark brown dress. We attended service three times on Sun. A.M. at the St. James Episcopal ch. the funeral services of a young [?] were held there, P.M. we went to the Presbyterian ch. & at eve attended the Bethel, there were good discourses at each of these churches and the congregation were quite large.

[. . .] In the eve'g we attended a lecture with Mr. Thompson the Publisher of the Communicator at the Catholic ch. col'd. given by Mr. Wm. A. Williams, a young man of color who obtained his education in Rome, Italy where he was studying nine years. The subject of his lecture was the Negro and his progress, which is to consist of a course of 6 lectures, the one we attended being the first. We are all endeavoring to induce Josephine to write a criticism upon it. I doubt whether she will do so or not. Mr. Cook is very anxious that she should, he is coming up here tonight or tomorrow & I anticipate having an interesting time as he's going to get Mr. W. to accompany him.

Mr. Simpson, the artist from Boston is here, we visited his studio this noon, he has some fine paintings on hand, all of which he has produced since coming into this city.

There is to be a great mass meeting of the Johnson party here tonight, they have erected a very large stage on Monument Square, I suspect it will be a gala night with them. There are to be five thousand troops to guard the city during the coming elections this Fall. The rowdies have threatened to burn down or out, I don't know which, the Communicator office tonight, the ed. did not seem to be much alarmed. It's only upon the next street from where the assembly is to be gathered. Yesterday it rained here very hard & steadily all day. Two more teachers arrived here yesterday P.M. & went away this morning[. . . .]

. . .

Upon returning to Royal Oak, Rebecca's primary concern is raising money for the schoolhouse. All of her letters through the end of the year report her progress in this endeavor and encourage her family to organize fund-raising activities in Hartford. These letters also relate her growing familiarity with the area and the development of her relationship with the local people.

> Royal Oak, Talbot Co., Md.
> Oct. 1, 1866
> Mon. A.M.

My Dear Parent & Sister

[. . .] Mr. Thomas did not get my letter informing him of my coming, & therefore had made no preparations for meeting me. I was told on the Boat that he was very sick & I expected to find him in bed, but he was not at home when I came. He has been very low & last Wed. week he was not expected to live. He was taken with a shaking ague which resulted in a Billious Fever. Yesterday was the first time that he's been from home. He's looking miserably being so very thin & pale. He complained of his head's aching all the time. Mrs. Thomas had not been very well either. I suppose its from waiting upon him so much. They are both delighted with that bottle of wine, Mr. Thos. says he's not had anything to taste so good. Mrs. Thos. desires me to tell you that he thinks it's all for him and don't want her to have any. They send a great many thanks. She is very much pleased with his collar and also the things Mrs. Freeman sent her. Emily[5] is delight with her sack collar & apron. After my arrival here yesterday, eleven persons called and only one was a female, since I've been writing this letter five of my old pupils have called upon me, & now it's all quiet here again, three of the girls have gone to sweep out the school house this A.M. & Saturday it's going to be thoroughly cleaned & white washed, it would have been done last week but the stormy weather prevented, & they would not have it done before because the said it would be all dirt again before I came[. . . .]

It is rather sickly here, a number are having the chills very badly, and are very sick. I learned while in Balto. that it was very sickly here on Eastern Shore. It is the season for the chills & then at some places the small pox is raging.

Eight teachers were to leave Balto. Sat. besides Josephine and myself, & I don't know but there were more. Miss Dickson is sent to Cambridge, Dorchester Co. on Eastern Shore, a couple of white teachers formerly taught there & it is said to be a good place, she is very well pleased with the change; most of the other teachers are, or have returned to their old situations. There is much dissatisfaction felt on the part of the teachers with Mr. Israel. I could not get my note cashed in Balto. because none were acquainted with the Bank in New York on which it is made. I shall therefore enclose it in this having endorse it, & will you please get it cashed in Hartf'd. out of the money please take $7.00 for expressing my baggage, give addie $9.00 which I borrowed of her, & with the remaining $3.00 please pay for my shoes.

I thank you father very much for the crackers & ham, the receipt of which I neglected to acknowledge before I left. Also mother you will please accept my thanks for the gum drops you place in my trunk I discovered them to my surprise Sunday A.M. as I was taking out my dress to wear to ch. I shall be as choice of them as gold dust, however I did not want you to get them, for I feel that I've been a great deal of expense to you and father as it is.

Give my love to everybody, every thing around me is clean & comfortable, the house has been white washed inside & out, and everything is in order. I hope this will find you all well & that you have rec'd. the two letters I wrote you in Balto. Mr. & Mrs. Thos. send a great deal of love.

Give my love to Aunt Em & Sarah, and accept a very large portion to yourselves. I hope to hear from you this week. Your affectionate daughter & sister.

Rebecca

P.S. I forgot to mention that these people have had a festival here to get coal etc. for the school & they realized $37 & [?] they have bought two tons & a half of coal at $8.65 cts. per ton. I judge they are very much interested in the school question. Give my love to Jim & take good care of him—little Jim is well.

Addie writes of picking up a bag of Rebecca's letters and rereading them. This certainly suggests that she saved Rebecca's letters. One hopes they are waiting to be found.

Hartford Oct. [n.d.] 1866

My Dear Sister

[. . .] A Mr Fairbanks spoke to the Methodist church congregation[. . . .] He was in prison for 17 years for freeing some slaves he was very interesting indeed and quite amusing at times. He went to Oberlin in 1839 and received his diploma in 1844. He then went and met with a colored man name Lewis Haiden. He tried to free him so he was put in prison for four years and six months and his father came and several other distinguished gentlemen had him pardoned out. Few months after that he put in again for the same and remain 13 years his statements about his life while there made a deep impression on the people hearts. After he got through they took up a collection for him he received $16.00 and some cents which he seem to be very much please. He will speak tomorrow eve at the Methodist.

[. . .] Saturday Eve I had to go to market so I thought I stopped to see Aunt Emily they went to Miss Ward prayer meeting I got my bag of letters and return home. I then peruse a great many of your letters while in New York. It was a balm to my aching heart[. . . .]

If Miss Booth succeed in getting the school in Oxford she will be near you will she not? I should like to see her fashionable bonnet. I think she would look well[. . . .]

Royal Oak,
Oct. 6, 1866
Sat. 9 A.M.

My Dear Parents & Sister

It is with pleasure that I resume my old custom of writing to you Saturday morning. It is the only real leisure day that I have to myself, that is, in which I can call the whole time my own to use solely for my own purposes.

I continue to enjoy good health though there is sickness all around me, there are no less than seven persons on this road sick, two children four men & one women, the children are getting better also one of the men, but the others are considered to be very ill. I think they have the chills & fever. During the present week there have been three fatal cases of cholera in this county, two at St. Michaels and one below Bayside. All were intemperate men who had been eating and then drinking to an excess. One was a colored man & he leaves a wife and six children[. . . .]

I have seen old Mr. Moore once he's been very sick this summer but he's to be about again. When you come on if you can get any old clothes to bring him or some shirts I hope you will do so. To obtain a livelihood he has caught fish and sold them this summer. Only one little child has died among the colored people since I left them, but a number of the people have been sick.

Than Easton murderer has never yet been caught and never will be now I don't think. I suppose the circumstance is well nigh forgotten except by those most nearly connected, by this time. Tis shameful that such things are allowed to go on with impunity.

I rec'd. a letter from Josephine Tuesday which I will send on. She was well and I think she bids fair to do well there, as you were informed concerning the distance from this place to Oxford you were correct, for by water tis only about three miles, but to go by land there it's sixteen miles, so Mr. Thomas informs me. The colored people are said to be a very respectable class of people and they are getting along very well I'm told. When you've read her letter you can judge for yourselves what the state of her mind was when writing and also what her future hopes are. I answered it the next day.

The women are at work at the church today I expect to find it in excellent order tomorrow, and shall endeavor to see that it is kept so while it is used as a school house. As far as building a school house is concerned nothing has been done as yet, for they've not been able to get the land yet. Mr. Benson has it still under consideration I expect we'll know about it one of these days & just as soon as we can have any satisfaction about the matter I'm going to push it ahead.

I opened school Wednesday. The rain Tuesday prevented my opening it that day. I've had fourteen scholars this week but shall have more next. They will not all be able to come now on account of so much sickness among the different families. Those that came have lost nothing during the vacation, and I have bright hopes for their future course.

The Sunday School has not been attended well this Summer, it will be resumed under my auspices tomorrow A.M. & I requested the children to tell <u>everybody</u> to come.

I rec'd. your's & Addie's letter Thurs. noon sent for them, and I was happy to know I was not disappointed by not rec'g. them. I did somewhat look for a letter previous to this one, but then I thought you might be at a loss how to direct it and therefore I gave it up. I rec'd. Addie's while in Balto[. . . .]

I am pleased to hear of the success of those freedmen you wrote about, and I think they commend themselves very highly. I hope they may be as successful wherever they may go. I think I've heard of or read about that other man who has been in prison so long[. . . .]

Henry Ward Beecher (1812–87) was one of the most influential religious figures of the nineteenth century. He was the charismatic pastor of the Plymouth Congregational Church in Brooklyn and the brother of Catherine Beecher and Harriet Beecher Stowe.

Addie's commentary on Henry Ward Beecher's speech demonstrates her intellectual independence. In spite of his stature, she is not too intimidated to challenge his interpretation of history. She is beginning to read more critically and is displaying a greater degree of confidence in her ideas.

Hartford Oct. 16, 1866

My Dear Sister

[. . .] At eight o'clock Sarah and I went down and the boat was just coming in the dock we staid until Mr. Tines went to the Post Office and back and then he accompany us home[. . . .] I went home or rather to Aunt Emily to see Mr. Tines for the last time for sometime the boat is going to leave here on Saturday at 2½ oclock P.M. Tomorrow he go to Phila. His sister is married at 8 o'clock tomorrow eve. He said he would like to had me to accompany him he also wish me to give his kinders regards to them and will answer your letter the first opportunity.

[. . .] There has been a great fire [. . .] 18,000 people homeless 2,500 houses burned to the ground. The steamer evening Star was last said hundred seventy five on board only sixteen were saved to tell the news ain't it dreadful.

I have been reading the speech by Henry Ward Beecher the duties of the hour he is very plain. He says the recent history of the nation may be divided into three periods. Discussion, martial conflict, and reconstructing I should think it was four. The paper spoke of being 30,000 people to hear him. Rebecca Camilla Vaso is coming here the 21st I would love to go and hear her again will be at the Allyn Hall this time.

[. . .] I am very much please to hear such incouraging account of Miss Booth and her letter she seems to be perfectly happy. I hope we will get along nicely yes I receive both of your letter while you was in Balti. and also answer them. I don't think anything about going to Middletown. I received the $9.00 last evening fr[o]m your mother and gave her the receipt today no doubt they was glad to have the Sabbath School resumed under your [. . .] I suppose you will get so attached to them that you will not leave them you ask will another be found to take the same interest in them as you do so they won't be any friend like you.

Addie finally admits that she "loves" Mr. Tines. This does not seem to have an impact on her relationship with Rebecca. Carroll Smith-Rosenberg asserts that in the case of Victorian white middle- and upper-class women, "their heterosocial worlds and their homosocial worlds were complementary."[6] This seems to have been the case with Addie and Rebecca as well.

Hartford Oct. 25 1866

My Dear Sister

[. . .] I dreampt of you and a <u>friend</u> I suppose it quite encouraging and to know and feel that your pupils improve. Your labors not in vain what a pleasure it is to know that your are a gem to be appreciated. Its rather strange you did not receive your mother letter I hope you will received all my letters[. . . .]

Yes Dear Rebecca I am very glad that I am not married this year I would have to suffer as will as the rest I expect.

[. . .] I was telling Mr. Tines that John [. . .] wrote to me and he wanted to see the letter so I let him have it. I also told him what you said he wanted to know if I was going to ans the letter I would not give him any satisfaction about it. I said that Rebecca was a fastidious young lady—was indeed she was.

[. . .] Mrs. Crowell gave me a ticket for the concert at the Allyn

Hall on Friday so Bell and I went and was very much please we took a reserved seat I think Camilla played better then she did the first time. It rained the eve and was not a great many there [. . .] circle was full we was the only colored up there Mr. & Mrs. Harris was aging I did not see them I heard he has left the college he was discharge for stealing I think it really too bad I dont know how I will feel if it was husband of mine.

[. . .] The boat did not commence to run early until Friday 26 so I had the pleasure of seeing Mr. Tines twice last week he accompany us as far as State Street on Thursday. I shall miss him very much if your not here I should not care very much he seems to be rather doubtful of my love for him I do love him but not fasinated and never will I shall retain the same feeling as long as he prove true to me[. . . .]

Hartford Nov. 3, 1866

My Darling Sister

I wish I could exchange pen and paper for a seat by your side and having a pleasant chat with thee. It will be many months before I will have that pleasure so I must resort to my pain.

[. . .] While in church last evening Julia braided Mr. Freeman hair and it stood out and course that set the choir to smiling all surpress their smile but Ella Henry after church Mrs. Clara Mitchell had conciderable to say and would give five dollars to have the choir make up I must smile even now Bell told her before the five dollars came out of her pocket it would [. . .] she did not like that very much.

[. . .] I understand they had a ball Thanksgiving night. Lydia Jackson and her husband was there and both inebriated. Jim Nott was there and fell down three pairs of stairs and never hurt him he laid so quite that they suppose he was dead. Some of them afraid to go down to him. We ask for his umbrella and that his mother gave it to him and did not wish to have it Mr. Harris inform Bell and I of it as we was going home it really strang that he don't kill himself it would break my heart if I had a dear friend like James Nott.

[. . .] Dear Rebecca I dont think I would care to hear those baby and screech owls you have there. Are you not afraid that they will come near them you why should I ask such a fearless young lady as you are such question. As you say your hope I am well and happy and in the best of spirits I am well but far fr[o]m being happy. I should like to see them killed his hogs and seen them cut up. I am quite surprise hear you weigh so much[. . . .]

Mr. Crowell says the turkey was cooked handsome oh I had called fr[o]m your mother that day. Miss M. was so please that I done so well that she gave me a silver dime on Saturday and a pair of gloves think her not kind. I shall have to get something to wear this winter for my neubia[7] is about gone I wear my hat yet but it is rather cold. I am please to think you like my picture for I had it taken expressly for you no I was not feeling very well at the time I had it taken why Rebecca I dont think it make any difference about me speaking to them about the working for if I did and they got any one they would deduct my wages and you know it is small.

[. . .] I read your mother the last letter fr[o]m you what is the matter that the letters has got to be sent to Easton? Nothing very serious is there? I have promise Bell that I will accompany her to the sewing society wednesday evening I have not been yet not many goes dont seems to have any interest in anything be of any benefit if it was gossip now everybody would be there[. . . .]

Hartford Nov. 4, 1866

My Dear Adopted Sister

[. . .] I see in Boston the Republican have nominated a colored man for the legislature no one but Mr. Charles B. Mitchell. I am delighted our color will be a people get a few more states like Mass. Mrs. Mitchell smiles more then ever perhaps Peter Nott think he will be nominated too I should like to take a peep at him I expect it will hurt the [. . .] feelings very much to hear of that its the theme of people conversation now.

[. . .] Mr. Tines says in his letter if the boat does not lay over here Sunday before the river closes that he will take a Sunday here I never said a word one way or the other if he does stop back it will not be by my asking although I should be very much pleas if he will.

Charles Mitchell, a former resident of Hartford, was elected to the Massachusetts State Legislature, where he served for two years.

Hartford Nov. 11, 1866

My Dear Adopted Sister

[. . .] Mr. Aker took me to the Allyn Hall Friday. You remember you took me two years ago I did not like them as well as the first did not have very full house quite a number of colored their.

[. . .] In speaking of Mr. Tines knowing little of your ways perhaps he know more than you think for last week he sent me two of his Sister picture. They both are very nice looking. I cannot write any more so good night[. . . .] The community in all excitement. The Grand meteorie shower to accur between the hours of 12 p.m. and 3 a.m. there bells are going to rung by the police moment the star's commence shooting so to give every one and opportunity to see them that wish too.

The freedman aid society meet Wednesday evening in the Pearl St. School house.[. . .]

Hartford Nov. 18, 1866

My Dear Adopted Sister

[. . .] We have not seen those shooting star yet great many set up for two night to see them the paper had quite a piece in it this A.M. I did not lose my night rest on this account.

[. . .] The quilt you gave me I fix it today and I shall put it on tomorrow. O Rebecca the ring that Henrietta gave me last Saturday I put the tub back in its place and smash the ring all to pieces I am so sorry for I had it so long. Dear Rebecca the clock is striking the hour for retiring rest of the family doing so I will have to follow good night my Dear Sister.

Interestingly, Addie sympathizes with Emily, the young woman about whom Rebecca writes in her letters. Emily twice conceived a child out of wedlock and consequently the Thomases, Rebecca's hosts, prohibited her from working for and living with them. Here Addie compassionately reminds Rebecca not to be too harsh in her judgment of Emily. Though Addie is often critical of such behavior in Hartford girls, one senses that she also empathizes with the young servant. She seems slightly critical of Rebecca's regional biases.

·   ·   ·

Hartford Nov. 18, 1866

Dear Sister

[. . .] So poor Emily is in trouble. You did not tell me exactly but I guess it was something that kind you spoke of her in one of my letter I feel sorry for her but my Dear you must not be to hard on her. You must remember how they regard such things and just think for a moment how the girls act here. They dont seems to have any shame here. I am please to hear the people interested about the Schoolhouse as you say I they will do little more then talked about it you spoke of receiving two papers fr[o]m Mrs. Little once that live were to Aunt Emily if so she was ver <u>Thoughtful.</u>

[. . .] received a letter fr[o]m Thomas Sand is oblige to remain in NY this winter Aunt Emily she would like to come up here but she is not going to give any incouragement for she will not have his wife up here I feel sorry for him. I dont think live together many years. I must come to a close I feel very tired the friend send their love to you except my best love and remember me to Mr. & Mrs. Thomas.

I am your affect Sister
Addie

Henry Highland Garnet, renowned African American abolitionist and advocate for black rights, was best known for his "Address to the Slaves of the United States of America" of 1843. The address encouraged slaves to use whatever means necessary to free themselves. Disillusioned with Reconstruction, Garnet accepted the post of American minister of Liberia. He was buried there in 1882.

From here on, Addie will frequently mention what she is reading in the newspapers and seems to be much more informed about current events than she was while living in New York.

Hartford Nov. 28, 1866

My Dear Adopted Sister

[. . .] Some of them gents of Hartford expect to give a ball night after Thanksgiving Ellen talks about going some think it will be a grand affair I hope it will not to dissappoint those anticipate going I dont know whether Bell is going I have not heard her say.

[. . .] I saw in the paper Rev. Mr. Garnett lectured [Talcott] St.

church Aunt Emily said she went and was very much please I suppose tomorrow paper will speak of it. You remember Julia Woodbrige that attended the Young Ladies night school Miss Primus was the teacher of it several winters ago well I believe she married a Mr. Porter and now she has a daughter[. . . .]

I suppose you have commence your night school have you many I hope you will not forget to tell me your dream you had are you going to preserve it until we meet if so I shall mark the letter so to remind you of it dont you think I had better?

[. . .] Yes I think they are very kind to get you a chair not only that but very thoughtful we have had little money. Thursday a.m. it snowed a little and also Friday and last night about a half inch tonight is very cold[. . . .]

Rebecca gives an especially humorous description of a local wedding. She also relays the hospitality of the local black community and reveals herself to be a kind, if distant, recipient of their hospitality.

The Royal Oak postmaster, Richard C. Lane (1852–61), a prominent citizen, was Rebecca's nemesis, who appears to have been a hardcore Confederate patriot.

Royal Oak, Dec. 1 1866
Sat. 10 A.M.

My Dear Parents & Sister

It is a cold, clear, but very pleasant morning, the first of December & no snow upon the ground yet. It has grown cold since Thurs. A.M. and last night & the night before the wind blew terribly, today it is more calm. I was out last night with Mr. & Mrs. Thomas till near one o'clock. There was a social gathering rather a tea, at the house of one their old friends, which was given to Rev. Mr. Cole who has resided among them many years, though not wholly in this district, and who was married to a lady in Balto. last Monday night. It was a very pleasant affair. The minister is a fine looking man, but the bride is the homeliest woman I think that I ever met with, and she has very masculine features, still for all this she may possess many virtues & fine qualifications. I did not discover any however last night. She is said to be a very successful woman in getting up these

146

Good Samaritan Societies. She's been twice married this making her third husband and she seems to be considerably advanced in years—he is 48 yrs. of age was a widower & is the father of thirteen children, ten of whom died in their infancy. They are to take up their residence in Balto. All of his relatives were present & his oldest child a young woman about seventeen yrs. old. The house was full and it was a very merry gathering. Mrs. Thomas is very lively in company she kept them in a roar of laughter almost the entire eve'g. The Bride wore a light stripped silk.

Thanksgiving day or at least a portion of it, I spent from home. And it's the first real visiting day that I've taken since I came upon Eastern Shore, I enjoyed it too, very much. It was so pleasant Wed. that I told Mrs. Thos. if it was a pleasant Thursday I would walk out & see some of these people where I had not before been, whereupon Mr. Thos. was informed & he made it his business to notify one the party whose house I proposed calling at, he then spread the news & great preparations were made for my reception.

[. . .] Word came that I was expected up in the neck—every road here is called a neck,—& that every preparation was being made for me. I hurriedly changed my clothes, & attended by a guide I made my way up to the Neck arriving at about one P.M. at the residence of Mr. William Gibson the principal man among our school trustees, where I dined an hour later, & remained till about three o'ck. then with his wife called upon three other families in the neighborhood with one of whom I took supper. The father of this family Mr. Williams has ten children & three of them are deaf & dumb, his wife is a fine looking woman but her health is not good. One of his sons brought me home in his own team. These families are among the most comfortably situated that I've ever visited on Eastern Shore, they getting along very nicely. They were all so delighted to have me visit them, & only wished I had let them known sooner that they could have been better prepared to see me. I told them I'd not purposed to let them know as I was only going to call, but this did not satisfy. These people desire to make a great time over one they like & I did not wish to put them to any trouble or expense for me,—they don't know me, at least they do not quite understand my ways etc. They seem to labor under the false impression that I'm an uncommon personage—that there's no one like me, but what should lead them to think thus is beyond my comprehension, I endeavor to make myself very sociable with them all, but I keep them at a certain stand point treat them with due respect & I in return, am rec'd. with deference on every side. I mean to visit more of them too, now I find they are so neatly & comfortably situated & they are so desirous to have visit them, it will not do to slight any. My food Thurs. consisted of cabbage & bacon, Fried chicken, sweet potatoes, apple-sauce, bread, biscuits, ginger, pear & peach preserves which were very nice, and a cup of tea. I relished my food because everything looked so neat & clean.

At the tea last night we, for the first course, had coffee, tea, bread, biscuits, cheese, cold meat & crackers, this we partook of standing around a long table in sets, the second course was passed around an hour later as we were seated, in another room—it consisted of some very nice cake, lemonade, and confectionery, this same course was passed a second time at a still later hour, making a third course I suppose. Before departing the Rev. lined the hymn of "A charge to keep I have etc." in which all took part in singing then followed a prayer, at the close of which we put on our wrappings & departed to our respective homes.

Mr. Thos. was the only one who saluted the bride with a kiss, & he only did it for mischief—he told me to tell you she was the homeliest woman he believed that lived or ever lived. You should hear him go on about that poor woman, he says if he'd seen how ugly she was before he got so close to her to kiss her, he should never have done it. He says he looked at her head & he believed one half of it has been cut off. They are all reproaching Mr. Cole for getting such a looking woman. I only wish you all could hear them & their expressions, it's really amusing.

[. . .] I have written so much I had forgotten to tell you about the little difficulty I've had with this poor old secesh Post-master here. It's all on account of the papers you've sent me and which he & his old jebusite wife have taken the liberty to open. Not sending the last to me with my other mail, then he asked if there were no papers, they said not any then afterwards said a bundle of stuff through the office, and adding twas $20 fine to do so & to write anything upon the inside of the papers. He also charge 33cts. postage. Mr. Thos. asked how they could have come without any directions whatever, he replied that he did not know but that they came just as they were then. They had some words with Mr. Thomas & he left them, they are still there and there they'll remain for all my sending for or paying that postage upon them. He says he's had more trouble with the d-m niggers papers than have with any one's else. But I do not intend to trouble them with them hereafter. I wrote a note to the Post Master at Easton to take charge of all my papers & letters hereafter and he sent me word that he would. Mr. Thos. is personally acquainted with him. A friend living near the office has promised to call for my mail & send it to me so you see I'm all right and P.M. Lane & his companion are all wrong. So please do not forget to direct all of my mail to Easton.

[. . .] Now I will turn my attention to your epistle which I rec'd. with its contents all safe, Thursday while I was dressing for my walk. I am delighted to know that you are all well. I do not think the people ought to be alarmed for my safety here, it is very quiet all around me, and I feel as safe here as any where else. I do not apprehend danger. I hope they'll all lay aside their fears & feel that I am on the hands of the same Supreme Being that has the charge of us all everywhere. You must not think I've had no seat to sit upon at school—ask Mrs. Freeman. Of course I've had a seat. I owe Gertrude a letter, I shall try to write to her this week. I am pleased to hear so favorable an account of her Brother[. . . .]

Tell the ladies that are my friends, to arouse up and interest themselves as much as they can in behalf of our school house for its very much needed, & these people are becoming hopeful again.

I hope Nelson's Pictures may be sold at least a part of them & that he may not be disappointed about coming to Balto. & I hope you will put them in Brown's store. I don't see how it is there are so many fairs going on at once.

I should liked to have heard Rev. Mr. Garnet's lecture, where did he stop? And I'm glad so many came out to hear him.

You must give my love to all of my relatives & friends and accept a very large portion to yourselves. I will not add any more for I've already written a very long letter of which I hope you'll not weary reading.

Rebecca

The enclosed check I rec'd. Sat. eve'g. from N.Y. Please get it cashed and then retain all excepting ten dollars in your hands until I send for it. Send $5.00 in one letter & $5. in the next, that I may have some money by me in case of emergency.

[. . .] It is election here & hereabouts tomorrow, but it's very quiet in tis vicinity. I hope you've all well I've a cold from Rebecca. Excuse hasty penmanship. Mon. P.M. I've had a fine bunch of monthly roses sent to me this afternoon.[8]

Mr. & Mrs. Thomas send all of their respects to you. Hope Jim is well, he was not mentioned in your last.

How was Sarah pleased with her letter?

Your expenses to Balto. will be just $8.65 each & in my next I shall send you all the directions that you may come straight through without any difficulty.

Rebecca instructs her family regarding their visit to Royal Oak. Using her own behavior as an example, she suggests that they not accept segregated seating. This is just another example of the struggles that confronted black Americans in public accommodations and in other aspects of their daily lives.

> Royal Oak, Dec. 6 1866
> Sat. 8 A.M.

Dear Mother, Sister & Brother

Your expenses to Balto. will be as follows—$2.00 on the Boat or $3.20 on the Cars. Then to Balto. $6.65.

Get some one to conduct you from the Boat to Jersey City Ferry, & express your Baggage to the same place, it will cost less than to get a carriage, the chambermaid will instruct you.

When you arrive at Kensington station the cars stop & you leave them and take the Horse Cars for the Southern depot—you'll have a long, long & tedious ride through one portion of the city of Philadelphia—but keep up good courage. The Conductor will tell you which cars to take after you arrive at the Phila. depot, & if you find he puts you in the smoking car & the door of the next car is locked watch the opportunity & as soon as the door is unlocked get up & go into that car. I did not occupy it either time, as soon as I found out where I was I improved the opportunity and changed cars.

> Your daughter & sister
> Rebecca

Hartford Dec. 7 1866

Dear Sister

[. . .] That Mr. Lane[9] and wife will find they have got somebody to deal with and is not afraid of any one or any things.

I will close hoping this will find you well fr[o]m your loving adopted Sister

Addie

Royal Oak Talbot Co. Md. Dec. 8 1866
Sat. 8 A.M.

My dear Parents & Sister

[. . .] I had school at night and most of my scholars were present. I have upon my roll book 27 names now for this night with your letter. Mon. A.M. I rec'd. a call at my school from Mr. Graham, he has been in Easton several days, & at A.M. he'd been to see the St. Michaels school & on his return he stopped to look at mine. He said it was ahead of that school, and that there was more interest shown by the people in sending their children etc. He returned to Easton gave a lecture that night at one of the col'd. churches, and I'm told he gave this school & people all the praise.

Now I tell the children we must keep ahead, & encourage their parents to keep ahead too. The attendance at the night school is not so good as that of the day for this reason, there are a series of pro-tracted meetings going on at Ferry Neck four miles from here, & every other night the greater part of this neighborhood go down to it, I judge nearly all went last night for I went out to school as usual, and only three scholars came, at 8 oc'k. we returned to our homes.[10] Mrs. Thomas & I rode down there Wednesday eve'g. but did not remain long on acc't. of the meeting being rather dull, on our return we stopped at the church here. Prayer meeting had closed, they had just begun to talk upon the school house subject, they were all wide awake for it and among the men with a few of the women $23 of the $25 or $30 was subscribed towards having the lumber brought here from Balto. They seem to be quite active about the matter now, & I think they'll make an effort to go through with it with what aid you can send us. I mentioned it in my letter to Mr. Burton[11] which I have sent him this week. I hope soon to be able to inform you what it will cost to build it, Mr. Thos. thinks we can not get it erected for less than a hundred dolls.

The one that's being built at Easton will cost nearly a $1,000. It is a large building & very nice one too. I'm told Mr. Graham has the supervision of it. He is also one of the trustees appointed for ours.

I've not yet got my chair. Mr. Thomas has the money in hand & has postponed going to Balto. till Christmas, he is very anxious to see you and Bell & I believe if the truth were told, that's the principal reason he's not gone before. He, as well as I, will be greatly disappointed if you do not both come, particularly if Nelson can not come on. It's been my theme every since I arrived on Eastern Shore, but I don't want either of you to come on alone. I will be responsible for Bell's board during the time we remain in the city, then if it is pleasant we'll take a day & go to Washington, the fare is only $1.50 from Balto. Miss Knowles was to come on but I've not heard from her yet, although I've written once since I came back.

[. . .] I had another fine bunch of monthly roses & box, with another kind of flower interspersed, sent to me Mon. on my return from school. The leaves of the roses have nearly all fallen off now, and I've preserved them in one of my books. O yes, I was always fond of flowers but do not care to work among them. By your being so fond of them Mother, I cherish them more highly, & because it reminds me of home & of those that constitute it. I'm glad you sent no papers last week for I don't want any more to pass through the Lane's hands. I've written to have the Independent sent to Easton too. I'm really surprised to hear that any of those freed women had been sent on. If we should go to Washington you can go & see that Mrs. Griffin if you bring her address with you. I'm pleased to know they all will be supplied with homes, which I trust will be good ones for them. I hope Miss Fellows will have those books in reserve for me I shall be disappointed if not. I'm going to allow a portion of my night scholars to use them too. I weigh now same that I did several years since, the very first time I was ever weighed. That time I went down East I only weighed 118. I've gained all since then, and enjoyed better health too ever since my return from there. The down east air & [?] agree with me. I had on the same clothes that I usually wear[. . . .]

I've been informed today that they are going to have a festival here during the holidays, the proceeds of which are to be divided between the church and the school[. . . .]

We are having company this P.M. one old man has been in here talking & arguing ever since I took up my pen, he's just gone out & I'm so glad, but here's another one come to fill the room made vacant by his predecessor, oh, these men are the greatest cases for talking that I ever met with. Sunday's their only leisure day, they make it a point to go from house to house and hold long arguments, & it's so very annoying, to me in particular[. . . .] Mr. & Mrs. Thomas wish to be remembered to you all.

Accept my best love to yourselves.

Rebecca

I'll ans. Jim's letter next time.

Here, we have Rebecca's letter to her cherished cat, Jim.

Royal Oak, Dec. 11, 1866

My dear Jim,

I have been mending & reading the papers this P.M. but becoming tired of the latter employment, I thought I would take up my pen instead, & write you a few lines in ans. to your letter which it gave me so much pleasure to me. After reading my self I read it aloud to the folks, & Mrs. Thomas don't believe you wrote it to make your hand tired.

I'm delighted to know you had such a nice Thanksgiving diner, & are so well cared for by your Auntie, Uncle, & Bell. I only wish I could see you myself. Your being so full reminds me of the time you got upon the table & drank up half of your Auntie's milk out of the pail one day—do you recollect it?

I suspect you do really look finely now my noble fellow, for I imagine you are very fat.

The night of the day I rec'd. your letter I dreamt about you, & I thought you looked so large and was so very clever. I know you can not be beaten in the whole U.S. Tis too bad poor Major & Kittie Smith had no Thanksgiving, and I don't believe you gave them a very strong invitation to partake with you.

Little Jim, Jr. is well and his mother & brother write with him in sending lots of love to you, he says he never saw his father. He would liked to have shared your nice turkey with you for he seldom gets such nice food, but he catches a good many mice.

Mrs. Thomas & Emily wish me to give their love to you, Emily was delighted to think you sent your love to her.

They all think you are a very wonderful creature but will not believe you are so superior to others of your race—but I tell them you are.

I would like to see you when I go up to Balto. very much, but I would not have you brought so far from home for anything, you'd be so frightened with the noise you'd hear & the new & strange scenes that would meet your eyes, that you'd very soon become wild, and then I'd be afraid you'd die.

You must strive to live and keep fat & good until I return home again. I think of you every day I believe, and I often tell little Jim about you, he listens, & sings, & seems much pleased. He is very timid & runs from every strange cat or thing he sees.

I must stop writing now, give my love to all & to Major, his mother & Sarah. Accept a very large portion to yourself and write again some day.

From your own mistress.

P.S. Addie must be more particular in applying epithets to you my boy.

Royal Oak, Dec. 14, 1866

My dear Parents & Sister

[. . .] It's been another great hog killing week. I guess fully one hundred of these quadruped animals have fallen victims to the butcher's knife since Monday A.M. for one white man alone was to have 28 killed.

Mr. Thos.' brother-in-law killed 8 yesterday weighing respectively 225, 208, & 199 lbs. each, all for home consumption. Mr. Thos. also killed his two shoats one weighed 156 & the other 120 lbs. the latter he's sold intending to get beef instead.

I've not had so good an attendance at school this week on account of the great hog sacrifice, both parents & older grownup children all go out to hog killing. I think they are all hired, the younger children are detained at home housekeeping. With this exception the school has gone on as usual. There was a gay old wedding here among the whites last week, & it's created considerable sensation, an old dame 52 yrs. of age was married to a youth 18 yrs. old. Mark the disparity if you please,—he is a dutchman, which probable accounts for his choice of a wife.

[. . .] Will you please get me a nice little turkey for [Nelson] and send it on immediately that they can have it for their Christmas dinner. Benajah dined with them Thanksgiving day. He's got the idea of going to Europe again upon his mind.

I'm glad he's succeeded in getting a good tenement to live in. I guess they find it much more desirable and comfortable too. Don't forget or neglect to send the turkey. Make out my bill & bring with you that I may know just how much they all cost.

Gertrude says she'll assist you all she can when you have the Fair if she knows when it's to be. I think you will do better by postponing it for I see there's so much going on in Hartford now it would be almost useless.

The last papers you sent I rec'd. Sat. & they've afforded me a mental feast all the week. The others Mrs. Thomas will call for tomorrow.

That old Mr. Moore has been very ill during the past two weeks. I hope you'll not forget to bring him something from the Society, he needs clothes.

[. . .] You need not have sent any money for those papers for I apprehend no danger. I got Mr. Thos. to inquire of the former Postmaster, he informed him that there was no such fine imposed in fact, that he know of none whatever, he'd often sent papers in that manner himself, all that is required is to pay the postage at the office from which they're mailed. No, I shall never trouble Lane or his wife for the papers.

[. . .] The col'd people home must be having & overplus of money this season, there being so many Balls among the class that attend them.

I hope you may be successful in selling Nelson's paintings yet.

I am glad to hear the Supt. is endeavoring to make the S.S. present a better appearance. I think he must be interested in the school[. . . .]

Given the consistency of her requests to Rebecca, Addie is perhaps envious of the pending visit to Maryland of Mehitable and Bell Primus.

Hartford Dec. 16 1866

My Dear Sister

    I suppose this time nexe sunday you will have the company of your Mother & Sister. I hope you will have a pleasant time is the wish of your adopted sister.

    [. . .] your letter was rec last Wednesday P.M. and it found me very well. I shall try to act upon some what the same principle Miss Booth present. So you had a visit from your friend Mr. Graham doubtless was please to see him. There was a freed girl at your Mother on Saturday. Look and act like Bell Sands. I would like Thomas to see her. I must ask your Mother if she didn't agree with me I do not know those persons that was at Mr. Firds She keeps the bakery in Main St. thank you I do not care about taking pattern.

    Dear Sister you mistake me. that I doubt your veracity and uncertainty upon the subject of <u>love</u> in your letter you pen as your expected it from what other have said and what you have read I doubt you then I think you know more about from your own feelings[. . . .]

Chapter Eight

"We must have a school house"

1867

REBECCA'S letters document the truth of historian Eric Foner's assertion: "In 1867, politics emerged as the principal focus of black aspirations."[1] Throughout Maryland, the rights of the freed people were being debated. They were the objects of physical violence, their churches and their schools were burned, and teachers who came to assist them were threatened by violence as well. Barbara Fields notes: "Black churches attracted violence as velvet attracts lint. . . . The most common reason for attacks on black churches . . . was that the freedmen conducted schools in them."[2]

It is in this atmosphere that Rebecca writes: "These white people want all the respect shown them by the col'd. people. I give what I rec. & no more." In spite of the danger, she maintains her dignity and is fearless in her commitment to educate the freed people. Those of the Eastern Shore joined their counterparts throughout the South in a quest to gain and exercise their rights.

As for Addie, her most stable employment during this time is at Miss Porter's School in Farmington, Connecticut, where she begins work in the spring of 1867. Miss Porter's was a private boarding school for white girls, founded by Sarah Porter in the 1840s. Just as blacks established their own schools, this period also witnessed the rise in educational institutions for women and girls. Prior to the Civil War, only Oberlin and Mount Holyoke accepted women. Following the war, the colleges known as the Seven Sisters opened in rapid succession. Miss Porter was ahead of her time when she established a curriculum that included Latin, French, German, chemistry, philosophy, rhetoric, mathematics (up to trigonometry), history, geography, and music. There were daily Bible readings, as well as rowing, riding, and tennis. Famous authors such as Mark Twain gave readings, and there were frequent concerts and dances. Addie writes of all these activities.

Miss Porter not only supplied secure employment but also encouraged Addie to take advantage of the library, which she did with a great deal of relish. During these years, Addie becomes determined to create a life for herself above and beyond that allowed by her circumstances.

Hartford Jan. 9 1867

Dear Sister

[. . .]Saturday night I went to N.Y. and return to N.H. Monday night I had a very pleasant time indeed. I went to Phila in the P.M. in the evening[. . . .] It is a beautiful church. Monday Mr. Tines took me to Barnum I enjoyed it very much.

I had a very [nice] time at N.H. although it rain and snow. But part of the time New Years day Mrs. Cummings invite Mr. Tines to tea and threw a fire. And then about eight o'clock we all attend the Temple street church festival. Mr. T met Mr. Green there and left for the boat ten P.M. it was very pleasant we start quite late. Friday Tiller gave a surprise in her Laver house. Mr. Tines was invited and also was requested to bring two or three more. Had a very nice time some was disappointed about the music they played several games past of the evening very nicely indeed the Gent seem to enjoyed themselves very much. That same evening Mr. Tines made me a New Years present a set of sleeves studs they are very pretty. He ask to claim my hand. I don't think I shall let him claim until nexe fall.

[. . .] Doubtless you attended Mrs. Adams grand affair. No doubt Bell look very charming. Has she made any conquests while in Baltimore? Aunt Emily and I been speaking about. New Years day it snowed all day in N.H. all the girls had several calls.

[. . .] Mr. Tines wish me to ask you if you had received his letter he would like to know he also send his regards to you.

Except my best love from your Adopted Sister

Addie

. . .

A letter from Addie Brown, dated 1867, to her "Beloved Sister," Rebecca.

Royal Oak, Jan. 11, 1867

My Dear Parents & Sister

[. . .] I settled my bills with Mrs. Adams—Mr. Israel condescended to give me $10—I told him I had not rec'd. my check, had no money, etc. & I wanted very much to return to my school therefore he opened his heart to give me that amount & Miss Hoy the sum of $5[. . . .]

While at Easton I spent an hour or so at Mrs. Armstrong's school, I am rather disappointed in it & she is also, for she expected to find it farther advanced, none write or study Geog. & she has 66 pupils. She was delighted to see me, after this week she expected to board with Mrs. Thos. Sister, she inquired very particularly after you all.

They raised over $200. at their Fair in Easton all of which is for the school house.

At the Festival here during that week I'm told they did not do so well for it was so very cold.

"Home Weeklies" to Rebecca Primus's family.

Mrs. Thomas is not well & not been since I left them, Mr. Thos. was taken sick Christmas day & was ill the rest of the week, which prevented his coming to Balto. as he intended, he kept his bed for he had no use of his limbs, & one day he said he did not know that ailed him, —he's quite well again now—but oh! he regrets so much not meeting with you & Bell. I told him you did not know but you'd come on here just before school closed they are both in hopes you will do so, rest assured you'll not lack attention among these people; they've all been anxiously awaiting my return. Mrs. Thos. says every day there have been calls here to know whether I'd come back or was coming[. . . .]

Emily is not here & I had no opportunity to see her in Easton—
Mrs. Thomas says she cried when she went away. Poor girl I expect
she feels badly enough. I feel real sorry for her, her family are very
poor but she has two older sisters who are as bad & lazy as they can
be, all are home now & their old mother is an invalid, I don't know
as she's scarcely able to help herself, & the father is of no account
they say, and older brother & his wife partly sustain the family.

There have been a number of changes here by removals & by
which I've lost some of my very best scholars, their parents having
gone out of the place. Oh! I do regret it so much!

In Mr. Graham's letter which was among those I rec'd. yesterday,
he desired me to encourage that lame young man that attended my
school, to prepare himself for a teacher & then to come to Balto. &
enter the Normal class, but to my great & sad disappointment this
can not be effected by me, for his folks have moved to St. Michaels.
I've been very proud of him.

Miss Dickson has also written and has been adopted by some
society in Boston, & now she has three reports to make out. She can
have some idea of what I've been doing all along. Mr. Burton has
written to Mr. Israel concerning our contemplated school-house, I
was informed at the Rooms.

[. . .] Give my love to every body & Jim & accept my best to
yourselves.

From Rebecca

Mr. & Mrs. Thomas send a great deal of love to you.

Hartford Jan. 14 1867

Dear Sister

What shall I attribute to your silence to? You are not punishing
me for not writing last week are you? I am at Mrs. C again. Came
last night and today I have been washing and back ache like a
toothache they all seem to be glad to have me return to them even
the cat[. . . .]

Gertrude Plato was out to church yesterday she has a new-look
she is getting ready to visit Boston nexe month I hear she is making
great preparations I dont think dress became her what do you think
about it I guess she would not like to hear that.

There is quite excitement amongst the upper tier here. Mrs. Wor-
burton is contemplating marriages [. . .] with Mr. Williams I under-

stand that he waited on her before. Mr. Warburton and then rejected not only once but twice now to think she is going to take him up after all that and he also has a living wife out west I wonder what Mr. Mitchell will do. her friend want to hear it up I don't think they will succeed now days many go the fourteenth well I am glad my love is not quite so strong as that when it is refuse one that is me for all with any one.

Dr. Green has put his wife in the retreat I heard it was for indulging in the intoxicating beverage I ask Mrs. Crowell if it was so she said yes and also Marshall Jewell wife for the same crime. I guess that nexe will be Mrs. Huntington on Clinton Sts I would not be surprise.

[. . .] I suppose your Mother is return home by this time Mr. Primus expect them this eve. Miss Addie Babcock in a great story about the fair think it time they had it. I called on her Saturday P.M. and was showing me some of the things she has made for the fair enough to fill a small table.

They have arrested three men in Farmington for murdering the Mr. Johnson of that town they have put the trial off until March they think one more is concerned in it. I hope they will get all of them[. . . .]

Royal Oak, Jan. 19, 1867

My Dear Parents & Sister,

I am all right side up again now and I'm feeling as well and brisk as ever I did[. . . .]

There is a plenty of snow upon the ground now and it's being improved, & if this weather continues 'twill last sometime. Mr. Thomas says it's seldom they are favored with such a season of sleighing. I only wish you could see the various and many styles of jumper sleighs that have been fitted up for the occasion by both white and black, some of them look hard but nothing for that they answer every purpose.

I guess the poor horses will rejoice when this snow is gone. I've been favored with two or three short rides, & Mr. Thomas purposed taking me out last evening but he was disappointed about his horse, some others had been driving him without his knowledge & he was in no condition to be driven any distance again. I did not regret it much for it was so very cold, & windy also. He owns one of those basket sleighs.

I suppose Mother you and Bell have reached home again ere this, I rec'd. your letter last Tuesday and I was delighted to hear you were both enjoying your visit to Phila. so well. I only wish I could have accompanied you. I am glad you met with Amanda Robinson & also that she paid you so much attention[. . . .]

I've had a school every day this week, but no night session, the largest number that have attended have been nineteen, the severe weather has kept the children at home. Four of my night scholars are attending the day school, they are out of employment and so improve the opportunity of coming to school. I wish they could all come so as to dispense with the night school entirely, but many are hired out by the year & therefore can not attend during the day.

I gave the old man his clothing & he was perfectly delighted with it all. He says he'll try to pay me for it. I told him I did not wish him to do so but hoped they'd be of service to him.

The people here think you are the kindest woman that lives and they're all anxious to see you and desire to know if you're not coming to see them. I tell them I guess you'll come on before I return home.

It is a very dull time with everybody here now, and sleighing is the most that's thought of. The mill cannot run on account of the weather therefore Mr. Thomas is out of employment. As soon as the weather moderates they'll all go into the woods chopping.

[. . .] Why did you not write to Father again seeing you continued your stay. I guess he thought you had gone for the winter surely. How did you find Jim upon your return? I hope he is well[. . . .]

Royal Oak, Talbot Co., Md
Feb. 2, 1867
Sat. A.M.

My Dear Parents & Sister,

It is very cloudy with us this A.M. and I think 'twill rain before long. Within the last two days the moderate weather & the sun's rays have nearly cleared the fields of snow & has done very much toward removing it from the roads. I can tell you it's wet and muddy enough here now, and will be until we've had a good rain to settle the ground.

This week I've made out my reports for Jan'y. finishing last night, and now they're in Easton—went early this A.M. I began them Thurs. P.M. I had 44 pupils in all during the month, the bad weather and bad traveling have prevented a number of my day scholars and nearly all of my night pupils from attending school this month, and five of my night scholars have attended the day session so that it has numbered 33 pupils.

The present month I expect to have a better attendance, the winter has been very hard upon us as with you, for it's been very cold here and we've had a considerable snow. I took my last sleigh ride—partly upon mud and partly upon snow—Thurs. night but to & upon my return from school, being drawn by a <u>mule</u>.

Quite a serious accident occurred in Easton last week, I think. A horse took fright ran away and with the shafts attached to him jumped or fell into a sleigh that was standing by the side of the road containing a man & his wife, broke in the breast bone of the latter besides doing other injuries, from which she has since been insensible, and seriously injured her husband about the head nearly tearing off his scalp. There are no hopes of his wife's recovery, but some for himself. He is a livery stable keeper there[. . . .]

Mr. Thomas has gone this A.M. to dig a grave for an old white lady 88 yrs of age, who died yesterday & is to be buried at 2 P.M. today, she was not sick long, and a younger sister who has been bedridden for 22 yrs. and whose death has been expected for years, outlives her. She was the oldest person here and also was a widow.

[. . .] Mr. Benson is exerting himself to get the land for us, and very soon I expect the money will be forwarded to Balto. for the transportation of the lumber, $5 or $6 more has been subscribed. The schoolhouse is my theme in school and out of it, and I'm striving to induce those living upon farms to ask their employers who are favorable to the school, to give something towards it and they've promised to do so. They're all very anxious for me to return to them this fall. I tell them that it only depends upon the school house, and it must be completed before school closes for the vacation. Their invariable plea is we're all poor, just out of bondage and times are hard with us etc. My reply is, very true, nevertheless we must have a school house; and then what the consequences will be if it's not built this Spring. I want to raise their ambition and survive & increase the interest. In my last letter to Jane I told her to do all she could for us. And wherever I think I can get any aid I shall put forth my plea. I hope the Fair will be successful in realizing a good sum. I shall keep account of every $1 and cent that I rec. for it from whatever source it may come, and I'll transmit a full acc't of the whole amt. to all the donors when it's completed.

[. . .] I am glad to hear Jim's living so highly upon the fat of the land, I can imagine how his fat sides stick out after eating, but I think it's too bad he should rec. such unkind treatment every now & then. His mistress will be there to protect and defend him one of these days.

You must give my love to Henrietta and her husband always.

[. . .] I paid my visit out today and enjoyed it, a portion of the P.M. I read aloud to the family. We had a nice dinner & tea also, the former consisting of the following articles, so that you can judge whether 'twas a good one or not—Pork & Cabbage, a Roasted Possum, Fried Oysters, Baked Sweet Potatoes, Mashed Irish do, Fried Parsnips, Stewed Apples, Pickles, & Wheat Bread—for Dessert Mince Pies, Peach, Apple and Quince Preserves & Cheese. For supper we had tea Biscuits, Bread, Sausages, Crackers, Cheese Preserves and Tea. I enjoyed both meals greatly, though the host & hostess complained of my not eating & kept urging me to do so, but I ate very heartily at dinner and had no appetite for supper[. . . .]

Mrs. Thomas made Mr. Thomas and myself some nice potato pudding yesterday, & today besides eating half of his own which was in a good sized Pudding dish, he's eaten about two thirds of mine today. I told him as I was writing to you I should mention it; he's a very hearty man, was weighed last week and weighs one lb. of being 200lbs. We tell him it's because he's not been at work this winter[. . . .]

In this letter Rebecca reveals a black community that presents one face in the company of whites and a very different, more relaxed one in their absence.

Royal Oak, Talbot Co., Md.
Feb. 8, 1867
Fri. 11 A.M.

My dear Parents & Sister,

Today we are having a cold rain-storm, or as is a more common expression here, —"we're having failing weather," and in conse-

quence of which I am at home today,—privilege of which I am
highly glad to avail myself, for the reason that I did not retire till
about two this morning, and I am feeling very dull & rather
sleepy[. . . .]

Mr. Thomas & I attended the wedding last eve'g., the ceremony
took place at 6½ o'ck., the bride wore a Delaine skirt—brown and
figured—with a white waist, and her head was decorated with flowers, artificial, as were also the heads of the two bridesmaids, who
were likewise attired in delaines. The groom wore a full suit of black
his vest being velvet I think, and his attendants wore the same; all
looked plain, neat and well. Rev'd. Trantum married them, afterwards congratulated them and eating a small piece of cake very
soon retired. The man with whom the bride lives was present with
two other white men, they all came & went with the minister, 'twas a
relief too, to have them gone, immediately following which the
entire company a large number of whom had assembled relapsed or
collapsed I don't know which would be the most applicable term
here, —into a long and painful silence. I was glad to have some
refreshments passed for a relief & a change of scene. The refreshment at this time was iced cake in thin slices, cookies & lemonade,
after an interval of an hour or two the tables were arranged for supper, upon which was placed two large Turkies, Cold Boiled Chickens
with drawn Butter turned over them, Shad Ham or Bacon &
Sausages, Bread Biscuit & Butter, Tea & Coffee, & Scallop Oysters
or something similar—they were very nice. I tasted them ate part of
a Turkey leg & two flat biscuit cakes, I suppose they're called here,
and drank two cups—very small—of tea. At supper a different spirit
pervaded the guests which continued till we left which was about
1½ o'ck. After supper & the tables had been removed, played upon;
which created much amusement. I did not participate in any of
them however, but remained a silent & interested spectator. Mrs.
Thomas did not go. We were the first to make a movement to
go home although 'twas so late. I can't tell at what hour the rest
separated.

While we were at supper a number of men both married and
single, came to the house surrounding it making the most horrid
noises with cow and sleigh bells, horns etc. added to their yells &
songs, firing of pistols & guns, that you ever heard, and I judged they
kept it up full an hour, to the discomfiture of all present.

This is a custom here upon such occasions among both black and white, and is considered very annoying, still it has to be endured though now & then I'm told, at the expense of law, for they go too far in their demonstrations sometimes. Just before we came away the bride's loaf which had occupied the center of the table during supper, was cut & passed around with confectionery. Everything seemed to be nice & was enjoyed the meats here decorated with evergreens, also three of the side walls of the room which was quite large & nearly square & warmed by a fire in the fireplace, the floor was uncarpeted but white and very clean.

I think I've now given you a full and fair description of the wedding, and you'll probably infer that 'twas a very pleasant affair upon a whole, which is quite true[. . . .]

Mr. Thomas thinks of going to Easton tomorrow, so I thought I get my weekly epistle ready to send by him. I rec'd. your letter & one from Josephine yesterday, Addie's has not come yet.

The mail driver has very kindly offered to bring my mail from Easton every Thurs., and stop at the church so that I can send out one of my scholars to get it[. . . .]

Tell Gertrude to take a position as clerk in the Fair, and act in my place. I am glad you're going to have it soon, and I really hope you will realize a handsome sum of greenbacks at its close, then I shall have something to write to Mr. Graham & Mr. Janney[3] concerning a portion of what we expect & from a reliable source.

I would like to see the various articles you have made and recd. for the Fair. Have you made any of those Gen. Putnum pen-wipers Bell? I suspect "Jacob's Well" will create a general sensation.

I hope the white friends will add to their interest therein liberality, has Miss Wells given you that ten dolls. her sister gave?

Mr. & Mrs. Snell must have taken a great interest in our School, I think it must present a fine appearance now every Sunday. I hope our church as done well at their festival this week. I think you could select something of value at the Fair and sell votes on it for Mr. Snell & our minister keeping an accurate acct. on paper of each name & vote sold, whichever of the two gets the largest number, to rec. the article.

I think Jim must eat too much. You must allowance him. Has he got so that he can shut his eyes now while he is sleeping. I would like to see that picture of the Cat and I think Jim, Jr. would be pleased

to look at it. He sends his love to Jim, Sr. & to you all. He was
delighted to have me back again.

[. . .] Remember one & all accept the best portion to yourselves.

From Rebecca

P.S. I sent you a copy of the Annual Report of the Balto. with the
last letter.

P.S. I enclose $7.00 the balance of my <u>contract</u> $3.00 of which you
already have in hand.

Royal Oak, Talbot Co., Md
Feb. 16, 1867

My Dear Parents & Sister

[. . .] Will you please tell me what Boneset is for? I made a tea of
it & drank hot at night & cold during the day for my cold, but not
knowing the nature of it I've not continued it. and I don't know
whether I was benefited or not. I've taken sage & hop tea, and now
I'm drinking wormwood again for my stomach has felt very weak
and bad all this week. I'm also making a <u>faithful</u> and <u>daily</u> trial of
your <u>snuff</u> now, which is doing my head & cold more good than anything else I've tried, at least I'm impressed to believe it is[. . . .]

Miss Dickson is in their new schoolhouse, and who's delighted,
she has 68 day and 3 night pupils, she feels that tis more than she
can do justice by and she'd applied for an assistant. She's enjoying
good health and has recently visited Mrs. Rogers, who is well but
much dissatisfied with her present situation. I think she's at the same
place where Mallie Gordon was sent.

Miss Smith retains her health and spirits, and she's getting along
finely with her school. The Assoc. agrees to furnish her with books
upon the same terms with the other teachers, they also desire her to
send them monthly reports for which they will furnish blanks. I shall
endeavor to persuade Josephine to have her school brought under
the protection for the Asson. in the same way if she will.

Miss Carrie writes that she has 42 scholars now and seems to be
quite elated, she returns you many thanks for your kind wishes etc.
She has rec'd. your letter Bell, sickness prevented her going to Balto.
as she anticipated[. . . .]

I hope you had good luck with the Fair & also favorable weather,
twas pleasant here those days, in fact all the week up to yesterday.

That young man is attending school with his sister in St.

Michaels. I say him the last time I was there & told him what Mr. Graham recommended, he said it would take too long to prepare him for a teacher. I told him I thought differently. I presume he'll think upon it and make what advancement he can[. . . .]

I rec'd. a very friendly letter from Mr. Burton Last Sat. he also gave me the financial standing of the Society and cheered me considerably by saying how willing the members seemed to be to aid in building our schoolhouse. He says my letters are read at their meetings & they are just what they need to keep up the interest in the cause. He adds "I do not know any sort of labor in the world more interesting just now than this teaching the Freedmen at the South." And he wishes me all sorts of success, he says, "at the present rate of work we shall in a few years have so many of them taught to read, that all of the Andrew Johnsons in Creation will not be equal to the job of keeping them down in the dirt under the white man's heel."

You wish to know whether those who attend school exhibit the same interest in it, I wish you could see for yourselves & then you'd think they had. The school is the topic at home & abroad, among the children as well as adults.

I'm invited to two "Pancake Toss" Parties this eve'g. but I shall decline attending either. One is given by my scholars & the other by some old folks—our neighbors[. . . .]

I hope the society will not employ those persons of whom you write unless they know who & what they are both in politics & principles[. . . .]

I had a full school this morning at the close of it we had singing. I had another name entered upon my Register—a little boy who's never been to school before, he has a hair lip which disfigures his face very much. His mother has the same[. . . .]

Rebecca

Boneset is an herb taken as tea for insomnia, fever, and the elimination of intestinal worms. Hop tea is believed to relieve insomnia, flatulence, and intestinal cramps. Sage is taken as tea for nervous conditions and depression, as well as for relief from diarrhea.

.   .   .

Rebecca's family and friends hold a fund-raiser fair for her school; Addie describes the event.

Hartford Feb. 16 1867
Saturday 4 P.M.

My Dear Sister

[. . .] Now I shall tell you about the Fair monday PM Bell and I went up to the Hall and found the table all arrange except the refreshment table had some difficult in getting something for the tables at last they succeeded every thing look very nicely indeed great many handsome fancy articles the White people was very friendly indeed.

Tuesday night we had the colored band it made it very lively and great many would like to participate fantastic time. I will tell you who was the table tenders doubtless you would like to know. Mrs. Champion and Sounds Harden Mason Hammer Bell and Julia Addie O yes Mrs. Andrew Mitchell Tuesday or Wednesday eve your Aunt Mrs. T look very pretty indeed O a royal purple dress and a white apron with a ruffle on and that was fluted she put some of us in the shade that night. Mrs. C Freeman made the cream it was very good but the best the night Mrs. Hammer made it and it excellent. Mrs. Hammer cream it was very very nice. I will say extra nice Mrs. F tried to find fault but she could not get any one to agree with her.

Eliza Smith and Miss Daniels was up from Middletown and also Mr. Lloyd. I have not seen your mother since Thursday night I do not know how much they realize as yet Your Mother must be tired out she was the most prominent person. Aunt Emily made me a present of a very pretty scarf Thursday night. Bell made me a present of a pair of boots from cowskin[. . . .]

Mary Champion[4] is very wild. I am afraid she is going to be like Emily[. . . .] Sarah Sands very uncouth in her manners but she was out every night while the Fair[. . . .]

I am very glad that you have written to Mr. Tines he has spoken of it tow or three times. My Dear allow me to inform you that Mr. T does not hear but once a week from me. I am very much please of the interesting account you gave of the wedding you say the guest forgot that the Bride and Groom would like to retire do you think they done much sleeping when they did retire[. . . .]

I think the table must of look very nice but sunsoyes? must be in the place of chicken salad. Do you not think so too? Rev Mr. Burton wife was at the Fair and their son they spent their money freely. Gertrude was out one night and your mother got her to assist with the refreshment table.

[. . .] I told Aunt Emily I glad I dont run after the men. She said I would if I love them as she did—as Mrs. Mitchell does I mean.

[. . .] Anne Francis has lost her baby made a great mourn even kept crape on the door only 10 days old Bell and Julie and I went to see the corpse it was very pretty is was born with a veil.[5]

[. . .] Miss Margaret has just told me they had cleared $200.00 at the Fair I think they have done well. I must not pen any more for I do not feel like it. Miss M is going to mail it for me this P.M. they wish to be remembered to you.

I except my love from your
Affectionate Adopted Sister

Addie

Royal Oak, Feb. 23, 1867

My dear Parents & Sister

[. . .] Yesterday A.M. I suspended two boys from school for the day for fighting, one went home & rec'd. a severe whipping, and I've not yet learned what has bestowed upon the other.

As a general think my pupils behave very well, but now & then an evil spirit rises among them, and I introduce different methods of punishment to quell it.

[. . .] The man with whom we've contracted to build ours says, if we'll get everything ready for him by the 20th of April he'll complete it by the 1st of June. The trustees have the desired amount for conveying the lumber over, and Mr. Thos. says they'll make arrangements to have it brought next month; aside from this they have all the materials such as nails, hinges, windows sashes etc. to get, and one of them will go up to Balto. so as to get them as reasonable as possible. We are to know this eve'g. whether we can have the land or not.

I rec'd. your letter Thurs. and I'm delighted to hear of the unexpected success of the Fair, I think you've amply repaid for all your labor.

Your assertion that we're sure of $200 for our schoolhouse certainly exceeds my highest expectation, and when these people are informed (which will not be until after they've all given what they've promised towards it, and the building is completed) I imagine they'll not know how to express their gratitude or what to think of the liberality of my Northern Friends. They've all been wide awake upon the subject since knowing that they were actually to be assisted in the matter. They've also agreed to raise a certain sum by the 1st of June to settle all minor expenses, which is a good idea. Mr. Thomas proposed it, the others approve and agree to it.

I've rec'd a letter from Josephine this week, she is well and complains of the mud & mire with which she's had to contend since the snow left. These country places do certainly excel all other places for mud, there is such an abundance of it. It is very springy here which I suppose accounts for it, out when the roads are in order they are excellent.

[. . .] I've devoted my leisure hours this week, to reading Mrs. Sigourney's[6] book, which I think & find exceedingly interesting.

From a regiment of colored soldiers recently disbanded in Balto. three have returned to their families and homes in this place this week and they've been warmly welcomed. Some of these poor fellows ran away from their masters and return free men. They seem to be very happy. A great many joined the Union forces from this county which has deemed a great loss to their owners, and strenuous efforts were made by some to get their portable & uncertain property restored to them, but all to no purpose. One poor fellow—some one's son who went from here has died [. . .], & he's the only one. there are a few others expected yet, whose time of service has not yet expired.

Some of the young women gave a "Pancake Toss" here Thurs. eve'g. and gave me an invitation which I did not accept. The young men to return compliment I suppose—are to give one next Saturday night.

The whites are also giving a round of parties now, and it's first here then in Easton. They have regular Balls on so private scale, and employ a colored musician to play the fiddle for them.

The P.M.'s wife here is confined to her bed with the Rheumatism. They are very particular of late to send me word when there are letters at the office for me if I've not previously sent to enquire. And they will not send them by any & everyone, for they say I'm so very particular about my mail. I don't know what led them to be so considerate. I've not had more than one letter mailed from their office since our little difficulty. I suspect they feel the slight. These white people want all the respect shown them by the col'd. people. I give what I rec. & no more.

I am quite pleased with Pussy's picture and shall deem it mine from this time henceforth.

Little Jim does not care anything about it though he looked at it. I do not think he understood it as old Jim did, for he's not favored with the good sense that his namesake possesses.

I am very glad you have paid Mrs. Thompson, and I hope the members of the society will agree to have the remaining portion used as you propose, it will be so good to have the poor creatures cared for in this way. And I think it will be such an encouragement for the poor girls, Now do those get along that have recently come to Hartford?

[. . .] You desire to know why I did not introduce conversation at the wedding—simply because I had nothing to say, I went merely as a spectator. I sometimes think they're almost afraid to talk or move in my presence. I always do what I can to remove their apparent embarrassment[. . . .]

Hartford Feb. 24 1867

My Dear Sister

[. . .] Dear Sister I am delighted to learn that you approve of me going to Farmington should Mrs. Jefferson leave I shall certainly inform you all of my arrangements should I go. Mrs. Crowell send the money for the Fair.

Rebecca I did not say anything to Mr. Tines about coming I have not forget last summer I did not return a fond imbrace. Rebecca I have to smile but I do not mean to say that we were courting as long as you think for I shall tell you all about it when we meet So you think I do queer thing every now and then.

[. . .] Colonel Trimble of Tennessee is going to lecture at Talcott street Church on Wednesday evening the subject is the capacity of colored men; I think I shall go for I would like to hear him providing I will have company there. Rev Mr. Dranes preached his farewell sermon yesterday at St John Church. He goes to Albany at St Peter Church. I am very sorry for I intended to have him marry me I must hunt some one else. I must come to a close. They all send their love except my love your adopted sister

Addie

On the back of this letter Rebecca wrote the following: "Addie, please give this to mother." This was probably enclosed in one of Addie's letters.

Royal Oak, Talbot Co., Md
March 2, 1867
Sat. 9 A.M.

My dear Parents & Sister:

[. . .] I will give you a statement of my school report. I have had 38 day & 22 night scholars during the month, with an average attendance of 30 for the former, and 12 for the Latter. The largest number in attendance at any one session was 34 pupils. I've had 2 new day & 4 new night scholars.—13 are reading in the 1st reader, 28 in the 2nd, and 16 in the 3rd; 18 are studying Geogr; and 20 are perusing Arith; 16 write in Copy Books and a number of others upon slates. The general health of the school has been good with the exception of colds.

I shall fill a blank and send to Mr. Burton with my letter next week, it will be [?] change to be rehearsed in the audience of the Society at their next meeting. Amount of sales for books during the month $5.18. I was adding up the amount of sales for last year and I found I had sold $65. worth. I keep a strict account of every book sold as well as all those I receive from the Asson.

We have secured the land for the schoolhouse & I've enclosed the bill of it which is $50. with my report, to the N.Y. Soc'y. & as soon as the money is rec'd. it will be paid for, then a deed of the land will be obtained & we shall also have it recorded at Easton.

As soon as the house is built we intend to have it insured, & my object is to have an exhibition to raise the means for its insurance.

Mr. Thomas or one of the other trustees will go to Balto. this month for the lumber & other materials. I shall be delighted to see the building fairly commenced. Whatever amount is further needed above the $200 which you have for us, the people have agreed to raise it among themselves and their friends.

A young man who was married here during the holidays has been very sick with the Typhoid Fever for the past two or three weeks, was supposed to be dying early this morning, [t]he doctor says he can't recover. He has been quite a steady young man and is a native of Virginia.

The young woman whom I think I mentioned in my last epistle is thought to be getting better she can sit up I'm told.

There are others here who are sick from colds, the old man Moore is also quite ill.

[. . .] My little Jim hurt his foot last night and this A.M. I've been bathing it with Rum, and he thinks it's awful, always making a terrible time. I hope old Jim is well.

[. . .] That young man died at 8 o'ck. last night, he has experienced religion during his illness, & gave his friends to understand that he was perfectly willing to die. He said to one of them yesterday A.M. that he should die that eve'g. He has been buried this afternoon.

I rec'd. your letter, the papers, and a letter from Gertrude & Mr. Tincs yesterday P.M. None from Addie I hope she's not sick. The one you enclosed was from Mr. Silvia, he is very well sends his love to Bell, wishes to be remembered to you. He enclosed one for Aunt Em he says he rec'd. my letter but not hers. —which were written when I was home. He has shipped for home & expects to reach N.B. if spared in five or six months. His letter is very brief as usual, I've not penned Aunt Em's.

Those daises & the corn starch were rec'd. safely, I made a custard of a portion this A.M. and Mr. Thos. & I ate it for dessert this noon, reserving a part of it for supper. I can tell it relished well. Mr. Thos. likes it so well he's going to buy a paper of it to use in the family. Mrs. Thos. does not use milk & therefore can not eat puddings etc. in which it's used.

Those daisies I will keep for future use, as I am rejoicing in my accustomed good health again, which I shall endeavor to preserve.

How well our church must have looked last Sunday being so well filled, I should liked to have been there too.

[. . .] I have just spread a plaster to put upon my chest which has recently become very weak, and today has began to pain me. It is so strange whenever I have an ailing of any kind & recover from it another is sure to follow.

I suppose that Tennesseean delivered his lecture, I have no sympathy for any of them, I think they would all be glad to be restored to their former power and slaveocracy.

[. . .] We shall have our schoolhouse built in a substantial and comfortable manner. When do you think you can forward the money? If you can send us $50. which we desire for immediate use soon, I will oblige us. You can send it in a fifty doll. bill. I think 'twill come as safely in a letter as that I've sent on. We're determined to begin upon it next month, another man desires to have the job of building; but Mr. Thos. told him we had one engaged. I will enclose the proposed dimensions etc. of the building, & one of these days I will send you the plan so that you may be able to [?] all in a measure. It will be a little larger than the white schoolhouse here, and just half the size of the new schoolhouse at Easton, only that has two stories. I intend to superintend its erection etc. the trustees are very willing that I should.

I am glad the <u>mere</u> rolling of the Pill in Jim's mouth effected the cure. I hope he'll be fat when I come home.

[. . .] The <u>Church</u> in which I now hold our school is two or three feet smaller both ways, than the schoolhouse will be. Then more books are being given, I'm very glad, for if we do not need them all I will share with Josephine. Tell <u>that</u> woman we're in the <u>country</u>, & the S.H. will be erected in accordance with it's surroundings.

Dimensions of School House as Drawn by Sam'l Benson, Carpenter and the Contractor.

20 by 25 ft.—width & depth.
16 ft.—height. cor posts.
to be weather boarded up & down and stripped, the inside sealed up to the joice.
Materials required.
3 sills   6 by 8—25 ft. long.
2 "   6 by 8—25 "   "
2 plates 4 by 6—25 "   "
2 "   4 " 6—22 "   "

5 scant 3 "   4—10 "   "
20 "   3 "   4—16 "   "
4 cor posts 4" 6—10 " "
26 rafters 3"   4—14 " "
16 Joice 3"   7—20 " "
13   "   3"   7—22 " "
750 ft. plank—12" × " 1 in. thick
60 pieces stripping 16 " "5 " wide
1400 ft. flooring
3500 shingles—Cypress
3 window frames—sash & shutters
    " 10 by 14—12 lights
2 door frames & doors 6 by 10—3 wide
1 keg 10 penny nails
1 "   8   "   "
40lbs. 6   "   "
1000 bricks
1lb. lime
    Royal Oak, Talbot Co. Md.

Give my love to all of my friends & relatives, & accept the largest portion to yourselves.

                    from
                    Rebecca.

Addie continues to attend lectures and concerts, and to keep Rebecca up to date on the variety of cultural events in Hartford. The two friends also share gossip that proves incest and sex outside of marriage are not only contemporary occurrences.

                Hartford Mar. 3 1867

My Dear Adopted Sister
    I have been perusing the Standard having a few moment to spare I thought I would answer your letter. [. . .]
    They are having great rivals over to the Methodist Miss Sills wish to have me to accompany them to night she has never been in the

church since she has been here. Miss Babcock called Wednesday eve and gave me invitation to attend the lecture at the church Col Trimble. His subject was Colored Mans Capacity. He spoke very well, there was not many out. He wanted to have the White people those that are against our race. He had been brought up in the south with all the prejudices of the southerners against the colored race. He did not think them fit for anything but servitude or capable of any great mental or moral improvement. Since the war his opinions has changed. He thinks there are in the equal of with the white. He also spoke of Garnet, Douglass and other distinguish men. The day would come when states would allow every man vote he also said that he was going back to Tennessee and take two blackest men one on each arm and go up to the ballot box. Now Dear Sister I must lay aside my pen for I must get dinner and prepare for Sunday School adieu.

[. . .] Miss Sills and I went to the Methodist it was crowded of course she likes the appearance of the church they had prayer meeting after church we staid a little while they are having great times. Mary Champion is one of the converts[. . . .]

The Mason contemplate giving a Banquet the 26 of this month they are not going to have a dancing the first part of the evening I am told so I suppose they will have more than would have if they did.

[. . .] Bell & I went to the Allyn Hall last friday evening to hear Mr. & Mrs. Howard Paul we was very much please with them Mrs. H has a fine voice the Hall was crowded to excess your Mother Aunt Emily came in after nine o'clock they went to some meeting. [. . .]

I am surprise to hear about that young man to think with his own Sister. I should not think that he would ever seek the company of a respectable people and to think that you respect him so much your Mother was speaking about him few weeks ago having him educated for a teacher. He is a fit subject for a teacher one I think I would not trust any one with him I hope the Young men will not give him any peace about it.

I am afraid Dear Sister the people will think you dont appreciate the invitation to the Pancake parties. who does Jane expect to hear from here when she dont write to anyone. Mr. Griffin does not take after his brother he cant go without a companion.

[. . .] I heard yesterday a young girl in New Haven went from there go south to teach her health was miserable so her Mother sent for her to come home since her return she present her Mother with a grand child. That is a new method of teaching.

[. . .] I am delighted to hear that you anticipate having the School house done so you can enjoy being a little while in it before you leave.

I do not know much about Chas Jackson he trys to get with Bell as often as he can. She dont like him any more she says I dont think she encourages him very much you know how men are sometimes. I dont think I should like any one come up to my bed room and see how my Husband and I was lying. It was a very good thing they both was asleep. [. . .]

Addie

Prompted by Rebecca's report of a young man's deathbed repentance, Addie here initiates an informed theological discussion of the possibility of such contrition.

Hartford March 8, 1867

My Dear Adopted Sister

[. . .] That young man has not enjoyed married life long. I am glad that he experienced religion before he died. I read in one of the Congregational paper speaker death-bed repentence he has not much faith in it. I will describe it as much as I can remember if it is a minister was sent to visit a Young Lady she had no hope that she was a Christian and was afraid to die he prayed with her from time to time and she was also sincere in her prayer after a few days her terror passed into hope bright delighted hope in Christ He had never met with a clearer case of conversion of anyone had she died he should of treasure it up as a beautiful example of death bed repentance but she recovered and was able to attend School again and he visit her and see if she continued the same delightful frame of mind. To his amazement she remember no such experience during her sickness nor even that the minister had visited her and was living the same life she was before she was taken sick so my dear what do you think of this not please tell me what you think or what you view on Death-bed repentance there is a knock at the door[. . . .]

your affectionate Sister
Addie

Again, in this letter, Rebecca expresses her disdain for the emotionalism of some southern blacks as well as her doubt of the religious sincerity of those who convert to Christianity during emotional revivals.

Royal Oak, Talbot Co., Md
March 10, 1867
Sunday 1 p.m.

My Dear Parents & Sister,

[. . .] I was favored with a visit from Josephine Friday eve'g. and she remained until this morning. She came very unexpectedly and I was quite as pleased as surprised to see her, she is very well & appears as usual. Mr. & Mrs. Thomas look upon her as a very peculiar being, he says he does not think her equal can be found & I think he's about right, —they both like her very much, she brought each of us a little <u>gift</u>. She came in the steamboat & returned in the same early this morning. Mr. Thos. carried her down to the landing & I accompanied them. She inquired after you all her school occupies so much of her time & attention that she does but little writing, which I presume accounts for her having never written to you. She has been out to school every day since the 2nd or 7th of Jan'y. with one exception—& that was last Thurs. it rained so hard she remained at home. She heeds not storms or mud, distance or cold, —they're all one & the same to her.

[. . .] I went out this A.M. to see that poor sick young woman, it is thought she has the consumption. I read to her from the New Testament & one of the Psalms, also a very interesting piece in the Inde't. She seems to be very resigned & expressed her hope in Christ. Some of the church members held a meeting with her in her room last Thurs. evening. She does not sit up now and has a bad cough. We've had rain more or less all this week, & for two days in succession Wed. & Thurs. I was unable to have school, & there's not been a single night session.

[. . .] I took Josephine to see the little structure in which I teach & pointed out the site of the new building, and when it is finished she's coming over to see it.

[. . .] Yesterday I rec'd. a check for $50 from N.Y. society to pay for the land for the schoolhouse. Mr. Thomas saw the contractor again yesterday & he says he'll commence work upon the first of April if the materials are ready. We've engaged to have the lumber brought down the next trip of a schooner that runs between Eastern Shore & Balto. The Capt. has engaged to bring it for $2.00 per hundred ft. his usual price being $2.50. He's a very clever man to col'd. people though a rank secessionist.

[. . .] I suppose you refer to the revivalists of last fall's meetings. I'm told they are all or nearly all of them lost sheep during the holidays, the excitements, pleasures & parties occurring at that time, cause their fall, so I'm informed. The converts here are like those we have home—they're only for a season.

I regret to hear the girls who have lately come on there have got into the habit of attending those night meetings, but the Southerners are so emotional & so fond of excitement that it's nothing more than could hardly be expected from them.

Jim and his little chum must have become excellent friends. He should not be called a "little heap," I suppose whether I accept of the explanation given of those pictures of mine or not 'tis all the same. All right—"all's well that end's well"—I suppose it will lead to the selling of the object itself next.

That Lincoln Institute must be a great and good enterprise. I hope that man may be successful in collecting funds for it but I think his demand upon the Conn. people are rather exorbitant. Is he a white man or one of the pupils?

Jim is increasing in importance I judge, & I'm very glad to hear it. I've no doubt he takes the best of care of your little birds Sundays. Tell him he's always remembered by his absent mistress. Little Jim lies stretched out upon the bed. He seems to feel he's of some importance too, for he stands upon his dignity like his namesake.

Mr. Perry Davis[7] is so interested in the welfare of the freedmen perhaps on account of the pecuniary returns that he may re. He understands how the thing is done!

[. . .] All nature is re animated—people, creatures, birds, and also the vegetation, —everything today wears a cheerful aspect. I hope 'twill continue many days. I shall have a night session this evening. I expect the night scholars will be very glad to be able to meet again.

I've just been informed of the illness of another col'd. woman here. The Dr. thinks she has inflammation upon the Lungs. She is a married woman & has children, her husband is a real shiftless man. Old man Moore is better, and I understand that young woman is better today. She's not in any pain, had bad cold, and has hot fevers followed by chills almost continually. She's very weak, her appetite has come again and the Dr. says she can and may eat anything she desires. [. . .]

This letter reveals the complex relationships between some freedmen and their former masters.

> Royal Oak, Talbot Co., Md
> March 16, 1867
> Sat. 10 A.M.

My dear Parents & Sister

[. . .] So then Nelson's little girl has finally arrived does she walk yet? I don't see what he's sent so many rules to govern her by for, he goes upon extremes. How did Gertrude endure the "cross." Is Benajah going to return to Dr. Brown's? I suppose his education is now completed and I've no doubt he feels himself to be somebody of consequence now. I presume Nelson will miss his society very much. Can Leila talk much? How does he [Jim] appear to like her, don't let her plague him.

We could not get the place of land we at first made application for although the owner gave every reason to believe that we should have it. He is a hard-headed old Negro-hating secessionist and looks like an angry bulldog in the face—which is his most pleasant facial appearance.

Mr. Thomas sold us the land though he would not have disposed of it for any other purpose upon any consideration. The $50 note that you enclosed came safely to hand & next week Mr. Thomas will go up to Balto. for the various articles needed for the building. You can send the remainder of the money in the same way—that is fifty dolls. at a time, we shall reserve that to pay for the house being built. I don't know as yet how much money has been collected here. Mr. Thomas has begged two trees from his former master for the sills, which he very readily gave & spoke very much in favor of the school & expressed his hope that it might be the means of improvement among the col'd. people. The Trustees purpose getting the sills here on acc't. of their being so heavy to move and so get the Asson. to give us something else instead. Mr. Thomas has spoken to someone to draw up a deed of the land for him, & when that is done one of the trustees will have it recorded at Easton.

[. . .] The young man that died had been in the service and was among those who were disbanded a year ago from Texas, & has been very steady ever since he's been here, his employer said he was the smartest hand upon his farm.

[. . .] Addie told me she assisted in the Fair. I think she overdid which I've no doubt is the case with Miss Babcock, you must give my love to her.

[. . .] Tell Jim I want to see him very badly too, & he must not hurt the little girl, also to keep out of her way so that she may not hurt him. [. . .]

I should like to see those rules of Nelson's. Have you seen Harriet Jackson's baby yet? [. . .]

Give my love to all the friends; it continues to snow very hard & it is fully a foot deep now.

Accept my best love to yourselves and overlook bad writing.

From Rebecca

[. . .] I forgot to tell you Saturday that one of our best young men here was beaten & badly stabbed in three places last Monday night, by some drunken white rowdies at St. Michaels, he with his brother & one other man were walking down to the landing to meet the steamboat, they were all attacked by these fellows & badly beaten. This young fellow fared worse than any, & could not be brought home, he remains there with an aunt under a Dr's care his parents go down to see him daily, & his mother has been there attending him. He can not be moved and he can not talk on account of his distress. One gash is three inches deep; his employer & friends have taken the matter in hand & have commenced a trail upon it. It was an unprovoked assault. There a great many low white fellows in St. Michaels.

I see in the Independent the death of Artemas Ward, which occurred at Southhampton, Eng. the 8th inst. I also noticed the statement of Dr. Livingstone's death in Africa, it seems he was murdered. He was that renowned African Explorer of which we've all heard and read so much.

The Independent contains a great deal of interest, there is always an article relative to the doings of Congress in it.

[. . .] Mr. and Mrs. Thomas unite in love to you all. they are as well as usual. He has today begged two more trees for sills, and they were freely given.

With much love to you all & my best wishes for you health & happiness I remain.

Your affect'e. daughter & sister.

Rebecca.

Artemas Ward (real name Charles Farrar Browne) was an American humorist who took his pseudonym from the American revolutionary general. He wrote for the Cleveland *Plain Dealer* and *Vanity Fair,* and also published several books. Ward died in 1867 at the age of thirty-three.

Dr. David Livingstone was a Scottish physician, missionary, and explorer. His *Missionary Travels and Researches in South Africa* documented the cruelty of the slave trade and greatly influenced public thinking in Britain. He died in 1873.

Royal Oak, March 23, 1867

My dear Parents & Sister,

[. . .] I should like to see Nelson's little girl, I suppose she's quite contented with you, he ought to let her stay as long as he could, for the change of air might improve her so far as strength is concerned. It's very good she's so hearty. Bell you had better write to Nelson to that effect, how do the rules work—well or otherwise?

The money you sent came perfectly safe, also that which you enclosed in your last letter, and I'm very thankful to the donor for it.

I am very much pleased to hear of the happy state of mind that Benajah is enjoying, and I trust he may be enabled to influence the minds of his associates so that they too, may follow his good example.

[. . .] Can Henrietta's husband play the guitar or has she taken it into her head to learn again? Give my love to both of them. Tell her not to forget she's owing me a letter. I shall be glad to hear from her whenever she can make it convenient to write.

So the Methodists are keeping up their exciting meetings, when they get tired I suppose they'll stop, and in the end have the pleasure of seeing the fruits of there labor, two thirds of which when the excitement has worn off, will have forgotten all about their professions. There's something said about starting another one here, but whether there's any reality in it or not I can not say.

I'm glad to hear from Jim & to know he's enjoying such good health, & continue to exhibit an interest in his Auntie's welfare. You see, he wants to impress upon your mind his desire to see the meat is unharmed when it's brought into the house. Little Jim Jr. is well and sends his love to him and to you all.

[. . .] Nearly all of my boys were at school & just about half of the girls, the road is settling fast & the traveling is quite good. I had the pleasure of a ride out to school. I always improve such opportunities, it saves one walk through the mud, & I appreciate it as highly as one could under the circumstances.

[. . .] I rec'd. a letter from Miss Cummings last Tuesday. She sends much love to you, she tells me that Miss Anderson the teacher at Havre-de-Grace, persecuted a fellow for pushing her off the walk this winter, and was defeated so she carried the suit up and beat him.

[. . .] I have today put my second class into the third Reader and they're all delighted. They have just finished the Second R. for the third time. There are six in the class & with one exception they have kept together ever since the school first opened. The other classes are doing well. Every now an then I make promotions which always produces a stimulating affect. I've recently excited an interest in them to write letters to me upon their slates, & occasionally one comes inscribed with pen & ink; when they have made more advancement I will send on some specimens. They are very amusing & in some respects contain very sensible expressions.

[. . .] All the afternoon we had company—two men, the eve'g. we were left to ourselves & I began the "Life of Lincoln" & read aloud till nine o'clock. I think it's very interesting.

[. . .] Your wish to know what's become of Emily—she still lives and now has a daughter a week old who is as homely as herself we're informed.

[. . .] Mr. Graham was over last week. They're going to build a house for the teachers there adjoining the schoolhouse. Mrs. Armstrong has gone to Balto. I suppose it's on business connected with the school. The other teacher likes there very well. They take charge of each session jointly, which must make the burden lighter upon each, and still more pleasant for both. This arrangement would suit all of us who are teaching much better.

The postmaster said he'd send my papers to me as soon as they came. I shall watch for them with interest.

A man accidentally shot off one of his arms in Oxford a few days since. We've not heard whether he was a col'd. or white man.

This is all the news I can now relate, & I'll close this poorly penned sheet. Give my love to all the family connections and remember me to all of my friends.

Accept my best love & kindest wishes to yourselves, an with much affection & a daughter's & Sister love, I remain as truly as ever, Rebecca.

P.S. I enclose $10 for you Mother to get me a piece of unbleached muslin with. The seven dolls. was the balance of Bell's board bill you know I agreed to pay it.

Hartford Mar 25 1867

My Dear Adopted Sister

[. . .] Gertrude was in Church she walk up the hill with me and spoke of the party of course her Ladyship is not going to attend and dont want them to come to her house she also dont approve of them this something new a Masquerade surprise perhaps I shall go.

[. . .] Please dont mention what I am going to inform you Mrs. Babcock told me that Mary Evens was in the family way by Mr. Snyder lost his wife last summer. Mrs. Swan told her I saw her in church last night she look rather suspicious. She is one of the young converts. Mr. Tines went home last Wednes to see his brother Dr. has given him up I received a letter from him Saturday saying he is no better. The Granite is running here on Sunday for the present on the account of the great storms in NY none of the boats could leave if Mr. T. had of been on the boat yesterday I would had the pleasure of his most agreeable society instead on that we had Mr. Ladure company Mrs. Fuller well acquaint with him I had them both come home with me first do you see through it my Dear Sister now I have pen all will be of any interest I hope this will find you enjoying good health all send their love to you except mine from your loving

Sister Addie

Royal Oak, Talbot Co., Md.
Mar. 30, 1867
Sat. 9 A.M.

My dear Parents & Sister,

[. . .] This is a delightful morning only rather cool & windy, the little birds have been giving us some of their sweetest songs. I see there are a great many Robins around here this Spring, and Black birds are very numerous.

All of the sick people here at least in our neighborhood, seem to be recovering, some of them more rapidly than others. One woman has been taken with the chills this week, it is the only case as yet.

That young man who was hurt at St. Michaels, was brought home this week at his own request, he is recovering from his injuries quite fast. His employer offered $500 reward for the apprehension and arrest of the one who stabbed him. He's a <u>secesh</u> in principle, but a kind man to col'd people and to his hands.

We've had trees given to us for all the sills for our schoolhouse, and all of them from southern rights men, which I think shows they have no real hostile feelings towards the col'd. school, but are rather in favor of it.

Hearing there were some apples in <u>Oat town</u> I have sent this morning to purchase a dozen. It is the first of my trading there since taking up my residence here. I thought I would indulge myself for once, they're the only thing my appetite craves. I've still left some of my other <u>luxuries</u>, only this week have I eaten the last of that loaf of cake Mrs. Homer sent me, there being fruit in it, it kept well. The beef I keep for an occasional relish when bacon is all the vogue & my appetite turns from it. Mrs. Thos. has sent to Easton for some fresh fish this A.M. I really hope there'll be some in market. I've sent again for the papers which I take for granting are enroute now.

I rec'd. your letter also Addie's with the Independent Thurs. that is quite a cunning little paper which you enclosed. I should like to see one of those skirts it makes such an ado about.

I was surprised at first to hear that neither of you had rec'd. my letters, but the reason for it soon came into my mind. I hope both last and this week's have been rec'd. 'ere this and eased your minds.

The money came perfectly safe and a portion of it has been expended for nails, the remainder Mr. Thos. took to Balto. to lay out for other materials.

[. . .] I rec'd. a letter from Nelson this week, he wrote that he was very lonesome without Leila, and that he'd become a book agent for a while upon trail. He also told me about the sudden death of Amorett's sister. Poor girl! I suppose her mother will miss her very much for she had her with her so much. Nelson ought to let the little girl remain as long she possibly can, that she may have the benefit of the fresh air and sun's rays to shine upon her. I really hope she may walk soon, and I should like to see her very much.

There does not seem to be any more excitement here than usual upon politics. I see by the Ind't. that next Mon. is voting day in Conn.

I am pleased to hear that the meetings at our church are being better attended, for Mr. Halman seems to be so kind and interested too, that they ought to show in some way that his labors are appreciated.

Yes, I've no doubt the Methodist are having a real exciting time, and I really hope the impression may not soon pass away. I'm surprised to hear all those young girls are among the converts. I wonder if they so really realize any changes of feelings or not?

[. . .] I suspect Bell has fixed Leila off so well that she looks very nicely attired in those articles. What do the people think of her, and how is she pleased with the sound of the piano? I can not add any more lines to your letter now for I have my reports to prepare. I made a beginning yesterday so adieu until tomorrow or Monday.

[. . .] Mr. Thos. returned as we expected, our lumber is to be sent down Wednesday, they were not satisfied at the Room's with the size of the building which the trustees had decided upon and require it to be ten ft. longer and four ft. wider making it 24 by 34 and 13 ft. high.

Now I shall exert myself and use all my influence to get it into operation as soon as possible, my chief means will be through the children. I made a beginning today and shall continue every day this week.

[. . .] One of our principal school men is down with the rheumatism & he can scarcely use his limbs.

I sent to Balto. & got old man Moore some crackers and gave them to him yesterday, you don't know how thankful he was. He's very feeble but able to go about. I told him I did not know what else to get him. If your rather <u>our</u> F.A. Society can send him a little change now & then I've now doubt 'twould be very acceptable, for he says he's not able to work any & he is not truly.

I've just learned today, that two little babies were born here last week. There will always be a prospect for the school's being continued & needed here, so far as supplies are concerned.

[. . .] Our schoolhouse will cost us something more I expect now. I shall first see how we make out here 'ere I ask further assistance. With much love to you all I remain as ever affectionately,

Rebecca.

Give my love & kindest regards to all my friends. Mr. & Mrs. Thos. wish to be remembered.

Hartford Mar 31 1867

My Dear Adopted Sister

This is the last day of March and it is certainly a beautiful A.M. we can call it a spring morning I heard the birds singing very sweetly before I got up. I was lying thinking of you my thought reflect back several years ago you remember how we use to take Sunday A.M. walks how we enjoyed them most exceedingly what a pleasure it afford one to think of these happy moments. I shall not go out this a.m. I shall devote it to you SS concert this P.M. I must prepare myself to repeat my verse which it is this 5 cha of Romans and 11 rec doubtless it will be well attended every one is able cannot remain at home today.

[. . .] This evening Mr. Tines and I are going to spend with Ellen Harris. He is to meet me at Aunt Emily at half past six his brother is no better.

[. . .] I went to see Mrs. Smith at US hotel she was telling me about Selina. A Gentleman in NY wanted to have her very much because he did not look very stylish enough for her she would not receive his attention. Christmas night he was married to young Lady in Brooklyn and took her in one of his houses furnish from top to bottom they have found out he is very wealthy. Selina feel very sorry. I am glad of it when she could have two good offers she would not have them. Mrs. Smith made me laugh said Selina went to Church and just as she was coming out her waterfall curls came off. Her brother pick them up for her she must of thought great deal of him. I think I should had to smile myself.

[. . .] You know I was telling you about a Masquerade surprise A. Cross was getting up I did not attend for it was at Mrs. Effs and you know I do not visit there I heard it come off very nicely so much so with some for Mrs. Saunders was there and also Elizabeth I guess they have got tired being retired from Colored people going into the society I must tells them about it I was really surprise when I heard of it nexe evening Mr. Hector gave a festival at Talent Post Hall for the benefit of the Colored band to get a concert I heard they had dancing and never broke up until morning.

[. . .] Mr. Chas Fuller that was arrested last fall for taking some bonds out of the Hartford Bank belonging to Mr. Wilcox his trial came off last week in Friday paper pronounce him guilty and he is to have his sentence under they put it off a superior court they will know Tuesday of this week his family is feeling badly your mother I suppose will send you the papers I wish Mr. Fuller had Lawyer Chapman great many thing the bonds was never put in the hand of the employees in the bank dont recollect ever seeing them but Mr. Perkins time will tell all things.

[. . .] I see your letters are mail from Royal Oak now how is that have you got reconcile to the Post Master now.

[. . .] I dont know about being Mr. Tines hearts Idol. I dont think I am I have a rather a Singular human nature to deal with I tell you I have great deal to tell you when we meet.

No I have not had the pleasure of sitting or lying in his arms all night as yet.

[. . .] The little girl remind of some of your peculiar ways of yours I dont know about looking like you only her eyes remind of yours years ago. She dont like little dirts. She is a sweet and interesting child. I see your father seems to think a great deal of her. [. . .]

Addie mentions the *Christian Recorder,* a publication of the African
Methodist Episcopal Church, in which Frances Ellen Watkins Harper
often published articles and fiction. She also mentions Miss Still, who
may have been of some relation to Harper's colleague and friend
William Still.

Hartford April 9 1867

My Dear Adopted Sister

Tuesday A.M. find me writing to thee It rather strange I suppose
well I will tell you Sunday A.M. I was reading the Christian
Recorder a Phila paper which I find quite interesting. Miss Still lend
them to me and it afford me more pleasure to know what a going on
my home in the future now smile Dear Sister. [. . .] In the evening
Mr. Tines & Miss Fuller and I went to the Methodist and was
crowded of course it was SS concert I can tell you it was quite interesting to hear them repeat verses in the bible some trying to see who
could repeat the most. Doubtless you wonder at Miss F being in our
company you know I am used to a third party as for me I did not
mind it well I tell you Miss F seems to like my society very well

[. . .] Mrs. Pennington is dead was to be buried on Sunday a
great loss to Timmy I can tell you I received a few lines Saturday
saying excuse correspondence for the present it cause a smile from
my lips.

I will turn my thought to something else. Last evening Bell and I
went to Allyn Hall to see Cinderella played we was disappointed for
we thought it was going to be some thing grand. Mrs. Crowell gave
the ticket to me so you see nothing lost in my pocket. The hall was
not crowded as we suppose it would be. [. . .]

Royal Oak, Talbot Co., Md.
Apr. 18, 1867
Sat A.M.

My dear Parents & Sister,

It is now past ten o'ck. I have been variously employed this morning so that I've only just got through to take up my pen, the last of
my doings was to wash out my Nubia, which I always prefer to do
myself.

It is a most delightful day with not a cloud to be seen in the sky, it was quite cool early this A.M. but it's quite warm now. I went out to look at Mrs. Thos. little chickens while she was feeding them this A.M. She has now 56 in all, and has 5 hens still setting, two hens she's set today; of the five one has duck eggs under her, one hen has hatched out every one of her eggs this week, she had fifteen. The raising of fowls is Mrs. Thomas' delight she watches over & cares for them just as you do Mother for your birds. [. . .]

The Carpenter has been up and examined our lumber & finding there's not enough & that much of it has been ruined by rough handling, we have had to send for more & he can not commence work until it comes. It's a disappointment on all sides. It will probably be forwarded without delay.

My school has continued without interruption ever since this month came in, & I hope I may not have any lost days to report for the month. The children having taken advantage of the warm days by taking off their coats, shoes etc. during play hours many of them now have bad colds. It's useless to advise to the contrary, for the adults are no better themselves, like black snakes, as soon as the sun shines & it begins to get warm they come out, one young woman was attired in a black silk basque & a light summer dress last Sunday.

[. . .] Josephine says an old colored woman from the alms-house was found dead there on the roadside last Fri. she was left there overnight until a jury could be summoned, & they build up a pen around the body to prevent the animals from disturbing it. I've no doubt if it had been a white person there could have been a jury found that day.

The copperheads[8] had a convention of some kind at Easton this week, and last Sat. night they had a political meeting at the Oak. The principal topic under discussion was the "Nigger" of course, & in the midst of one speaker's harangue he cried out "put down the nigger schools etc." I expect it was a <u>gala</u> meeting with them.

[. . .] Yesterday was delightful day & I had an interesting S.S. and at the close of the exercises I read Mrs. Child's[9] sketch of "Benjamin Banneker" with which they were much pleased.

[. . .] I rec'd. your letter Sat. containing the $50. It came very safely.

[. . .] The fruit trees are putting forth their leaves & blossoms quite rapidly, a cherry tree in the yard is already blossomed out fully, & some peach trees are nearly blossomed out.

There have been robins here for several weeks in flocks, there are also numbers of other kind of birds around us who fill the early morning air these fine mornings with their clear voices, & richest notes.

You must keep Jim in doors that he may not see where the poor little birds roost nights, tell him his absent mistress requests it & he must submit. I expect he thinks they are for him. I suppose he remains on amicable terms with your little birds, eh?

I guess Nelson will not regret having sent Leila on although he's deprived of her company longer than he intended. Gertrude wrote that she was no trouble whatever. [. . .]

Rebecca.

There are some mysteries that require a little teamwork. One of Rebecca's references in the above letter forced me to enlist the services of my mother, my aunt, and all of my own sister-friends. We solved it, but only by a process of elimination:

> My dear Parents & Sister,
>
> It is now past ten o'ck. I have been variously employed this morning so that I've only just got through to take up my pen, the last of my doings was to wash out my Nubia, which I always prefer to do myself.

Nubia? Judging from the context I thought she might have meant her hair. I could very well see it taking some time to wash her hair, especially in the days before the enterprising Madame C. J. Walker, who became the first African American woman millionaire by creating hair straightening products and tools for black women. But I had never heard of hair referred to as Nubia. What a lovely, Afrocentric-sounding name for a black woman's hair, I thought. I began to imagine the implications: Upon publication of the letters black mothers might begin to refer to their daughter's soft, kinky mane as Nubia.

However, I consulted the definitive *Oxford English Dictionary.*

> nubia niu.bia. Irreg. f. L. nubes cloud. A soft fleecy wrap for the head and neck, worn by women.
>
> > * 1881 Confessions of a frivolous Girl, Emerging therefrom, five minutes later, in my nubia and snowy wrap.

* 1885 Van Voorst Without a Compass 34 The bracelet of
a lady . . . became entangled in the nubia of Agnes.

Then, for *Nubian*

1. Nubian, a. and sb. A. adj. 1. Pertaining or belonging to the
country of Nubia. 2. In the specific names of certain animals.
B.sb. 1. pl. An Eastern sect of Christians. 2. A native of Nubia; a
Nubian slave. 3. A Nubian horse. 4. The language spoken by the
Nubians. 5. A kind of black dress-material.

So Rebecca is writing about a wrap for her head. She often talks
about pieces of clothing and her maintenance of them. At one point
Addie also writes of her Nubia. On November 3, 1866, she writes: "I
have to get something to wear this winter for my neubia is about gone. I
wear my hat yet but it is rather cold."

A soft and fleecy wrap for the head and neck might also be a
metaphor for her hair. *Nubian* has come to be a synonym for "of
African descent," as in "Nubian slave" or "Nubian queen."

One of the women I consulted about the meaning of *nubia* is poet
Harryette Mullen, who was inspired by Rebecca to use the phrase in
the book-length poem *Muse and Drudge:*

> lady redbone señora rubia
> took all day long
> shampooing her nubia[10]

There are those things about Rebecca and Addie that remain mysterious. Hopefully they will continue to be taken up by readers, historians,
and poets, and other such mythmakers and image weavers.[11]

Spring has finally arrived, as is indicated by Rebecca's changing from
wool to calico.

> Royal Oak, Apr. 28, 1867
> Sat. A.M.

My dear Parents & Sister,

It is with pleasure that I begin my weekly epistle to you this
delightful morning hoping it may find you all the participants of
Heaven's richest & best of blessings—that of health. I have attired

myself in a calico dress this A.M. it being the first that I've worn since Dec. I tell Mrs. Thomas it seems good to put on a clean, whole dress once more. I've worn my woolen one all winter and I can tell you it's about thread bear now & full of dust & dirt. Mr. Thos. brought Mrs. Thos. two very pretty calico's from Balto. Her sister is making them. If you should come across any good pieces which you think I should like please have a couple laid aside for me.

I presume yesterday was recognized as Good Friday with you all & set apart for a holiday, but not so with us for as far as I could learn labor went on as usual, and I continued my school having a full attendance. It rained very hard here last Tues. & I told the children as we'd. lost one day this week we'd. better have school and they were very willing that it should be so.

Next Mon. & Tues. they have for holidays, which days are generally recognized as such by both black & white. The white school was closed yesterday & it seemed to be uncommon only still throughout the neighborhood.

[. . .] One of our neighborhood men is very sick with the Pleurisy this A.M. He is worse & they've had to send for the Dr. who is attending him. He has recently joined the Sabbath School. His employer says he'll do all he can for him & that he shall not suffer for want of any thing. He is a young unmarried man and very steady.

I rec'd. a letter from Mr. Estes last Tuesday in which the committee wished me to give them all the particulars of my school & our contemplated new schoolhouse. He said they were anxious to prove that the freed people had made sacrifices to educate their children. I nearly filled two sheets in reply, which I told him I hoped would prove satisfactory. He added that 'twould be very gratifying to me to know what pleasing statements the asson. sent them relative to my exertions to get assistance for building our schoolhouse here etc. However it makes no difference to me so long as I meet their approval. I've rec'd. no pay from them since Jan'y. & I desire to be knowing something about that. I shall make inquiries when I send my next report. I don't know but Rev. Israel has decided not to pay us until at the close of the term, which will ans my purpose as well as any other. We've been expecting the agent for the asson. —Mr. Janney—to come & inspect our lumber this week but he's not yet made his appearance & I look for him today. He wrote that he sent the lumber in a good condition & was surprised to hear it had been so badly broken up. I hope we'll get the amount we've sent for next week. This delay is putting us to a great disadvantage. Our contractor has other work engaged & if we can't employ him soon we'll lose him I fear. He's the best workmen around here & has as much as he can do all the time. It will be a bitter disappointment on all sides.

[. . .] Mrs. Thos. has shown me your hens one's name is Rebecca & the other, Bell—they having been named according as they characterize the individual whose names they bear. The latter being more gay than the former wears a crown, & this is the distinguishing feature. But the <u>former</u> produces the largest eggs & is the more <u>independent</u>.

Why was only Jim's name inserted & nothing further said of him either "pro or con?" I might have known 'twas some of your work Bell.

[. . .] The letter you've expressed to me is not yet rec'd. and I think you'd. better make inquiries at the office. We've sent regularly every mail day & made diligent inquiries. Your other letter containing the $50 note came safely & directly. I will not write any more today so adieu.

[. . .] We rec'd. the unexpected intelligence of the death of Emily's baby yesterday, it died last Mon. week, in consequence of which advent she's expected to return to Mr. & Mrs. Thomas this week for they'd. agreed in case of its death to receive her again & she's very disirous of doing so promising at the same time to be a very different girl, & I'm told she is very anxious to see me.

[. . .] Remember me to all of my friends and accept my best love to yourselves & Jim tell him to be a good boy till I come. From your absent daughter & sister

Rebecca

Here are some mock orange seeds Mrs. Thos. sends you to plant around the house for shading the windows.

Hartford April 28 1867

My Dearest Adopted Sister

[. . .] Mr. Tines brother is dead he went on to Phila Tuesday and his brother was buried Thursday I feel sorry for them all the family seems to be very much attached to each other I received a letter from Mr. T and he will be down to see me this evening he expect to leave Phila Saturday A.M. in time to take the boat. Mr. Green called on me Tuesday I wish you could of seen my head I was busy sewing I thought I would not stop to comb my hair until the P.M. [. . .]

Mr. T. expect to go to the Springs in the last of June I understand they are not going to run in the new boat it is called the State of New York they say it is very handsome. Mr. Green told he will not go head write on it and if he dont go—Mr. T will not. [. . .] No I have never allowed Mr. Tines to visit me at Mrs. Crowell he has escorted me to the door and that is all.

[. . .] I suppose Bell will have all Mrs. Pennington clothes I heard she had very nice one she ought to have some one clothes. She got none of her own. She is worse then I am for I have got two or three pieces. A few more weeks I will hear My Dear Sister is home. wonder when I will have the pleasure of seeing her. Please to direct your letter to your Mother and she will forward it to me to Farmington[. . . .]

Addie moves to Farmington, Connecticut, to begin working at Miss Porter's School for Girls.

Farmington May 5 1867

My Dear Adopted Sister

You see where I am and I like it very well so far. I left Hartford Thursday 3 P.M. and arrived 6 oclock Sarah accompany me and expect to return Tuesday A.M. I had rather a tedious ride the stage was so full in side and out something happen I will not tell you until I see you it made me rather low spirited since Friday A.M. I have been in rather good spirits since. I have not been out any so I cannot tell you much about the place. I like the house, and the grounds are very pretty. I have had excellent appetite ever since I have been here. Mrs. Jefferson reported that the work was very hard it rather discourage me coming out here what I have to do is nothing. I have great deal of time Mr. Sands is very kind. Any thing is very heavy he lift off the range. Some of the cooking utensils are as large as I am. Some of the help are quite sociable one girl I like very well she ask me quite often if I was homesick I seldom feel that. Last evening I saw the young ladies dance not many of them graceful.

I hope I may have the pleasure of seeing you out here when you return home. Mr. Sands was speaking of you this A.M. you the <u>best</u>

<u>one</u> out of all the family and you was a lady now what do you think of that.

Now about Election day it rain of course which I did not care very much I did not intend to go out in the A.M. I promise Ellen that I would come over then in the P.M. [. . .] We seen the parade Main Streets was crowded not withstanding the storms if you could only seen the styled. [. . .]

The Granite never reach Hartford most 5 oclock so I did not see any one. I spent a very pleasant evening with him [Mr. Tines] and he also called Monday I suppose it will be sometime for I will have the pleasure of seeing him again.

I have been looking at the young ladies going to church. Sarah wishing she could go the only thing keep her she forgot her stocking and I would lend her pair I will not learn nexe time when she comes out to bring her things she grows worse instead of better. I had quite a time to get her off Sunday evening to church with your Mother I did not go out all day for I have nothing this spring to wear.

[. . .] I am please to hear that you spent such a pleasant time I am sorry you was disappointed not seeing the ceremony perfrom who know but the nexe be the Royal teacher dont tell her I said so seems to me nothing but marriage there.

[. . .] I have pen you all of any interest I coming to a brief close except my best love from your affectionate Sister Addie

P.S. Please to direct your letter

Care of Miss Sarah Porter

Farmington Conn

Rebecca documents a series of conventions at which freedmen began to exercise some of their newfound political clout. In the series of letters that follow, she details their participation in a mass meeting at Easton, the purpose of which was to elect delegates to the statewide convention in Baltimore in 1867. Rebecca's letter relays a sense of optimism and urgency, and one can almost feel the exuberance of the attendees. During this relatively brief period, blacks emerged as lawmakers and the black public crowded the galleries of state legislative halls. Rebecca also introduces us to Judge Hugh Lennox Bond, who supported black participation in the Union Army as well as other initiatives to grant rights to the freedmen.[12]

This letter also includes a tender expression of concern for Addie.

Royal Oak, Talbot Co., Md
May 11, 1867
Sat. 7½ A.M.

My dear Parent & Sister,

[. . .] The mass meeting convened at Easton per agreement, and multitudes of the col'd. race from all parts of this county were assembled there. I continued school as usual & as all from Ferry Neck, St. Michaels, Bayside & Broad Cr. Neck were obliged to pass the church enroute to Easton. I had a fine opportunity for sight see-ing which I enjoyed hugely; as many walked as rode I judge—both women & men. It was cloudy all the A.M. & at noon it began to rain here & continued very hard & steadily the rest of the day. Mr. & Mrs. Thomas went up they say it did not rain as soon or so hard there, however the meeting went on. A Judge Bond has charmed all the people of color, but the Copperheads are all raging & raging about it—him & his colleagues. Both col'd. & white delegates were chosen to attend the State Convention next Tues. Mr. Thomas is one, & he goes up to Balto. Mond. I've sent to Easton for a paper to send you with this letter, so that you can know the full particulars of the meeting. Some of the men who attended it have been turned out of employment on account of their going but notwithstanding this, they are all very hopeful & look forward to brighter days. I can assure you the col'd. men are all wide awake now upon political mat-ters & the whites are saying all they possibly can to discourage them, but in vain.

[. . .] I have 35 pupils attending school now & yesterday every-one of them was present all day. Every Friday P.M. the girls being sewing & some of them sew very neatly.

[. . .] We're again disappointed this week in rec'g. out lumber, and too, just by the dilatriness of Mr. Janney who failed to get it to the boat 'ere it left although the capt. delayed one day to accommo-date him. It is very trying indeed, & still more discouraging for we're to such a great disadvantage thereby.

I would like to be in Balto. now. I'd just tell them how meanly we've been served by them, & I'd. should endeavor to make every-thing appear in its worst form & light. Mr. Thos. says he'll tell them,

& he's going to ask Mr. Janney to give us the coat of the lumber—that is the money—& we'll take it & buy what we need here without further delay, by so doing we'll be spared the cost of transportation etc. so that 'twill be much cheaper for us. I hope Mr. J. will do so.

I rec'd. your truly welcomed epistle Thurs. & Addie's also. She writes me that she's very much pleased with her new situation, which I'm very glad to hear as she's going to receive such good wages. I've rec'd. letters from Ed. Randall & Josephine this week. I don't know whether she rec'd. her box or not, she's so peculiar that sometimes I feel real provoked with her. She seldom ans. any of my questions & I'm done propounding them now. I suspect she does cause much remark when she's from home & she'll never be any different from what she now is I know. Ed. Randall wishes to be remembered to you all. He is well.

[. . .] I forgot to tell you a teacher has finally arrived for Ferry Neck & yesterday A.M. He paid my school a visit. he's from New Bedford & is an acquaintance of Mrs. Armstrong's. He is young & I should judge quite smart, but he's very short in stature. He said he was quite well pleased with the appearance of my school. He opens school Monday. There are now seven col'd. schools in this county.

Geo. Carr is such a steady young fellow that I hardly think he'll have any trouble in getting a situation to teach, all he requires is to get some society to adopt him, pass an examination & the asson. will supply him. There's to be another school opened in this county as soon as a schoolhouse can be built, but twill not be opened this term. I wish Mr. Burton has known it. Miss Usher's sister is teaching under the Del. Asson.

[. . .] Now about the girl you have with you. I told Mr. Thos. of the probably connexion, he says it may be for he has an aunt that was sold away from here years ago & she's never been heard from since.

I had to smile at Jim's movements but I'm glad he did not hurt the child. I'm surprised to know he'll allow her to play with him at all. He has become remarkably gentle. [. . .]

In the following letter, Addie paints a portrait of Miss Porter's School as an intellectually, socially, and culturally stimulating place.

·   ·   ·

Farmington May 12 1867

My Dear Adopted Sister

[. . .] Mrs. Porter was asking me this A.M. if I was not going to
church I think I shall go nexe Sunday Mr. Sands is not feeling very
well this A.M. I will have to wear my hat I have nothing else and
dont expect to get anything for the present Miss Porter is very much
of a Lady. Her housekeeper cant step in her old shoe for all she is a
cousin to her. [. . .] You know I am not as fond of cats as you are.
<u>Babes</u> [are] my pets. [. . .]

I presume you have heard from Mr. Tines ere this he inform
me in his last that intended to write to you last Sunday I am getting
very tired receiving morning letters I hope they will come to a
close.

[. . .] Rebecca do you think you will return to the school again?
Rebecca I think I will ask a favor of you this summer which I am
always doing so and you always gratify me in every thing. I would
like you to lend me some money. I thought I would tell you in time. I
only wish that I could of come out there last winter. I must not complain. [. . .] I hear music all day there is a piano in the hall nearly at
my room some of the Ladies play nicely Saturday there is not school
they do what they choose some go out riding and walking there is 17
pianos? and their all going on Saturday in the winter they tea
evening in the week summer evenings Miss Porter read to them.
One of the Chamber Maid is very pleasant I was setting in my room
sewing she came and invited me in her room and staid until 10 P.M.
I have promise to go out some evening while I am here she came
from England a year ago last month. She likes Aunt Emily very
much and wants to go in see her with me.

I have free access to the library Miss Porter has two one for the
week and one on Sunday I have read two quite interesting books. so
I will have every thing to make it pleasant but society. I can depend
on that for a while. Now I must come to close

except my best love
from your Sister
Addie
Care of Miss Sarah Porter
Farmington   Conn

·   ·   ·

Rebecca the black Yankee reemerges here as she requests information about the young freedwoman who boards with her family and as she describes a spring church service in Royal Oak. The compassionate Rebecca gives an in-depth portrait of "old man Moore," an elderly man who is sustained by the Royal Oak community. For the remainder of her correspondence she will respond to her family's inquiries about him. Eventually the Hartford family will also send packages to him as well. This demonstrates the ethic of care and concern that maintains a sense of connection and community for struggling black communities North and South.

Royal Oak, May 18, 1867
Sat. 7½ A.M.

My dear Parents & Sister,

[. . .] Mr. Thomas returned We. morning. He says the convention passed very quietly & pleasantly the Republicans had the majority; the object of it was to add an amendment to the constitution in favor of "Negro Suffrage." The col'd. delegates numbered about two to one white man, the democrats would have been the victorious party but for that. All were allowed to speak ten minutes at a time, & he says some of col'd. delegates spoke well also some of the whites, both those who were for, & against the suffrage question.

The ambition of the col'd. men in this state is raised high I'll assure you, & they are confident of voting at the next election. It's the general topic of the day now among them.

Mr. Janney has again promised to send our lumber down by the first boat & we look for it next week, should he fail to do so we're going to procure it here & say no more about it to him. Mr. Janney & Mr. Thomas have applied to Gen. Gregory for assistance for me & he's promised to furnish our desks, & as they cost $3.00 apiece 'twill be a great help to us. Collections are gradually going on & I hope we may raise a sum sufficient to defray all of our intervening expenses.

[. . .] Mr. Mills with whom Josphine boards was one of the delegates. He went up Mon. night with Mr. Thomas. He says Josephine is the most singular person he ever saw. I have heard from her this week. She acknowledges the receipt of your letter. The box has not arrived yet, but she presumes it will come along by & by. She says "you know it takes longer for these heavy bodies to move south of Mason & Dixon's line than it does north of it." She deems the whites here only half civilized.

I rec'd. a very interesting letter from Carrie's sister last Saturday eve'g. She seems to be getting along finely with her school, has a good boarding place and likes very much. The church in which she teaches is made of logs & never possessed either a sash or window pane. She has a walk of two miles & has 39 pupils now, she has had more than this number, but they've been taken out of school and put to work as is customary in the South.

[. . .] I did not rec'd. your letter Thurs. but I've this morning sent to Easton for it. Addie's came as usual, she seems to be delighted with her new home & all its surroundings.

Old man Moore is quite sick both his feet are badly swollen & pain him constantly. The rest of our neighborhood of people are all well I believe & just as busy as they can be. [. . .]

As for that girl I judge she's one of Emily's make,[13] but why do you clean until Bell returns or why not leave it till I come home to help? Don't put yourselves to the trouble of cleaning my room. As it's not been much used 'twill not be much or hard to clean & I can do it myself as well as not. She would not suit me I know.

[. . .] I see Jeff Davis[14] has been released. His bond's men just esteem him very highly indeed, to go his security for such an enormous sum of money.

In this week's Independent, there is an account given of a grand presentation of a marble clock to Wm. Lloyd Garrison by a few of the col'd. citizens of Boston, also the presentation address by Wm. C. Nell, & Mr. Gis. reply. His white friends have presented him the handsome of $30,000 & purpose raising $20,000 more so as to make the whole am't. $50,000 on account of his real & unwearied labors in the abolition cause. The world truly moves. I want you Bell to write & tell me all about your visit to Boston & everything else you can think of to write.

How does that girl treat Jim is she for or against him? Tell her I say she must not ill-treat him upon any consideration.

Give my love to all the friends. Mr. & Mrs. Thomas wish to be remembered to you all.

[. . .] It was a delightful Sabbath and I see a number of the blacks attired in their new spring hats, bonnets & dresses some in the latest styles. I judge, & oh! such looks some presented! Some of these people do make themselves appear so much more ridiculous than they really are. I don't know what they think of my always dressing so plainly. I must close now as I've two letters to write for outsiders. So adieu.

Rebecca

I send you two papers with this the "Easton Gazette" Rep. Ed.

The Addie who refused to patronize a minstrel show also protests the segregated seating of a local Farmington church. Once again she provides evidence of racist practices in the North.

Farmington May 19 1867

My Dear Adopted Sister

Not been long since I have return for A.M. church I dont think I will go very soon again I am no advocate for white churches they have seats expressly for colored people and I do not like them but the rest are very much please they can be for all me. It a rather pretty church and have very good singing.

[. . .] I have been resting O Rebecca I am suffering with my back I can hardly set still I have had it three days. Mr. Sands think its lifting well what can do. Already he is very kind he help me all he can possible do. [. . .] I am with Mr. Sands in Miss Porter kitchen we are getting on nicely so far he would not let me do very much today. [. . .]

I sincerely hope I will not increase size but I would like to have my face little fully that all.

I did not leave Hartford for Farmington until the 2 of May so you see I was there on Election day. You ask how Mr. Tines bear the loss I can tell you only this much he said he was very sorry to part with me and he hope the day was near at hand when he can imbrace me in his arms say that you are mine until death separate us. Please dont say anything about it you can imagine my surprise at such language from his pen I have more to tell you but preserve until we meet. [. . .]

Sister Addie

Royal Oak, May 25, 1867
Sat 9 A.M.

[. . .] I have 40 scholars now & it's the largest number of day scholars that I've ever had. These new ones are all small & new beginners, & I return from school nearly exhausted every eve'g. so that I'm glad to seek my bed at as early an hour as possible. We breakfast by 6 o'ck. now every morning. The children are getting along finely in learning their pieces. I've copied off two dialogues for them. One in which five will take a part & the other for two girls only. There are 30 learning pieces, then I'm also learning them some new pieces to sing. They've got "Auld Lang Syne," "Dare & Do," & "Sister & Stripes" so that they can sing them well, & they've only been practicing them about two weeks. Whatever they like they soon learn & it's just the same with their lessons.

[. . .] Old man Moore continues quite miserable & his feet are very much swollen so that he is receiving some benefit therefore I called upon him one P.M. this week & gave him a dollar to get what little necessaries he most needed; the poor old man was delighted, he said 'twould last him two weeks. I wish you could see how thankful & pleased he is when one gives him anything. Mrs. Thomas often sends him his dinner. The people are I believe very kind to him. He is sustained by their charity; his deceased brother's children do nothing for him, & he says he's done every thing for them that he could do. These are his only relatives excepting a married sister in Balto. The general health of the colored people continues good, & they are all hard at work.

[. . .] I think I told you there was to be a bush meeting at Miles River last Sunday. I hear it was largely attended & that it passed off finely. They took up a collection of $16.00 & raised a subscription of $60. A Quaker gentleman there has given them a spot of ground upon which to build the schoolhouse, & he's offered to take the entire responsibility of it upon himself, until they can pay for the building thereof. I think immediate steps are to be taken to procure the lumber from the government. This is the farm that the famous Lloyd family once owned & where Frederick Douglass[15] lived in his childhood & youth. It was so bad a place for slaves in those days, that it has been named Georgia & still retains that name. This old Quaker was one of the delegates to the convention, & at the close of the services last Sun, he made an address relative to the proceedings of it, & also made known to them his gift of the ground etc. He's a strong Union man and his wife is a bitter Secesh.

Flowers have arrived & I'm beginning to receive my share of them. Two very nice bunches were brought me this week by one of my girls. Then yesterday or the eve'g. before Mrs. Young sent me a few carnations pinks & a large red tulip. I think very much of these little tokens of friendship and regard from these people. [. . .]

The remaining of our lumber has finally arrived, & we expect the building to be commenced this week. I'm quite encouraged again.

[. . .] Political & all of the matters appear to be going on very quietly here about now. The teacher's house in Easton has been commenced, & they were expecting to occupy their new schoolhouse last week, but I've not heard whether they did so or not.

Give my love to everybody. Mr. & Mrs. Thos. join me in love to you all. Yours.

Rebecca.

Royal Oak, June 1, 1867
Sat. 8½ A.M.

My dear Parents & Sister,

[. . .] The ribbon came safely but I think it's too light to put upon that dark hat, & shall reserve it for some other. It is a very pretty & delicate shade & was very cheap. Don't send any more for I can make this answer. I am very much oblige to you for sending it.

[. . .] Old man Moore will be very glad to rec. whatever you may send him. His limbs are better the swelling's gone down so that he can walk about a little now.

[. . .] I rec. letters from Carrie, Miss Dickson, & Miss Hoy with yours on Mon. The two latter have been sick they tell me, which has prevented their writing. Miss Hoy sends her love to you & Bell. She informs me that one of our corps of teachers has recently died at her home in Phila.—Miss J.T. Ellender, quite a young person & very pleasant & agreeable in her manners. I was acquainted with her; she contracted a severe cold while discharging her duties last fall, returned home during the holidays & died the 15th of April.

Miss Hoy's preparing her scholars for an exhibition to take place the 10th [. . .] Carrie's been to Balto. again. She's well, desires to know why you've not written Bell. She thinks she shall ask for a dis-

missal if the asson. require our schools to continue longer than this
month, on account of her school's being to small. She sends much
love to you both. She saw none of the Adams family. Mr. Simpson
boards at Dr. Hudson's.

Josephine wrote Thurs. She said nothing about the box. They're
going to have to fair there during the next holidays & she says she's
instructing a few of her pupils how speak some pieces she's learning
them. Their <u>gestures</u> & <u>articulation</u> she deems very important. I
should like to be a silent & unseen observer of her <u>mode</u> of instruc-
tion. She says "perhaps we'd. all like to come over to the fair." I shall
be oblige to forego the pleasure on account of previous
arrangements with Miss Smith. There's to be an all days meeting
there tomorrow, if I could make any arrangement I would go, but
Mr. Thomas being sick I can't very well. I've requested her to come
to my exhibition. Mr. Thos. says he'll take me round there by way of
Easton before I come home. That will answer every purpose.

The white people are going to give a grand supper at the Oak
next Friday night, to raise money to aid in relieving the suffering
poor at the South. Admission 50c, supper 50c & all confectionery
extra. It's thought to be rather expens[ive] by some. I tell Mr. Thos. I
guess it's only intended for a <u>certain</u> class. The wealthy circle are
getting up & have exclusive management of the affair. One man has
given a whole lamb as his donation.

A little girl baby was born in our neighborhood yesterday. She
has two brothers & four sisters—the youngest of these is a two year
old baby just learning to walk. It continues to be very healthy among
the colored people. Did I tell you in my last that I've 40 scholars? 25
are boys.

I must not forget to tell you that I've been the recipient of three
splendid bouquets this week. Two were brought to me by two of my
pupils & the other, one of our neighbors presented. I shall be supplied with flowers now so long as the season lasts.

[. . .] Late P.M. yesterday I rec'd. a letter from Mr. Janney
ordering our schools be closed the 28th inst. It is joyful news I can
assure you. I shall complete all my arrangements in the interval.
Mrs. Armstrong has rec'd. the same orders. Mrs. Thos. called upon
her & Miss Briggs. Both are well. Tues. in the holidays, Judge Bond
& Gen. Gregory are going to deliver addresses to the col'd. people of
Easton.

Mr. & Mrs. Thomas wish to be remembered to you all, accept my best love to yourselves & give my love to all the friends.

From Rebecca.

It's just begun to rain.

Farmington June 2, 1867
8PM

My Dear & Adopted Sister

[. . .] Mr. Tines will not be very long there. He leaves for the Springs the 20th of this month. I should like to spend the last Sunday he will have in Hartford. Mr. Sands says I can go if I wish. I do not want to use my money. I want every penny and more.

[. . .] I have received a letter from Thomas. He like Portland very much. He wish me to tell his father there is room for another druggist. [. . .]

Your mother sent me three shirts to make. Send few lines informing me of the death of Miss Ward. She has gone to her everlasting home where she always will be welcome. She has had her troubles as well as the rest of us. I received your welcome missive Wednesday evening the 25th. I was very much of cause if I had not I would of been much disappointed. I have received them so regular since I came here first part of the week. I am quite surprise to hear you have so many scholars. You are doing remarkable well.

You are worthy of all regards that Miss Booth. I think she would make a grand Procter. I suppose I will have the pleasure of seeing it. Bell making quite a visit in Boston. I don't suppose she care about Mrs. Jones for she dislike her so very much she has inform me.

[. . .] There is quite excitement last night. There was a man preaching to the people in the roads. One time he was nearly opposite Miss Porter. I rather think he was a little out of her range. Mr. Sands has let me make a cake turner. I had very good luck. He says I am getting along nicely. I have been here four weeks Friday last and think I have $12.00 and if had been to Mrs. Crowell only $6.00. What a difference isn't it? Rebecca I suppose by this time nexe month you will be winding your way home to your dear friends. Mr. Sands wish me to give his love. No more at present from your loving Sister,

Addie

When Rebecca here writes "One obstacle with which the col'd. people have to encounter here is in rec'g. cash payments for their labor which makes it very hard for them, & so too they're kept out of money," one is struck by the similarities in the position of the freedpeople of Royal Oak and that of Addie Brown in New England. Both struggle to be compensated for the labor they perform.

Royal Oak, Sat. 9 AM, June 8, 1867

My dear Parents & Sister,

[. . .] That little baby is dead that I mentioned in my last letter. It took cold I believe, had spasms & died Thursday eve'g. Old man Moore is considerably better, he has changed his residence this week & I've not seen him since.

[. . .] The supper came off at the Oak last night although the weather was so unfavorable & it's to be continued today & tonight. We are told they cleared $200 last night which was a good sum. Both black & white attended it. I don't suppose any suffering <u>blacks</u> will derive any aid from it's proceeds.

Judge Bond & Gen. Gregory are expecting to hold forth again at Easton next Tues. Also a col'd. gent. from abroad, I've not yet heard who it's to be. If it's pleasant I presume some of the neighborhood will go up to hear them. [. . .]

Your this week's epistle has not yet been rec'd. but I expect it this eve'g. Addie's came as usual, & she apprized me of the death of Miss Ward which was certainly very unexpected intelligence. Poor woman's better off now & all her troubles are at an end. She continues to get along very well out there she tells me, & I'm really glad she likes so well, hoping she may continue.

[. . .] Mrs. Thomas has asked me to give her love to you all. She permitted Emily to accompany me to S.S. last Sunday & she wore her new dress, which has made up very pretty indeed. She is delighted with it. She's getting along very well here. Mrs. T. gets very much tried with her at times, & a terrible commotion follows continuing perhaps an hour or so, & then there's dead calm again. Emily is pertinent & cares as long as the storm rages, but as soon as it's fury is expended she is the same Emily again. It's really amusing sometimes.

[. . .] I've been making out school bills this P.M. of the taxes which have not been settled up. Some keep it paid up by the month which makes it much easier for them, but it don't seem to be in the power of all to do this. One obstacle with which the col'd. people have to encounter here is in rec'g. cash payments for their labor which makes it very hard for them, & so too they're kept out of money. Their employers readily give them orders & desire their hands to take up all in orders, but some will not agree to it.

[. . .] You must give my love to all of my friends & accept the largest & best portion to yourselves. I hope your letter will arrive Mon. or Tuesday.

From Rebecca.

Farmington June 18, 1867

My Dear Adopted Sister

[. . .] Mr. Tines sent a letter last week asking me to come in before he leaves the boat. I went in Saturday AM and return last evening. I did not enjoy his society as much as I expected and I guess he was disappointed as well as myself. I shall tell you all when you return home. [. . .] Nevertheless Bell and I went down to see the grand boat called the State of New York. Josie[16] return home with us and remain until I took my departure for Farmington which I was very glad to do he has change very much they say and is very dark. [. . .] Why should that Mother feel the death of her babe? All of her children are very dear to her even she should be bless with a dozen. You ask my opinion of the man think and if his wife did not have any children he would bear her he is not worthy of any and ought not to have any. Mr. Tines sends his regards to you. He leaves for the Spring the 25th and says he is not going on the boat any more.

[. . .] Mr. Sands send his love and is looking for your letter to know what you will say about the message he sent about me. Except my love and I shall remain as ever, your dear and loving Sister

Addie

In this letter Addie expresses her disdain for President Andrew Johnson.

Farmington, June 23, 1867

My Dear Sister:

[. . .] The picnic came off last Friday. Most every person and their grandfather was there. It was a beautiful day. Had amusement of all kind. Dancing, boating, swinging and ball playing. Every one out of the house went but there Miss Wood one of the young ladies and the two was Misses Jane Lawrence and Addie Brown. The latter had a very severe headache kept for bed part of the day. Towards the evening she felt better and then she went to sewing and sew until most ten and I thought she had better retire.

[. . .] I hear the President Johnson expect to be in Hartford the 26th. I suppose his <u>friends</u> will make a great time over him. I wish some off them present him with a ball through his head. It would be better for him. Well dear sister two more Sundays and then you will be home. How long will it be before I can have the pleasure of seeing you? Now I must answer your very kind and interesting letter.

[. . .] My fat is all right [. . .] should I be incline to any other kind of fitness I should not have the opportunity. [. . .] Do not Rebecca consent to teach another month. O do come home, won't you? I should think you had quite a large Sunday school. Mr. Sands went to church this AM. I just look out of the window I see he is in his room. I guess he will not go this PM. The bells are just done ringing. I heard Miss Porter is going to close her school the 24th of nexe month.

Mr. Sands wish whenever I write to send his love. He was anxious to know what you said about my fat. He says I did not tell him at all. I am going to dress myself now so I am coming to a close and hoping in the nexe you will tell me when you will be home.
As Ever
Adopted Sister
Addie

Farmington, June 31, 1867

My Dear Adopted Sister:

This is your last Sunday for the present in the southern clime. I have been quite happy since I received your last Thursday letter. You say you did not expect me to ans the letter but I shall do so and send it to Hartford and shall be waiting for your arrival. I only wish I could be there. I have been thinking the time you return last year.

[. . .] Mr. Norton [. . .] has a beautiful place. The young ladies went there last night. Strawberries party one of the young Ladies does not participate in any the pleasure. She expect to get married when she leaves this town. I wonder if her lover is the same—do not indulge in any pleasure. Well nothing like it. [. . .]

I should think the people was hard to get along with. I have got something to tell you that I have experienced in a few days. I am delighted to hear of the progress on your school house. I hope you will realize all you anticipate. We are well aware that your whole heart is in the work. If all was like you they would be more executed. I have had plenty of berries and cream this year. Not had any cherries as yet. You have been ahead of us. Gertrude has told me she was not fond of doing house work. she is sometimes like me—likes sewing the best.

I am going to lay aside your letter for the present.

Farmington July 7, 1867

My Dear Adopted Sister:

Where are you today? Are you any nearer home then when you was when you wrote my last letter. [. . .] The fourth was spent very quietly here. Some of the young Ladies help some of the teachers put lanterns in the Arbor. Have it illuminate in the evening but a storm came up about tea time. They had to take them down in a hurry so they will postpone until nexe year. [. . .]

Wednesday 4PM

Dear Sister I am realy glad that you have return home. I only wish I was at home Sunday. [. . .]

So Miss Levin has heard from Mr. Tines? Who know but they will get married. You know stranger things happens now a days. I should be much surprised. I thought Bell was going to meet you in NY. I suppose you did not let them know when you expect to leave Baltimore. I think you done nicely at your Exhibitions. Dear Sister I am afraid you expected too much from your pupils you had more strangers than last. [. . .]

From you
Sister Addie

Although Rebecca has returned to Hartford for the summer, Addie remains in Farmington. Consequently, while there are notes from Addie to Rebecca, there are none from Rebecca to her family. However, during her time in Hartford, Rebecca apparently gave an address about the work in Royal Oak, and the text of that address follows Addie's last letter of the summer of 1867.

Farmington July 18, 1867

Dear Sister

I feel rather tired and I feel as I like to be [e]mbrac[ed] in your loving arms once more. Perhaps I would get rested. You are aware by this time I have taken Mr. Sands place. I have got along very nicely. This woman that has my work to do is very pleasant and kind to me. What do you think, I made some ice cream for Miss Porter today and also some biscuits for tea. They all think they are very nice. I hope I will continue and as soon as Mr. S return I will bid farewell for the present. Rebecca if you have no company when Mr. S come back and you are quite well, will you come out here and return home with me? That is if you don't intend come before, if so come right along for I long to see you.

[. . .] I think those shetland shawls are very pretty. What bonnet are you wearing for Sundays? [. . .] O Rebecca one of the young ladies plaing beautiful piece. It bring your spirit near to me. Give my love to your mother. Tell her I shall let her have the shirt very soon. I did expect to send them this week. Under the present circumstances I am afraid not. Now Dear Rebecca I am going to close now. I have got considerable to do. Remember me to all except my best and cherish love and ever think of my beloved and only sister.

Addie

Farmington July 25, 1867

My Dear Sister:

[. . .] The school is close and I am delighted. 28 left Tuesday PM and the rest Wednesday AM and now it very lonely. The house is very quiet. Sometime nexe week we are going boating. One of the men propose taking Mary Reedy and I with his family. I am anxious to go as I have become very fond of the water through the influence of my Sister.

The Talcott Street Congregation, circa 1930.
Church Mother Rebecca Primus Thomas is in the second row, seventh from left.

Last evening two of the girls and Mrs. Edge and I took a walk was very pleasant so very cool that we enjoyed it very much. Sunday PM Mary and I went over Miss Porter grounds for the first time. Then we stroll along the river edge. O we had a lovely time at the same time you was the object of my thoughts. How I did wish that I was in your company [. . .]

Your very welcome missive came safe Tuesday in company one from Thomas Sands. I was expecting it as usual. I suppose you do not feel the effects and working and other duties you are with that as your and with other things heart and soul [. . .]
Addie

Farmington July 28 1867
My Dear Sister
[. . .] How kind and thoughtful it was to write me last night. I did not expect it until tomorrow. I would really like to be in the first of August. I will have to resign to my future as you do yours. [. . .] I

am very much please to think your Mother thought I done the shirts nicely. I feel quite encourage. You say you are keeping close quarters. Are you waiting for me to return home so that I can accompany you? I will be at your demand entirely nothing to call me home. It will be quite different from last summer.

[. . .] I have no explanation to give you for I have not interfered with Mr. Tines correspondence. He need to make me for excuse for not writing to you before.

[. . .] Good night from your loving sister
Addie

Farmington August 5, 1867

My Dear Sister
[. . .] We have had a great deal of rain. Wednesday eve we all went a boating and a delighted time. We was gone just one hour. I was thinking of you and wishing you was along in company. We anticipate going again this week. This eve Aunt Emily and I expect to take a walk. Perhaps we go down to the river. Not having her bonnet she oblige to remain from church. I have been absent for a while. Mrs. Edge call me to go with her to her room to see the people go to church. Wish to run my mind several times to be in Hartford. [. . .]

Rebecca, I have got to get something to wear outside. what do you think it is best to get and also a bonnet. I shall have it trimmed with blue I think. Miss Porter has her brother family here. One of the Daughters she is very pretty looking young lady. [. . .] Except my best love
I remain Your
Affec Sister Addie

Having been asked to make a few statements this eve'g. relative to my mission south during the past two years, I thought perhaps It might be interesting to my friends to do so, & therefore have taken up my pen to make the attempt.

I began my labors upon the eastern shore of Maryland the 11th of Dec. 1865 by opening a day & night school in the church under the auspices of the Balto. Asson.—an organization formed solely for the moral and educational improvement of the col'd. people of that state.

I began with 10 day & 26 night scholars. The number soon increased to 75, including persons of all ages. The adults attending the session.

But few, very few could read, others only knew the letters or a part of them. Yet, the greater portion know nothing about them. In a remarkably short time many learned them, & able to read in "Sheldon's First Book" quite well, Now they're using "Hillards Third Reader", can spell well, study Geog. & arith. & are learning to write. The children can make figures repidly & write upon slates legibly.

The actuary of the Asson. has visited the day school twice & expressed himself well pleased with the proficiency they had made.

We have a flourishing & a very interesting Sabbath School in operation numbering between 50 & 60 members who seem to take great delight in attending it. Two thirds of them read in the Testament & answer questions therefrom with readiness.

They take great delight in perusing the S.S. papers that have been sent them from this school & by others in the city, being something entirely new to them. They've ever been rec'd. with evident satisfaction. I have distributed them once a month but having now nearly disposed of my stock, unless I can obtain a fresh supply I shall be unable to gratify them with them very much longer.

I have also occasionally sent them to other schools where they've also been rec'd. with the same gratification.

We are now building a schoolhouse 34 by 24 ft. which is expected to be completed by the first of Oct. It is of wood & is being fitted up as comfortably and as nicely as other schoolhouse. It will probably cost a little of $400.00. We've already paid over $300 & $200 of this sum were furnished us by our Hartford friends & sympathizers. The recipients know not how to fully express their gratitude for this munificent gift. They are all just beginning life as it were for many of them were made free by the Emancipation Act—for which they revere the name of "Abraham Lincoln." But they are industrious, & hopeful of the future, their interest in the school is unabated & many of them deny themselves in order to sustain it.

The government has promised to assist in defraying the cost of the building etc. so that we hope to have no expenses upon it after it is finished.

The Primus Institute of Royal Oak, Maryland, circa 1973.

I have now given a sketch of my work South, which I hope may be approved, I for want of time I close.

Rebecca Primus
Hartford, Sept. 1, 1867

Upon her return to Royal Oak, Rebecca finally gets her schoolhouse.

Royal Oak, Sept. 30, 1867
Mon. 9 A.M.

My dear Parents, Sister, & Brother,
[. . .] The family are all well. A lady from Balto. is visiting them. I've rec'd. a warm welcome from everyone. They all say they're so glad I've come back to them. I've distributed the gifts. You can better

imagine their feelings & expressions of thanks than I can describe them. I will say more about them hereafter.

Our schoolhouse is looking finely. I only wish you all could just take a peep into it, the desks are to be forwarded today or tomorrow. I called on Gen. Gregory. The Govt. has taken the balance of our expenses upon itself & it will soon be entirely paid for. It is surrounded with a neat fence which has been whitewashed. The house is to rec. another coat of whitewash both inside & out. Next Sun. we propose to have it dedicated. Mr. Thos. is going to Balto. tonight to make arrangements for it. Gen. Gregory, or Prof. Day will come over I expect. I spoke to both of them about it one or the other is expected; —an extended notice of it has been circulated through the county already. Bishop Wayman is to be here also. I resume there'll be a large gathering if the day proves to be a pleasant one.

Yesterday it was fine and very warm also. A bush meeting is being held here now, which is to continue a week. I attended yesterday P.M. Seats are arranged in the woods & a preacher's stand. At night the meeting was held in the church. I tell them I think it's too late in the season to hold these out-of-door meetings. This A.M. it is very windy here & quite cool in the house but the sun is very warm.

[. . .] Carrie came to see me I went to see her. She's very well she sends love to you all also Mr. Mason. I had the pleasure seeing the whole family—all of whom are very fair & very clever, but it's very evident they do not live in much <u>style</u>. The son that's expecting to be married soon has just opened a shoe store in the city, & two other sons are in their father's store. I guess they're smart but not much for showing off, for the house is very plainly furnished. Carrie starts for her school this morning, it's in the same county in which she previously taught but at a much pleasanter place. She said she would write to you soon. Her sister was in the city also, enroute to her school. She goes by the way of Washington. She has far more zeal in the work than Carrie has.

[. . .] It is very doubtful about the city schools now. Judge Bond & some other state (Union) men are about to be removed, & conservative men are to be placed in office; 'twill be a sad change to the col'd. people. It is feared, however they're to make the best of it.

[. . .] Give my love to all. The family join me in love to yourselves. I'm not going to write any more now & whatever I've omitted in this I will enclose in my next Mr. Thos. will mail this at Balto. Direct your letters to Easton.

From Rebecca.

I'm going to write to the Independent today.

It seems Addie finally got to Hartford during the last weeks of August and was able to spend time with her beloved friend Rebecca. For the remainder of 1867 there are fewer letters, most having been written from Farmington during October. In September Addie made a visit to Philadelphia that seems to have solidified her decision to marry Mr. Tines. In the letters that follow she speaks of him with a great deal of affection, at times even referring to him by his first name and her nickname for him, Josie. Perhaps this is because he has promised to cease his correspondence and flirtation with the mysterious other woman. Addie's letters are now more mature and self-assured, and less anxious.

Philadelphia, Sept. 30, 1867

My Dearest and Adopted Sister

It is only 7 oclock and I am the only one up. I don't think we will have a very pleasant day. It is quite cloudy this AM I have had lovely weather since I have been here and only wish that you was here too. Friday PM I went out to Fairmount Part—quite pleasant but nothing compare to Central Park NY. On our return home we made two calls. One was on Mrs. Adams. They all appear very glad to see me. They made quite a time. I remain at home on the evening. I was very tired. I retired about half past 9 and Josie went out to see the torch light procession which he was very much pleased to see. Saturday I spent nearly the day with Amelia. Had quite a nice time. She said she would like to have seen you very much indeed. She has a fine babe only seven weeks old. I also went around to her brothers. I have not seen him for 9 years. He had not forgotten me. I would quite like to remain in Phila this winter.

Josie is going to New York to stay the winter. I had a talk with him last night about Miss L. Has promise not to be so friendly and cease correspondence with her. I think he will keep his word. Josie sister has a fine son and is doing nicely. Her mother still wait on her. It realy to much for the old lady to go up and down so much. One of the Neighbors is very kind and comes in two or three times a day.

[. . .] Josie will call for me to go to church in the PM. I then shall take tea here and attend church in the evening. It will depend on the weather. I am very much afraid I will have to remain in the house. We will leave tomorrow morning in the first train. I say we for Josie is going to accompany me as far as N.Y. which I am delighted. I have pen all about myself now I shall return to you. I hope you arrive safe to Baltimore and found some of the teachers there waiting. I suppose you are now in Royal Oak and thinking of attending S.S. this AM I hope you found Mr. Thomas family and please do take care of yourself. I shall come to a close for some of the family are up. So good morning my darling Sister

Addie

Whereas in the past Addie wrote only of missing Rebecca, now she tells of missing Mr. Tines as well.

Farmington Oct 6, 1867

My Dear Sister Rebecca:

A week ago today I was in Philadelphia having a delightful time and now where am I now. Here in my lonely room thinking of my two absent friends. I am sorry I did not rec your first letter in Phila. So thoughtful and kindly to send it to me. Mrs. Tines sent on to Joseph. He forwarded it on to Farmington.

I shall tell you how I spend the Sunday in Phila. I accompany Mrs. Micks and Mrs. Scaden to the Episcople church. I return home with them and dine with Mr. Parnell family. Amelia father. Mr. Tines called for me and we attend the Central Church where Rev. Mr. Reaves is the Pastor. He had an excellent sermon. Church was well attended and very good singing. I did not see but one or two that I was acquainted with in my childhood and they had forgotten me. Mr. T had a friend of his to stay to tea. We did not attend church in the eve but made several calls and then took a little walk and then return home and spent the rest of the evening in talking about the future. We have postpone our marriage again. I was thinking it all over. I cannot afford to get anything for winter as I would like to have and the Spring will suit me best. Don't you agree with me my Sister?

His father is going to have another room built on for us. They was talking about it in the presence of me Sunday evening. I am very much pleased with his family and they seems to be likewise with me. Mrs. Tines desired my picture I promised I would send it on I had some taken the same day I arrive home. That was on Tuesday. I shall send you one on and also one to Josie. He ask me for one. I would not promise. I shall surprise him. Further we left Philadelphia Monday 8 A.M. and arrived in NY a few moments after 12 and then he got me a lunch to the house he has a room and then went on to see the Albany boat called the Dew. It is superb. I only wish that you was with us. I then took the City Hartford. I had quite a pleasant time. All the Chamber Maids was very kind to me. Mrs. Seymes gave me a state room. Little Mary Asher came up the same time as usual. The City got a ground at Pratt Ferry so the passengers took a tun boat and arrive at Hartford 15 minutes.

Thusday I came out to Farmington. Mrs. Jefferson was married at 11 AM at the church. She look very nice indeed. A blue silk and white shawl and purple stripe and a white bonnet and veil. Not as many out as I expected to see Mr. R Mitchell and Mr. Douglass stood up with them. They all look very well considering being young folks.

Now I must lay aside my pen a few moments I am writing down in the kitchen—too cold in my room. I tell you a good fire feel comfortable. Miss Porter has 14 young ladies and I believe not all come yet. She is getting her winter provision. Her brother sent on from Washington three barrells of sweet potato we are going to have nearly a bushell for dinner. Two barrels of Cranberries and apples. Mr. Sands made ice cream for tea last evening. Very good. Young ladies had a dance last night. Miss Porter allow them two evening in the week. Now I must tell you a little Farmington news. Going to be two weddings this month. One party's be courting 15 years. I think they ought to know each other well and the other the gent was waiting on the mother and she get all ready to be married and left and court the daughter and now she ready to be married the 16th of this month. What do you think of that. It rather dangerous to place your affection on anyone nowadays.

A white woman married a colored man here sometime ago we received introduction to her at Mrs. Tyler and since I have been gone she has invited Mr. Sands and his wife out to see her. A party to be given at her husband family in Plumville so she extended invitation to Mr. Sands and his Lady. Cook Miss Brown I gave one of those smiles when he told me.

Now I shall return to your letters. One that was write in Bath you will not have any one offer an objection now perhaps not in the future I am sorry you had to cross the bay alone at night too. I see disappointment still follow you. I think you felt the low spiritness sometime before you left home. I hope you will have spirits ever up. [. . .] Rebecca I would inform you how long I should stay in Philadelphia if I had of known it depend on Josie and his family I would have staid until Wednesday if Mrs. Brown had not been sick. They did not have anyone and it was too much for Mr. Tines to do so I thought it best to shorten my visit. I presume you having grand time in Royal Oak today. I should like to be there to the dedication

Now it time for me to part for dinner. Mr. Sands send his love. Mr. T wish to be remember to you and wish you to direct your letters to 101 Lawrence Street New York. Except my love,

From Your Affectionate Sister

Addie

Once again, Addie is having difficulty receiving the wages that are due to her. This time, Mr. Sands is the culprit.

Most important, however, here Addie tells Rebecca of her plans to elope with Mr. Tines. Surprisingly, Sarah Cummings, not Rebecca, is to be her bridesmaid.

Farmington, Oct. 15, 1867

My Dear Sister:

I am writing to you in the kitchen for it is very cold in my room. I am entirely alone. Mr. Sands has gone home for a little visit expecting his wife & cousin to arrive last evening. I hope he wont be disappointed if they did not. I think they would but I will know when he returns. Before I proceed any further I must tell you some meanness. You with the rest of us thought I ought to have been paid extra for my work when Mr. Sands was gone and since I return, Mr. S. was telling me that Miss Porter paid him more than he expected. I thought then that she had paid him for absence impulse of that. I told him he said I guess not. I never thought any more about it until yesterday A.M. Miss Porter brought him down some money. He has been back just two months so she told him there was two mon wages and the last time she paid him up to August the 11 which of course he was paid for the weeks he was not here. So I told him about it and I said I would never stay and work as I did and get nothing for it. He did not like and we had a few words about it. I was speaking to Aunt Emily about it when she was out there and she told Mr. S what I said. I think it mean. I must expect it. I always been treated mean by some. If he stay or nay a week I should speak to Miss P about paying me extra if only stay few other days not say anything about it. I had Mrs. Griswald to help me this A.M. and she has promise to come this P.M. I can do it alone but I will not as I will not even get thanks. Rebecca I have not felt like myself since I have been out here. I am feeling low spirited more or less since I have been here.

Last evening the Young Ladies had a dance. They seems to enjoy it more than they did a week ago. Last night I was looking at them sometime. I rec a letter from Miss Lizzie Smith. She told me she would write but I hardly credit it. Don't you think I write to her while I was in Phila and never got it until I had been home nearly two days and had been open also and she say it was Miss Levinia had done it. Dont you thin that was more meanness? So now she wants me to direct my letter to Mr. James Green, then she will rec them without being open. Miss Lizze dont think she will stay on the boat much longer for it rather too cold. It only heat by steam

[. . .] I rec a letter from Sarah Cumming last Monday night. She wants me to come and make her a visit this winter. No one will see me unless they come where I am. Mr. Brooks is still paying his address to her. He is feeling quite badly. His youngest sister has become a mother—a daughter. Sarah says she feel sorry for him I wonder what ails the girls. Mr. T wants me to have bridesmaid so I shall have Sara Cummings. I have ask her she has promise. We are to be married at 6 PM and leave at 7 whenever take place. Please don't mention to no one.

[. . .] I think the school house has the appropriate name. I should like to see it very much. I was quite surprise to hear that you had such a large collection. You done grandly. Perhaps I may have the pleasure of seeing the <u>Primus Institute</u> some of these days.

[. . .] The young ladies are singing this evening. I have made one piece of garment since I have been out and one of my yokes is nearly done. Dont you think I am getting along nicely? I want to make some skirts while I am here so to have very little sewing to do when I go home.

I am getting sleepy. I have to get up so early now Mr. Sands is gone. Goes very much against me. I can tell you now I must bring my missive to a close.
From you affectionae
Sister Addie

Addie tells Rebecca about her "female lover," an "English" woman who also works at Miss Porter's school. (It is more likely she was Irish.) This letter begins the series in which Addie's discussion of her interaction with her coworkers further reveals the erotic nature of her relationship with Rebecca. It is also evidence of interracial socializing between working class women.

Farmington Oct. 20 1867

My Dear Sister

I am not feeling in the best of spirits today. If my letter is interesting you can account for it I laid down and took a little nap. Has done me very much good.

Last Wednesday evening the grand wedding came off. There was five waiters from Hartford. I knowed two: Harris and Rodney. I did not see them Mr. H sent me word if he had time he would called to see me. Had a band from Hartford. Three of the girls and I went to the house to hear the music. We also saw some of guests. Some look beautiful. We just had a little peep at the bride and groom. He is not as homely looking as the people wants to say. I think I got a little cold standing on the ground.

Your letter was rec Thursday at noon. Also one from Josie on

Tuesday. Rec two from Phila. One Mrs. Brown—Josie sister and the other from James Purell. Mrs. B is quite smart and her mother was very much please with picture she sent on to Newport for the other sister to look and I hope they wont get disappointed with me. Mr. Bantum sent for a picture—Josie friend. He said if I had no objection he would let him one of his. I sent word I had none. Josie has given me his watch. It was quite a pleasant surprise. I had it while I was in Phila. and while in Hartford some one had the impudent to take it out to see what it was. Mr. Sands return at the time He stated Aunt Emily arrive home the same night that Mr. S went home. Mr. De Silva is there too.

Gen [Sherman] will be in Hartford Thursday. [. . .]

I suppose it will be great time that day. [. . .] No I don't find it very lovely. I have three rooms. I visit all of the occupants visit me also. Two of them English—one of them I call her my female lover. She is a fine looking girl, quite tall. She take hold of my hands and look at me and hug me so tight she hurt me. She told me last night when she love anyone she love them with her whole heart. I thought first I would ask her if she loved me. I will some day. I am getting along nicely with my sewing. Sometime in Dec. I want to get some skirts. Will you lend me some money then. I don't want to go to Miss Porter for any [. . .] I shall come to a close. Hoping to have more news nexe week. Mr. Sands send his love. Except my love from you.
Affectionate Sister
Addie

While teasing Rebecca with the possibility of giving her "consent" to allow one of her coworkers to share her bed, Addie reassures her with "I am not very fond of White."

Farmington October 27, 1867

My Dear Adopted Sister

I am in the kitchen entirely alone. Mr. Sands has gone to church. My time would be better spent answering your letter. I rec Friday A.M. I look for it on Thursday. Mr. Brown neglected giving it to me. It was quite interesting. I will answer it before I give you any Farmington news or gossip. I please to hear that your children has not forgotten what the Royal Teacher has learn them It must be a great pleasure to <u>her</u> I presume. You do enjoy the School house very much. If the rest of the teachers were like you maybe comfortably situated like yourself.

You seems to be enjoying yourself very much by all accounts. I am quite surprise to hear the girl so sick last winter in trouble again. I should think her suffering would be enough for her. I think something ought to be done to that Dr. if he think the North is almost as bad as the South. If I was living in Philadelphia and had the ready money I think I should attend the festival. I suppose you would realy like to know what is making low spirited and perhaps you will learn before I finish my letter. Any one would suppose my visit to Phila would leave a very pleasant impression. When I think of that alone it makes me feel quite happy but for all a shade of sadness shed over in spite of all my efforts. Even I enjoy myself more this then I did the last.

The girls are very friendly towards me. I am either in they room or they in mine every night often and sometime just one of them wants to sleep with me. Perhaps I will give my consent some of these nights. I am not very fond of White I can assure you.

Dear Rebecca you would like to know the cause of Thomas and I cease corresponding. Well it with this. I believe I told you that Miss Lizzie had something to tell and also Joseph. After we left you at the cars on our way home I ask him to tell me what that was. He waited until he reach his home and while he was eating his breakfast he inform me what it was and it is this: That I had been writing improper letters to Thomas Sands. I ask him who inform him the news. Miss Louisa Smith said Mrs. Pennington told her so and made him feel very bad about it. Of course I don't blame him. We had quite a long talk about it. I would not if had of been the only one but several knows it and you know I could not let it rest after I return home. I ask Bell Sands about it. She denied it and said Mrs. Curtus told her that. Bell S went up in her room and told her about it and several other things. I went right home. I tell you I talk well this A.M. I was <u>angre</u> and she told me considerable what Henrietta told her even said the Mr. Tines would never marry me. If he marry would be Miss L. If I had of been on speaking terms with H I would of went to ask about Sarah being in the room while we was talking

so what she do but go and told what we said. The day I left Hartford
Henrietta came down and also her husband and we had a great
time. I will tell you about it should we ever meet again but one thing
more I write a very plain letter to Joseph about Miss L. He got to do
one thing or the other. Think he was not to go and see her or even
correspond with her, if so I should give him up. He could one or the
other so he has promise not to have anything to do with her. I will
tell the rest some of these days for I am tired and I dont want him to
know I told you about it.

[. . .] Friday evening Mr. B invite two of the girls and I into the
cottage and treat us some beautiful grapes and popcorn. We enjoyed
it very much so you see I ought to feel happy but sometime I cannot
feel so of course you know why I feel so. It time for me to see about
dinner. Mr. Sands send his love. Except mine from your
Affectionate Sister
Addie
you must excuse pensmenship today Addie

Farmington Nov. 3 1867

My Dear Sister
[. . .] Miss Porter head laundress Mrs. Lewis, her older daughter
was married six week ago. Has a fine son born Friday. Dont you
think she has been smart? Her mother feel very bad about it. It getting a very common thing.

I rec a letter from Joseph last Wednesday. He is not feeling very
well. I suppose he is feel little worried. He was disappointed in the
[. . .] He expect to have and several has come after to go on the
boat. Mr. Bruce ask he said if had not of promise his mother and I
not to go on the boat he would take some of the offers. I believe Miss
L must of ask Mr. Bruce to ask him I think she will do all she can to
have him near her.

I am glad you have written to J.T. He has spoken of you often.
Yes you have told me who made the opening prayer. I thought the
Royal Teacher would do so. Yes I do enjoy myself very much this
time and time passes very rapidly. I have been here nine months
[. . .]
your loving Sister. Mr. Sands sends his love. Except mine yours
with a <u>kiss</u>. Addie

Addie mentions both Frederick Douglass and Edmonia Lewis (1843–), the Oberlin-trained artist who was of African American and Chippewa descent. The date of her death is unknown.

Farmington November 17 1867

My Dear Adopted Sister

[. . .] Tuesday we had quite snow storm—nearly a foot deep. Wednesday night and Thursday AM Miss Porter had a concert in the house for the young ladies. She send to NY for the musician. It was quite a leisure day for me. I had but very little to do. The ladies look beautiful. You think it was a ball.

[. . .] That was very kind of Fred Douglass to remember his brother in the kind act. I wish there was more like Miss Edmonie Lewis.[. . .] Rebecca I would never say anything to Mr. Tines about going on the boat again. He can do just as he pleas whatever is my fate I will try and meet it.

Mr. Sands wish me to give his love to you [. . .] I have finish my chemise and drawers now I am making my night dresses that my sister was kind to give to me. I only to get some cloth for skirts and my limited under clothes will be complete. I must close. Bidding a good morning.
Your affectionate sister
Addie.

It is clear from Addie's next two letters that Rebecca has expressed concern over Addie's flirtations with her fellow workers at Miss Porter's.

Farmington Nov. 17, 1867

My Dear Adopted Sister

[. . .] If you think that is my bosom that captivated the girl that made her want to sleep with me she got sorely disappointed enjoying it for I had my back towards her all night and my night dress was button up so she could not get to my bosom. I shall try to keep you favorite one always for you. Should in my excitement forget you will pardon me I know.

Yes I had opportunity hearing to all the music & wanted too

enjoyed it very much last evening. The young ladies was acting. They took some pieces of well. Miss Porter told the help to go back in the study hall and we saw everything very nicely. What pleasure some people has. Great many of the Ladies going to spend the thanksgiving at home. It is a theme of their conversation. It 38 to remain there as their home is too far to go so short a time. Miss Porter is will give them a grand dinner here commence about is Yesterday. I hope to spend mine a little pleasanter than I did last I was at Mrs. Crowell. [. . .]
Addie

Farmington Dec. 8, 1867
My Dear Adopted Sister:

I have had company nearly all day. It is so very cold that the girls cannot keep warm so they come down in the kitchen. [. . .]

I thought I told you about the girl sleeping with me. Whether I enjoyed it or not I can't say that I enjoyed it very much. I don't care about her sleeping with me again. I don't know what kind of an excitement I refer to but I presume I know at the time. I can't recalled. [. . .]

This letter tells of the establishment of a Union League on the Eastern Shore. This is an important development. The Union League originated during the Civil War as an organization of white patriots who supported the Union. However, in 1867 Republicans began to use the league to help organize black people throughout the South. Eric Foner notes, "By 1867, it seemed, virtually every black voter in the South had enrolled in the Union League or some equivalent local political organization . . . The local leagues' multifaceted activities, however, far transcended electoral politics. They promoted the building of schools and churches to collect funds.[17]

"I really do like fast driving and quick movement, in anybody or anything," writes Rebecca, revealing a different side of this apparently conservative woman.

Royal Oak, Dec. 8, 1867
My dear Parents & Sister
[. . .] In the A. M. I took a ride to Easton with Mr. Thomas'

brother who had to go to the mill for some meal. I went up to see Mrs. Armstrong to carry her some large slates & to get some small ones in exchange, also to take her some books. Her mother is with her. She arrived last Sat. or Friday week. She's a real clever appearing old lady, but Mrs. A. does not favor her in the least. She likes over here very well, they want to remove their things there.

Last night Miss Smith rode up here for her desk—my old one which she ask me for. She had a long cold ride did not seem to mind it at all. She's a well disposed young woman & she is getting along very nicely at B'd. [?] 'twas after eleven when she started upon her return, but the moon shone here & beautiful & twas as bright as day. One of her pupils—a young man, brought her up.

[. . .] I rec'd. your letter from the office yesterday myself. I am very much surprised to hear you had not rec'd. those oysters & I was quite disappointed also for I felt sure that you would get them by Thurs. I really do feel quite discouraged about sending any thing to you or having any thing sent to me. I do think I am a most unfortu- nate creature in respect to some things, most particularly if I set my heart upon them. I shall certainly get thoroughly discouraged one of these days & attempt nothing only tha which I think I can with a certainly perform <u>myself</u>. I really hope however, that the barrel has reached you 'ere this & that you're enjoying them & when the next goes some one will go with them. Those oysters are all they're repre- sented to be & Mr. Tilghman selected some of his choicest. I shall tell him what you say.

I thought Mr. Seyms[18] would remember you as usual & I'm glad to hear you enjoyed it. I presume you remembered Jim so that he had <u>his</u> share. Tell him to send ma a letter all about it. Does he lie upon the little girl's sofa now-a-days? I like those pictures of his they're taken so dark, don't forget to give Aunts Em. & Bashy one, also Miss Babcock with my messages. I have given Miss Smith and Mrs. Thomas one & they're both pleased with it.

My money is not yet forthcoming but I'm not alone for the other teachers are as destitute as myself. Ive written to Mr. Janney about it & he says it shall be sent soon. I'm inclined to think it's purposely withheld & will be till Christmas to prevent any from visiting the city during the holidays.

I only hope you've not wanted your sacque Bell, & that my delay in rec'g. my money had not prevented your getting one. I will make you a <u>fair</u> compensation when I do pay you.

Mr. Thomas has entire confidence in me with his horses. He thinks I do first rate though he says he believes I like to go as fast as I can & want to keep it up—I presume it's something like my walking. But he is correct in this respect for I really do like fast driving and quick movements in anybody or anything. Still, I really have a great deal of feeling for dumb beasts. I'll not misuse them I'll assure you, but his horse does so little eats & grows fat so fast, that when he's geared up her don't want go only just as he has a mind. I see Mr. Thos. is sharp with him & I endeavor to act upon the <u>same</u> principle. His name is Sam & he's a real good horse. Mr. Thos. says if he's treated rightly he'll hurt no one & I agree with him.

I don't know what the people think about the carpet I'm sure but the children have contributed over fifty cts. towards it and now I can tell them all to ask their parents & friends to give something towards it. We, shall get second hand carpeting if we can, we only want 4 yds. the platform is just six ft. sq.

I shall expect to hear about the spoons in your next and please don't disappoint me. I hope to be able to send the money in my next.

Mr. Thos.' hogs weighed 712 lbs. The madam has tried out 12 gals of lard & made quantity of sausage meat, the livers are made into what they call puddings, & are very nice the rest is salted down in its first state of preparation for Bacon.

We have an abundance of fresh pork now & the spareribs are very sweet & nice. Mrs. Thomas has had several of her ducks stolen & she's so provoked about it she has put up the balance to kill. Her other fowls are thriving; how are Rebecca & Bell?

[. . .] I shall be glad to hear about that ball for I've been wondering what new affair it was etc. Probably some have had their feelings very much hurt thereby. I thought twas among the whites at first. Nelson said Henry was expecting to attend it. I hope they all had a good time that went.

I rec'd. a letter from Josephine yesterday. They're thinking about having a festival over there & if they do I shall certainly make an effort to go. She is well. I have permission from Mr. Janney to give her my old blackboard. She wants it. Twas so unpleasant Thanksgiving day she did not go out of the house, but on Sat. A.M. she went to Trappe. I presume she walked.

[. . .] Did I tell you a "Union League" had been formed among us? It was organized last Sat. night at the schoolhouse, and they meet once a week. They have one at Easton, Oxford & Trappe. The one here bids fair to prosper.

[. . .] There has not been so much wind today. We re all enjoying good health this cold weather. I expect Emily will heave us at Christmas. It's thought she's in trouble again & Mr. Thomas told Mrs. Thos. if she was so, she could remain in his family any longer & when she goes she's never to return. She don't want to leave but otherwise does not seem to care. [. . .]

Rebecca.

At a masquerade ball, one of Miss Porter's students dressed as Topsy, the black urchin from Harriet Beecher Stowe's *Uncle Tom's Cabin.* Mr. Sands took great offense and protected his young daughter from witnessing the stereotype.

Farmington Dec. 11, 1867

My Dear Adopted Sister

It is a very cold day but very clear indeed. Mr. Sands is preparing for church. I shall be the only occupant in the Kitchen. Thanksgiving has past. I am glad of it for I work quite hard on that day. Aunt Emily & Mr. DeSilva & Sara came out night before. Mr. & Mrs. Brown dine with us. It was quite pleasant at the table Dine at half past 3. I will give you the bill of fare: Turkey, Chicken pie and Macaroni. Oysters potatoes and wines. Apple, pumpkin, mince, coconut pies, ice creams, oranges, grapes, nuts, candy, raisin, prunes, dates coffee and cake. I left the company at 7 PM and went to my bed I was very tired. I [woke at] half past five AM you can imagine how I felt when night came. Some of the young Ladies went home. About 20 remain and some of them had there friends to visit them which made it fifty, altogether. Friday Evening the young Ladies had a masquerade Ball. They look very well. One of them was Topsy and Mr. Sands was quite angre about. Was not going to let Sarah see them. She was the only one remain until Saturday A.M. the rest went Friday A.M. Mr. DeSilva was going to New Bedford. Saturday. I did not get a chance to talk to him. Both of the female kept close to him while he was here. I am very glad that your Mary came down an hour ago and she is just gone so you see I had to stop writing in the meantime Mr. Sands ask me to fry some oyster while he was at church. I have just got through doing so.

Your interesting letter was rec Saturday noon. I was quite well and please to think you all had such a pleasant time at the Festival. I rec a letter from Gertrude too. Also for Miss Carrie Cummings. I had given up hearing from her. No I did not witness the great shower of meteors nor did I hear anyone speak of them in the house. Snow is all gone has been for some days. I am glad you wrote to Mr. De Silva for the first time that he was out here. He did seems to like it that you had ans his letter. He told me that you did Thanksgiving.

H. Brown was telling me that he read in the Hartford paper about the grand ball. Was as many there. Miss Downing from New Port was there. Mrs. Saunders brother took the Landy and Mr. Walter Mitchell took Miss Houston. I guess they had a stormy night for it rain very hard out here. I guess Thomas Sands aint very much please with his Mother for he has not written to her for sometime. I heard there was more money missing out of the house. I suppose they think it Mrs. B Sands. I hope they will find the thief. It was cold last night. Three of the girls came down in the kitchen to keep me company. One of the girls or rather three of them wants me to learn them to dance. I am afraid they will be disappointed. Mr. Sands sends his love. Says he's sorry there aren't any rich men there. Well he says you are a good girl and wants to see you do well. He say you are the best of the family. I agree with him. Good After Noon from your Sister Addie.

Royal Oak, Dec. 14, 1867
Sat. 9 A.M.

My dear Mother,

I am expecting to take a sleigh ride to Easton this morning, at the same time I am going to get my check cashed—which I have rec'd. this week, and enclose to you <u>twenty dolls</u>. for those spoons. Please pay father the $3.28 I am owing him. This is all I will send until I know whether it's been safely rec'd.

Hope you're all well. I shall write as usual next week. Time will not allow of my writing any more now. With much love to you all I remain y'r. affect. Daughter,

Rebecca.

Please have these initials H.J.C. put upon Henrietta's spoons & N.A.A.P. put on Nelson's.

Farmington Dec. 15 1867

My Dear Adopted Sister

[. . .] I received letter from Mrs. Tines and Daughter, Mrs. Brown. They both very well but not Mr. Tines. He keep about. I think he is rather too old to work. The other Daughter in New Port is poorly. She has a cancer in her right breast. Truly feel sorry for her. Mrs. Tines wish me to write to Joseph to inform him of his Sister situation. Wants him to go and see her. Mrs. Brown babe grows finely. Her husband is still home and expected to leave every day. The Ladies in Phila is preparing for a fair for Christmas. Don't I wish that I was going to be some where this Christmas and New Years in particular.

[. . .] Today I write two teachers in Norfolk for one is Amelia Adam sister Mrs. Miels and the other Miss Gordon. Perhaps nexe Sunday I will ans Miss Cummings letter. I have my night gowns done. I shall wash them this week. I am reading a book called <u>Our Old Home</u>, a series of English sketches quite interesting. I think you would like it. Now I am coming to a brief close. Hoping I will soon rec my letter. Good night, your affectionate Sister Addie.

Chapter Nine

"The people are quite cheered up & hopeful once more."

1868

THE spring of 1868 witnessed some of the most dramatic events of Reconstruction. President Johnson went on trial for "high crimes and misdemeanors," for which he was eventually acquitted. Ulysses S. Grant received the Republican nomination for president. Grant had been a war hero and was favored by the more conservative and moderate members of the party who wanted to weaken the influence of the radical Republicans.

Addie and Rebecca make little mention of the impeachment procedures, though Rebecca continues to document black participation in state conventions, and she and her family anticipate election day.

Addie continues to work at Miss Porter's School, but her letters cease after February. Apparently she left Farmington for Philadelphia following her marriage to Mr. Tines in April 1868. An undated letter that appears to have been written to her from her husband (see Appendix) suggests that she had a happy marriage and that she had children. On the back of an envelope, in Rebecca's handwriting, is written: "Addie died at home, January 11, 1870." She was twenty-eight years old.

Ironically, in 1868 Rebecca's letters start in March, after Addie's end in February of that year. Instead of providing a sense of the correspondence between the two of them, it is as if the surviving friend speaks for them both.

A mature, determined Addie speaks in the following letters. She welcomes the opportunity to leave her job as a live-in servant and to begin a new life as the wife of her longtime suitor, Joseph Tines. Nonetheless, though she views marriage as an escape from life as a domestic servant, she continues to express some ambivalence and fear about the institution.

Addie's letters also provide additional information about the elegance and intellectual stimulation Miss Porter makes available to her students.

Farmington Jan. 6, 1868

My Dear Adopted Sister:

[. . .] This winter only three of the young Ladies. Expect more this evening. We prepared dinner for them. It only 16 weeks more and then I shall take my departure from Farmington.

Mr. Brown gave us a New Years Eve Supper quite a surprise. I was up in one of the girls room about 10 o'clock. He called us down. We enjoyed ourselves very much indeed. Mary went to Watch meeting and staid a little while. Wanted me to go. I rather stay at home. I was quite busy. New Years day I was all alone too. [. . .] Rebecca, sometime ago I ask if you would lend me some money to get some cotton cloth to make some skirts. Will you send me two or three dollars in your nexe and I will send it to you in April? I don't want to take any money up until then.

I rec your letter Thursday at noon. I was little surprise but very much please. I think you had a very nice dinner. Almost went head Miss Porter dinner on Christmas. Well Rebecca I am getting tired of turkeys. I was just reading the bill of fare to Mr. Sands. I am thinking you are having a grand time there. [. . .]

Mr. Tines was telling me what nice time he had in N.Y. on New Years day. Mr. Dunsey from Phila and two other gent in company went out calling at 4 PM Some of them kept it up until morning. Mr. Tines left them at eleven P.M. for he was very tired. He had partly promise to accompany them night after to a Fair at Saint Phillips Church. He would have to disappoint them for he was not going to make any present this year. Whether they succeed in having him to go I presume I will know in my nexe. I am wearing my night dress that you gave me. I tell you they keep me nice and warm. I hate to

get up in the morning I am so comfortable. Mr. Sands joins me in love to you from your affectionate Sister
Addie

Farmington Jan 19 1868

My Dear Adopted Sister

My reason for not sending my weekly missive last week was on account of sickness. I have not felt well for sometime. I was taken with a severe headache and backache and sore throat. Miss Porter sent for the Dr. Sunday night and said I must keep very quiet and gave me some medicine they all was very kind to me. Jane took care of me. One that been here 16 years. Miss P came in three times in the day while I was sick and Miss Ran gave me my medicine. I am not intirely well yet. I am doing my work. Mr. Sand had some one to help him.

The School is together again. It quite lively and several new scholar comes this term. Miss Porter has Prof. Adrian J. Ebell to lecture on Geology for two weeks. He has been here one week. They go in the evenings at the School house. They had tea in the Study Hall last eve and dancing afterwards. I look at them a few moments.

Rebecca do you recollect me telling you a Mr. Bowen here died so suddenly. Well his Daughter and her husband both follow him in less in six week. Only the mother Mrs. Bowen survive. She is sick too and they are very wealthy farmers. Miss Porter and her Mother family attend the funeral yesterday of the daughter Mrs. Lewis.

The Methodist had a Festival Thursday & Friday night. Several of the help went the first night. Had a pleasant time. They cleared over a $100,000 dont you think they done well in this country place.

We are having very cold weather but I dont feel it very much only when I go to my room. It very good singing now. I have had two rides I dont suppose I will have any more this winter. I have told you all that will interest you about Farmington.

[. . .] Do not think Dear Rebecca when I say I have 16 weeks to stay that I am thinking of the change in life. I expect for realy I have very serious thought and make me feel unhappy at times. I often wonder if everyone feels as I do. I realy think I should be little surprise to hear you thought of marrying too. Well you will have a nerve.

One thing more, Miss Porter came to me or rather call me down in one of the music room and ask me pointedly if I was going to be married and when, where I was going to live, everything about it. Her object for asking, she wanted us to live with her like Mr. Edge and his wife is doing. I dont think Mr. Tines would and I am sure I would not. They dont care to have me leave here. I would not stay under no consideration for I am tired already. [. . .]

from your sister

Addie

Farmington Jan. 26, 1868

My Dear Adopted Sister

I feel quite well today. I felt miserable all the week. Mr. Sand favored me considerable and I am in hopes to keep well during my stay out here. I took a little walk with Mary Friday night up to the School house. They think I stay in the house too much but where am I to go. Nothing to see this time a year in the country and very bad walking so I think the best place for me is to remain in the house. What say you? Prof. Ebell is still here I believe is to remain until first of Feb. Miss Porter will have to pay something for his lectures. The young Ladies seems to enjoy it very much. They go up Saturday afternoons and the evenings they dance every evening through the week. [. . .]

Rebecca now please not say what I told you but Miss Porter went in to see if she could get Mr. Joseph Curtis to come out here and take charge of the dining room and she told Mr. Sands that him and his wife both are coming. She seems to be very much please. She said his wife took in her rooms remarkable neat. So you may have the pleasure of seeing Farmington in its beauty for it is lovely in the Spring and Summer. Joseph told me Miss Louisa friend Mrs. Henson expect to be married Feb. 6th to Mr. Hicks family of Phila. I hope Miss L will find some one also. I heard Mr. Bantum Josie particular friend was waiting on her. I ask him about it. He said it was not so. I rec your welcome missive yesterday at noon. I was afraid you would not write to me because you did not rec any from me I was agreeable disappointed. I presume by this time you know the cause.

You seems to have a great many wedding in that country. I hope you will have pleasant weather so not to prevent you attending. I suppose Leila must look quite pretty as she is a sweet looking child. I

am please to think your brother is doing so well I hope he will meet
with greater success. I think the Methodist done very well indeed I
can imagine how Mr. Ross must look. He walk more dignify as them.

Why I did not know that Miss Powers had [a brother] out to
Africa. I guess she dont take after him. Is she still at Mr. Ed Freeman.
Yes, you told me about the Saunders being in Baltimore. I dont know
what to think about that woman visited heaven or hell. I rather
doubted it. It may be so. It will do for a story. Mr. Sands send his love
and except mine from your
Sister
Addie

Farmington Feb. 5 1868

My Dear Adopted Sister
[. . .] Miss Porter has company came Friday eve. Last evening
they had tea in the Study Hall. At half past seven commence to
dance. I looked at them a little while. Mr. Sands received a letter
from his son Friday night. He was quite well but quite likely in
Saratoga. He sent his love to his sister Sarah and never mention his
Mother. Mr. S. feel rather bad about it so he wants me to writ for
him some time this week. A French teacher, Madam Carpenter gave
birth to a daughter Saturday A.M. at 4. She was at school day before
until 5 P.M. Apparently quite smart she very much disappointed for
she expected to be a Son she has three children.

O Mr. Sands rec a letter from Mr. John DeSilva Thursday. He
sent out his love to Addie Brown out there. I suppose they are quite
happy at No 12 Wadsworth Street now. (Well such is life). [. . .] My
invisible company came and made me feel pretty bad I should think
Leila would be miss very much. It rather strange about Miss Dickson
having these spasms I should think she would go to her friends perhaps some one has done something to her and has affected her in
that way.[1] I have no confidence in those people at the south or even
with some at the north. I rec a letter from Mr. Tines this noon the
boat he on caught a fire. Considerable excitement for a while but he
did not tell me all the particulars will in his nexe he says. Some of
the young Ladies commencing to go home to spend a few days this
week. [. . .] Except mine from your
Sister
Addie

239

Royal Oak, Mar. 16, 1868

My dear Parents & Sister,

[. . .] Labor is getting more plentiful now and the people are quite cheered up & hopeful once more. It continues to be very healthy among the col'd., the children have commenced to go about in their barefeet—they're as tough as pigs & I sometimes think they're getting more & more wild daily.

The Southern relief society throughout this county are now raising funds by means of fairs, concerts etc. to send relief to their suffering friends still further South. They held a concert at Easton one night last week, & the avails arising there from went over an hundred doll.

The boats have resumed their regular trips again through the day, but the night line is not expected till the last of the present wk.

I rec'd. a lengthy epistle from Josephine last Tues. She's enjoying her usual health & has recently paid another visit to Trappe. I presume she walked although she said nothing about it. It is eight miles from Oxford.

She says she rec'd. two <u>valentines</u> but from unknown sources. She thought they were out of date. She is always silent about school one would judge from her letters that she had none. I want to go over there as soon as the traveling gets good.

[. . .] Sun eve'g. I rec'd. verbal messages from the Easton teachers all were well. Miss Price sent me a couple of papers—"Harper's Bazaar" in which there is a very interesting but continued story, the previous numbers she baned me the time I was there.

[. . .] Was glad to hear that you were all well at home & that you hens are doing so well. Mrs. Thomas has sixteen & they seem to laying quite sharp now. Also all of our neighbors hens.

[. . .] I've no doubt the Soc'y meeting was quite interesting. Does Mrs. Saunders attend them? I wonder if Miss Elwell has the whole charge of her school? I have so many reports to fill out & prepare always that I've decided to be as brief as possible, though the one I sent to Auburn contained a sheet and a half. I think the Soc'y. does well to continue to support so many teachers.

I hope cotton is not going up again. I was really in hopes 'twas falling for I wanted you to get me a real nice piece of bleached. The unbleached I will keep as I shall want some chemise for next winter. I will send you my next <u>check</u> as soon as I rec. it. We're only paid once in two months now or I should have sent it before. Mr. & Mrs. Thos. borrowed a large portion of my last or I should have sent that. It would make no material difference with me about your getting the money, only I don't know but twould interfere with their arrangements with the Balto. asson.

[. . .] Mr. & Mrs. Thos. are quite well & unite in love to you.

Royal Oak, Apr. 4, 1868

My dear Parents & Sister,

It being a stormy night I am at home otherwise I should have been down in Ferry N'k. at this hour. I have been obliged to postpone writing your weeklie until now on acct. of being from home etc. Mrs. Armstrong is here & expects to return home tomorrow if the weather permits, so I thought I would write to you this eve'g. & thereby improve the opportunity of having her mail it for me.

I presume you would like to know how our exhibition has passed off etc. I have the satisfaction of informing you that it is said to have been the best we've yet had. The children all did remarkably well & enjoyed it greatly. The house was filled & the exercises began at 8 o'ck., closing at about 20 min. to ten. Two of the speakers were detained at home by illness. After the speaking was over I gave a general invitation to the refreshment table while I with the assistance of two or three others, distributed some cakes, candies, & cream among all the children that attend school. I have 42 this month & almost all of them were present. I think about thirty of them spoke. I had excellent luck with the cream & it has been highly commended. I made it Sat A.M. and got a young man to freeze it. We had about two gallons.

Mrs. Armstrong & Miss Smith came to my assistance Sat. P.M. which was very acceptable and much needed. I was very busy all day & felt very tired at night & 'twas late when we closed. We took a little over $40. I had a great deal of cake sent me at night & most of it was very nice. The day & night was very pleasant though the day before was quite stormy & very disagreeable. Sun. A.M. was like a summer day & Mrs. Armstrong, Miss Smith & I went out to spend the day with Mr. Gibson's family. Late P.M. there was a sudden change in the weather, it became very chilly & soon after a storm arose. We came home between 7 & 8 o'ck. in a hard rain storm, in a covered carriage so that we did not get wet or experience any inconvenience from it. We enjoyed our visit very much, but were all much fatigued from the previous day's work & rather dull from loss of sleep.

Miss Smith held her exhibition & festival last night & was obliged to return in the A.M. At her request I accompanied her to Dr. Cr. & lent her my assistance. It also passed off well & very pleasantly, some of her pupils were much embarrassed & could scarcely be heard, but generally the children spoke well & their singing was also very good. Miss Smith had the satisfaction of knowing that her pupils did far better than she'd. expected. She also had refreshments for sale, and took in $28.50 which was first-rate for that small neighborhood. Several white persons were present & seemed to enjoy the occasion as much as the colored people themselves. I remained there overnight & returned this morning. Mr. Thomas, Mrs. Armstrong and several others were expecting to come down in the evening, but was disappointed in so doing & went to Ferry Neck instead, Mrs. Thomas also went down. I reached home about two o'ck. & I'm feeling very tired having been up till three o'ck. before retiring. The people certainly do enjoy these occasional gatherings greatly.

[. . .] Give my love to all of my friends & accept the best to yourselves. From your absent

Rebecca

P.S. I don't believe & neither does Mrs. Thos. the tale about Miss <u>Rebecca</u>.

Royal Oak, Apr. 27, 1868

My dear Parents & Sister,

We have eaten breakfast somewhat earlier than usual this morn'g. so now I have a considerable leisure before preparing for school & I thought I would improve it in writing your weeklie—I style it "The Home Weeklie."

It is a fair & happy morn'g. the air is a little cool but I judge it will be warmer by & by. We're all enjoying health excepting colds, but this is nothing new or strange to me, for I seem to take up fresh ones about every third week. The wheat is coming on finely now all around us. It has been as wet and changeable thus far this spring, that the farmers have not been able to do much more to their fields than manure them & repair fences. I hear them talking about ploughing now so I presume they'll commence today as it's so mild pleasant.

[. . .] Josephine came over to see me Sat. arriving at noon. She walked & came quite unexpectedly, but we were all very glad to see her. She is in the bloom of health & is as brisk & active as ever. I could get her to remain no longer than over night, therefore I drove her down to the Ferry at 8 A.M. & then returned alone, and went out to the church to discharge my duties in S.S. It is about five miles to the Ferry and there are some quite bad places in some parts of the road, which impedes the traveling very much. I rested the horse a few moments & reached home at ten precisely. She has rec'd. the box & will write to you & Miss Fish very soon. She has been very busy like the rest of us, preparing for an exhibition & festival for the holidays, from which she says she realizes something over $30. She went to Balto. to get her things & that was the reason she did not come over to mine. Neither did she inform me about hers. She's as eccentric as ever. Mr. Thos. asked her for her picture sometime ago not thinking he would ever get it when to the surprise of us all she presented him one on a card Sat. & it is taken well too. She had it taken in Balto. She also brought Mrs. Thos. quite a pretty little bag of her own invention, & me a very neat little penwiper. I think she will come North this summer.

Mrs. Thomas' mother returned home Sat. A.M. & the niece went up Tues. The old lady is enjoying her usual health & she's as clever as the day is long. She & I always have quite a jolly time together whenever she is here.

My S.S. is fast increasing in numbers & I hope soon to have the whole quota together again. It numbers 45 now, & yesterday 34 were in attendance. We are to begin having S.S. concerts every month & next Sunday will be our first. Nearly all are learning verses. The object is to see who will learn the most. I'm to keep account & I purpose to reward them in some way. We had a very interesting school yesterday. I have put the most advanced class in the "number one question book" & they ans. the questions quite promptly & are learning to find the references quite readily. It is all a source of much gratification to me.

[. . .] I should have been glad to have seen all of you at our exhibition, you would have been warmly welcomed by the people & children also.

I am glad you're going to let "Miss Rebecca" set for I think she's deserving of it. I think it's going on two years since she's been allowed to do so.

I have rec'd a letter from Henrietta characteristic of her own peculiarities. I am glad she likes so well.

I was pleased to rec. a letter from you Bell, although it contained some unpleasant passages, which I must say only involves me in still deeper mysteries, for I don't know what to make of it. I presume time will tell however. I hope the sociable at Mr. Johns' passed off pleasantly & happily. I am rather surprised to hear of work bet. 2 & 3 P.M. so that he was in & out the rest of the P.M. & the hours did not seem so long.

Mrs. Armstrong's mother has washed & done up my striped skirt for me & sent it down by Mrs. Thos. Sat. You've no idea how well it looks, one would think it a new one for it's not faded in the least in the washing of it. I am really delighted with it.

[. . .] There has been no preaching here this spring by the preacher in charge & his appointed locals. I believe a little class meeting is held generally Sabbath morning after the school & a general prayer meeting at night, but I never attend either & have heard no preaching since last Fall; we want to attend ch. all day in Washington if the weather is favorable & I really hope it may be, for we're all longing to hear some good sermons once more. We want to visit three different churches if possible.

I have read last week's no. of the "Bazaar" I think the hero Brandon is doing the thing up brown. I long to hear the end. Mrs. A. is going to try to get the book she says it is in book form.

I see the "Courant" speaks of the return of Tom Saunders,[2] I presume he's more foreign in air, speech, & dress, than American now. I presume they're all very glad to have him return, & also have abandoned the idea of leaving their native land for the present at least.

How long has Ida Cargil been attending dancing school that she has become so proficient in the art? I see her name is upon the list of fancy dances in Mr. Rielly's soiree. How is Mrs. Cargil's health nowadays.

"The people are quite cheered up & hopeful once more."

I wrote to Henrietta last week. Have you heard from Nelson lately? He's so long answering my last letter I did not know but some of his family were sick. Give my love to them all when you write.

A few of our young men here are endeavoring to organize an instrumental band among themselves. One of them belonging to a band while in the army & remained in it until they were honorably discharged.

There has been another death among the whites here, it occurred last week; the deceased was quite a young man with five or six children. He had the pneumonia & some other disease & is said to have been a very clever young man.

Mr. Foster is in trouble—he came to inform me last Sat. A.M. before Mrs. Thos. had gone to Easton; he rec'd. an anonymous letter from an unknown source last week quite well but meanly written, warning him to leave Ferry Neck within ten days etc. He says he paid no attention to it at first neither said anything about it, but some young man has informed him that a plot has been made to shoot him which has put him on his guard & he has decided to leave, but not until after the 10th day for he thinks there's something in it. He will probably report to Gen. Gregory. It seems the white school children have annoyed him very much ever since last winter, he complained to the teacher twice but to no purpose & he has borne their insults patiently until recently when as they were passing one eve'g. one of the girls came round to the door & burst it open. He anticipating her desire caught her immediately by the shawl & held her firmly he says, for a few moments freeing his mind. I presume this letter is the result, as it is since learned to be the uncle of the girl who has taken the case up & he resides near Easton & is said to be only a mean, low, despicable villain.

Mr. Foster is feeling very badly & hardly knows what steps to take. All sympathize with him & the people dislike to part with him for he is very much liked down here. He does not feel safe to remain.

My head is inclined to ache now.
Remember me to all of my friends & give my love to Jim.
Excuse this ugly blot.

From Rebecca.

The family join in love to you all; I hope you're all well. P.S. In week before last's letter I enclosed a 5 doll. note. I hope you rec'd. it. Forgot to mention it last week.

Royal Oak, Oct. 18, 1868

My dear Parents & Sister,

I have now seated myself to inform you of my safe & pleasant return to this place. I arrived at St. M. on Friday at 11 A.M. & found Mr. Thomas at the wharf waiting for me. We reached home in about an hour afterwards. As I drove into the yard and alighted it seemed as if I'd only been away for a short time, everything looked so natural. He had one of my school boys with him to bring up my luggage in a cart.

Mr. & Mrs. Thomas are enjoying good health at this time & they're delighted to see me again also the rest of the people. They hardly knew what to think of my delay. It is much healthier here now than it has been, though the chills have not yet quite left the neighborhood. Last Sunday Mrs. Thomas was quite sick with one but has had none since. Mr. Thos. is looking quite well, he says he lost 28lbs. during his illness last summer.

I traveled alone from Hartfd. to Baltimore & was glad to do so, for I had the toothache & headache the whole distance & was in no disposition for talking much.

I awoke Thurs. A.M. to find it raining which it continued doing till about 11 o'ck. then it ceased & finally during the P.M. it cleared off.

I visited the Rooms A.M. & accompanied a young man from Vicksburg, Miss. & a stranger too, in the city, out on a shopping tour, & it was three o'ck. when we returned. I then dined & at 4 P.M. went out again & this time alone, making five calls—first on old Mrs. Lee, then on Miss Creek the old maid who was delighted to see me, she said, & had only been talking about me the day before. She enquired for you & Bell & sends much love to you both. Miss Fortune's parents reside in the house with her & it is the same apartment through which we passed the night we all called upon Miss Creek. I had the pleasure of seeing Miss Fortune & she said she'd been talking about me too, & was wondering whether I had returned to my school with-out calling as I'd promised to do. She was in <u>dishabille</u> apologizing for the same on acc't. of being busy. Her hair was in it's natural <u>frizz</u>, otherwise she was unchanged. She inquired very particularly after many of the Hartford people. She spent three delightful weeks in Philadelphia, & desires to return there this winter as some friend has

246

written on for her to do so. I afterwards called upon Miss. Cooper who was also very much pleased to see me & I spent sometime with her. Miss Williams rec'd. my last call & paid me <u>five dolls</u>. 'Twas just about tea time 7½ o'ck. when I returned to the hotel—(I could not be accommodated at Mrs. Forresters, her house being full,) & finding Mr. Ballard one of our former corps of teachers there, I accepted an invitation from him, in co. with a Miss Haskins from Pittsfield, Mass, to attend a concert at the col'd. Catholic church that eve'g., & went but it proved to be a very poor affair indeed. The large audience present exhibited much dissatisfaction. I've left at the close of the first part of the program. This Miss Haskins is an agent for Mrs. H.B. Stowe's last new book, "The Men of our Times" & I purchased a copy from her, & propose reading it aloud to Mr. & Mrs. Thomas & others this fall & winter.

I also succeeded in finding the question books I wanted, in a store on Balto. St. and at the same price they are sold in Hartfd.

I got some gum drops, and a lb. of mixed candy for Mrs. Thomas. They are both truly delighted with & grateful for their presents, & send you many thanks for them. Mr. Thos. wishes me to tell you that we rode 28 miles last night after sundown, & he wore his gloves. 'Twas a cold drive the wind was very high all day & did not fall till late in the eve'g. but I want to get inused to these things, so I did not mind it much. I wore my coat, & also my waterproof over it enroute home. We went down to see Miss Smith, she came over last Sat. week and came up here being much disappointed to find that I had not returned. So I thought I'd. go down & surprise her. She has had a more comfortable boarding place provided for her by the trustees & I think she will remain with them, though the people at Miles River are still very anxious to obtain her services. Still they're not yet ready to open their school for they've been disappointed in rec'g. some of their lumber. Mr. Cole has allowed her to take her choice.

Mrs. Armstrong has been on for her things & gone. Miss Briggs has not been heard from. Miss Snowden has charge of the Easton School. I shall open tomorrow & Miss Smith does the same.

Now I will close & what I've forgotten to state in this letter I will remember in my next. Direct to the <u>Oak</u> now as we have a daily mail. Give my love to little <u>Doll</u> & say to her—her Auntie would like to see her little old fat self every day, & tell her not to forget me. Give my love to Leila also & Jim accept the best & same to yourselves. From

Rebecca.

Remember me to all the friends & well wishers. My tooth has ceased to ache since Friday night & I am also feeling very well otherwise. Mr. & Mrs. Thos. join me in love to you all.
Rebecca

Doll, the little girl who is now living with the Primus family, makes her first appearance in the preceding letter. In the following, Rebecca mentions Frances Ellen Watkins Harper, the nineteenth century's most well known black woman poet, novelist, essayist, and activist. Like Rebecca, Harper also taught the freedmen in the South during Reconstruction.

Royal Oak, Nov. 1, 1868

My dear Parents & Sister,

[. . .] I have just written a letter to Henrietta in reply to one rec'd. from her last Friday. She says she's been frightened almost to death of late by what was supposed to have been a ghost story, which fact I presume you're all well aquatinted with now through Joseph. She said he was coming in Wednesday & told what she was going to send you. I imagine you're enjoying the turkey today. I've not yet tasted the cake I brought with me, but I've given Miss Smith some of it & she has given me a jar of preserves pear which are just as clear & white as they can be & a tumbler of plums. She put them up expressly for me she says.

[. . .] A little babe was born dead in our neighborhood last week, & the mother now lies quite sick. Her husband is one of our trustees. The girl that was taking a bottle of that chill medicine, has not the chills since, & she has taken all the contents of one bot.

I think it is quite healthy here now, & the past week has been a most delightful one. The saw mill has been rebuilt & was in working order when I returned. The boiler is a non-explosive affair and came from Phila. Mr. Thos. is engineer & the owner will not have the engine run unless Mr. Thos. is there himself. He offered him more wages to induce him to take charge. The old hands are all at work there again excepting one. The mill is erected in another place & very near the water this time. they are having all the work they can do.

Mr. Thomas has heard from Mrs. Armstrong since my return. She is teaching at Trenton, N. J. now. No one has been appointed over the Easton school yet.

Politics are very dull here there are no demonstrations, meetings or anything else thought the Rep. had a gathering with addresses etc. yesterday P.M. at which some of the rowdies endeavored to make a disturbance but the speaker silenced them we are told. I suppose there was a grand rally as well as a grand display in Hartford last Wednesday night.

I thought Mrs. Watkins Harper was to deliver her poem the week I left home. I am glad you heard her & liked the poem. They were so long dallying about the Installation while I was home that I treat it as a matter of indifference now, & had become to feel thus about it long before I left.

[. . .] I am glad Nelson reached home without any harm to himself, but they must have had a rather tedious time of it. I wrote him last week.

My trunks came safely but one jar got broken. However, its contents did not all get wasted only a part of the liquor run out. I did not know I had any <u>sculcap</u> with me. I will look for it some day. That lady was not a teacher. I gave $3.50 for the book.

Sam is all right & glad to see me again. Give my love to little <u>Doll</u> & tell her not to forget me for I think of her often. Does she creep much or any more than she did? Give my love to her & Leila. Tell Jim to be a good boy & to grow fat & good together. Mr. & Mrs. Thos. send love. The enclosed please return. 'Twas given Mrs. Thos. & she sends for your inspection Bell as the style of the Southern <u>G. Bend.</u> We think the Saratoga Belle rather the best. I am glad Nelson put that picture of Mrs. F's. on exhibition. She may conclude to take it. Has Mrs. Cargill paid for Kittie's?

I sent to Easton last Sat. week but there was no letter & I did not get it till Friday. The other I rec'd. on Thurs. as usual.

Remember me to all the friends and accept my best love to yourselves. From Rebecca.

P.S. Company has just come in. Please give Sarah Usher her book there upon the table the next time she comes down. I know not how this blot got on here or when.

In the next letter, note Rebecca's rather condescending description of the worship practices of the Royal Oak Congregation. She sarcastically suggests that "shouting" is of no spiritual value at all.

Royal Oak, Nov. 8, 1868

My dear Parents & Sister,

Mrs. Thomas & I being left entirely to ourselves this afternoon I thought I'd improve the opportunity and begin my "home weeklie."

It a very mild & delightful day, a little hazy this A.M. but now the sky is clear & warm, with a southerly wind. The meeting is going on here today, & this A.M. I attended & had the gratification of listening to the new preacher, but soon became tired of him. His text was, "Let your light so shine before the world, etc." After reading or I should say repeating it over once or twice, for the Bible was closed, he went directly into Genesis where he remained sometime, then he proceeded to John the Revelator repeating & dwelling upon several passages in the Revelations. From thence to Job, repeating the text again, went back to the Gen. & ended with the Gospels. 'Twas a great sermon,—he got the people to <u>patting</u> & if he'd continued much longer would have them all shouting I presume. Mr. Thomas has gone out this P.M.

Mrs. Thomas wants me to ride out with her after tea, so we're going out to make a call on the sick.

Last Thursday night Mr. Thomas carried me to Easton to attend a concert given at the schoolhouse by Miss Greenfield and three of her pupils. It was a fine affair but was not well attended on acc't. of there not been given a sufficient previous notice. I spoke with Miss Greenfield, she inquired after you all. The young lady's sister with whom you correspond Bell sang finely. She asked how you were and said her sister was very low with the consumption, & that she was not expected to recover. Miss G. said she missed her very much for she was their pianist. Her sister & Miss G. presided that night. Dr. Hudson was with them doing escort duty. They have been in Balto. nearly three weeks giving concerts & were to give another at the

Catholic Ch. upon their return. From thence they were going to Linchburgh, VA. I think Miss G's. voice has failed very much. She was attired in a rich black silk. I did not ascertain any of the young ladies names. They all seemed to be very much careworn & weary. They also sang at Cambridge last week on Tues. night.

We have learned of Grant's election & all the col'd. people's hearts about here have been made glad thereby. While on the other hand the Rebs. are quite down in the mouth. The day of the election her was as quite as any other day.

Although the result of the election was anticipated, still it a source of much real gratification to all parties concerned.

[. . .] My number of pupils has during the past week, been increased to nineteen.

Tell Dolly Dutton I have dreamt about her twice of late, & the first time I thought I came home suddenly, & found her occupying my placc at the table seated in the big chair, and as happy as a lark. In the second, I thought I had her in my arms vainly attempting to escape observation as usual. I thought Eliza Dickson was coming and was right in the room upon us ere we were aware of it, & a considerable confusion was the result. I can imagine just how little Doll. looks. I presume she'll forget all about me. I would like to see how she gets along creeping. I think of her often.

7 P.M. I rec'd. your letter on Wed. 7 P.M. & I was pleased to hear that you were all well. I am wearing the same camphorbag that I used last term. I did not forget to replace around my neck the day I left home. I did not see the papers you allude to, I only saw a small bundle with the books and those I took.

I am glad to hear that Ellen's health's is improving & that she has been enabled to return to Hartford. Give my love to her should you call upon her.

[. . .] Sylvia is all right now. I rather thought she push matters in her favor by her being so determined in persisting for her claims. I glory in her spunk for under the circumstances, I would have done the same.

I hear Josephine went up to Balto. last Wed. night and returned Friday. I suppose she went on business. She did make out to tell me that she had 15 pupils attending school, the neighborhood is very small in which she resides & does not afford as many children as this of ours. I did not tell her Doll destroyed her gift. I think Leila did it.

She wishes me to return you many thanks for what you sent her. I presume I shall never know what pay she gets.

[. . .] I am glad Dolly's so kind to Jim & I presume he too, feels very grateful to her.

I thought that torch light precession would be a very imposing affair.

I suppose Mr. Sands thinks someone will want his rooms now, when they'll be obliged to leave them so soon again. 'Twill serve them right if no one takes them.

That Mrs. Henderson must be a hard case & she look like it.

I've been told this eve'g. that the gent I listened to this A.M. was not the minister, but a local from Easton, appointed to preside in his place. So I live in hopes of hearing better. The speaker being a stranger to me, I took him to be the preacher in charge.

Mrs. Thomas & I took our little drive this eve'g. & returned a few minutes after six. Found Mrs. Williams quite convalescent.

Mrs. Thomas has just now retired & Mr. Thos. has gone out to church. Both desire me to give their best respects to you all. He has on one of his nero shirts, & says it fit him every way & it's just right. I finished both the next week after I came & have since made two night gowns for the madam. She got the cloth at Easton. It's past 8 o'clock. Good night. Remember me to the friends & accept much love to yourselves. Excuse poor writing for I been subjected to one of my nervous series for a few days past & am not quite composed again yet.

Rebecca

P.S. Send the <u>papers</u> to <u>Easton</u>.

Royal Oak, Nov. 22, 1868

My dear Parents & Sister,

Being alone this P.M. I am improving my time with the pen. Mrs. Thomas is visiting Mrs. Tilghman & Mr. Thos. has taken a ride to Quaker Neck to call upon some gent of color there, I declined accompanying him today, though had it been pleasant, I should have probably been spending the day in Broad Creek Neck. As is, I am at home & very glad to be here.

We have been having some real unpleasant and stormy weather for about three days. It has rained, hailed, snowed and blowed. Today the wind is high & very black & threatening looking clouds o'erhang the sky, & every now & then weather of some kind is falling, but has not am't. to anything more than squalls as yet.

I went out to preaching here this A.M. There were but seven persons there besides myself. I suppose the stormy appearance of the sky kept the people from coming out. The minister was here today & I think he's quite a sensible man to all appearance. And he is a tolerably good preacher for the limited means he's had for procuring what knowledge he possesses. His complexion is coal black, but his features are good, & he seems intelligent. He speaks far better than the one that pretended to preach last Sun. week, & he is quite an old time looking little personage, but not bereft of the common civilities of life. I think I must have been prepossed in his favor by his particularly asking me to visit his family when he removes it to St. Michaels, which he expects to do this week.

I have today rec. a letter from Carrie, She is now in charge of a school at a place called Port Republic, Calvert Co. Md. The Quakers have sent her out this time, & she's made the auspices of the Bureau. Her surroundings she says, are just the opposite to what they were last year. Many of the houses are mere hovels with neither windows or floors, unless she says, one can call a few pieces of board spread over the grown floors. The people are very illiterate & every thing by her statement, is below <u>par</u>. She has a schoolhouse in which to teach, but not to compare with those recently built by the Govt. She sends her love to you all, inquires very particularly after Leila, & says she'll be glad to hear from you whenever you see fit to write. Her sister has a school in the same County about 14 or 20 miles from her.

[. . .] Carrie met Miss Greenfield in Balto. & does not like her at all. Also respecting Miss Fortune, she says she only accidentally visited her house the day previous to Miss F's. starting on her visit to H. & told her she would meet me & Gertrude there. She's met with her several times but does not care much for her she says, nor does she consider her friend.

[. . .] Your very kind epistle was rec'd. Thurs. giving its usual pleasure & containing much of interest. I am glad to hear good health is still your portion, & that little Doll is enjoying her little life, & is willing to share with Jim her food when there's more than her own little stomach can hold. I would liked to have been the two eating from the same plate. I presume she was upon the floor at the time & crept to his plate. I can imagine just how very cunning she looked. I dreamt a few nights since that I was buying a little toy of some kind for her, & that it was a long time 'ere I could get suited. Tell the little creature she is in her Aunt's mind very much of the time. I wonder if she'd know me now.

[. . .] I'm not suffering from nervousness now, so that the hoptea & sculcap are not needed. I always bundle up well when I'm riding, but I do not intend to take many rides this cold weather. I regret to hear of so much sickness among you. I hope Mrs. Connover may recover & that Ellen might also. 'Tis too bad her husband is so indifferent to her welfare etc. I presume the poor creature feels miserably. I don't think Mrs. G. ever did care for him.

[. . .] If that <u>coat</u> you speak of is of the same quality of cloth as Bell's, & there's no <u>defects</u> in it any way, I will take it, & pay for it as soon as I rec. my money.

I wish you'd call on Miss Woodbidge & ask her if ther's been any money forwarded to the asson. for me. I told Mr. Core it would be sent directly to me, or that you'd rec. it for me & forward it ect. Please tell her this for I supposed 'twas so understood as my wish & also the desire of the Society. I shall forward my report & salary bill to her at the close of this month. They pd. me one month's advance salary & did not expect further pay till Miss W. heard from me & rec'd. my monthly report. Please do not fail to inquire for me 'ere you write again, so that I can write to Mr. Core about it.

Mr. Thos. <u>wears</u> night gowns but never's had any of the sack shape.

Now I will bring my lengthy epistle to a close. I've been writing steadily for two hours.

Mr. & Mrs. Thos. desire to be remembered they expect to kill their hogs Thanksgiving day. Remember me to all the friends & accept my love to yourselves.

Rebecca

Royal Oak, Nov. 29, 1868

My dear Parents & Sister,

This quiet Sabbath P.M. I seat myself with pen in hand to write my "Home Weeklie".

We are all well & enjoying good health & cheerful spirits. The day is a clear, sunshine one & not very cold although 'tis quite blustering. We've had no calls as yet today & have enjoyed the quiet to ourselves. But there'll be some one in 'ere the day's gone.

The past week has been a very pleasant one, we had rain on Wed. night & a part of Thurs. A.M., but the rest of the day was very pleasant only windy. We seem to have a great deal of wind lately which helps to dry up the mud & water so that the roads are kept in very good order all the time & also quite free from dust.

After it had cleared off I took one of my boys & Mr. Thos. <u>Sam</u>, and went down to Broad Cr. to spend the Thanksgiving with Miss Smith, intending to return the next day, but she kept me till yesterday & I reached home to noon. Mr. & Mrs. Thomas were wondering at my stay but as the horse had not been wanted they were quite well satisfied.

I had a very pleasant visit. Miss Smith is quite comfortable at her new quarters, but she is surrounded with a house full of children— all quite small, yet they do not disturb her or any of her things so that she feels quite well satisfied. She had school on Friday so that I spent the day in her school room. She has 19 pupils & is making preparations for an exhibition for the holidays.

[. . .] We've had considerable beef to eat lately. A butcher from Easton & formerly from Delaware, brings meat around every Tues. & Sat. supplying the people throughout the Oak & then at St. M. It is a great convenience & a treat too. He comes in a covered market wagon, stops before the house & rings a bell which certainly does sound strange in these parts. He brings along some very good meat & is very reasonable in his prices. Mr. Thomas is very fond of beef & therefore patronizes him about every Saturday. He says he's not going to eat so much hog meat hereafter so I live in <u>hopes</u>.

Some twenty hogs were slain among colored people just around us last week. And from this time until Christmas there'll be hardly anything else done in these parts but kill hogs. Women are employed to clean the entrails, prepare the sausage meat etc. so that some make it as much of a business to go out to <u>hog-killing</u> as the men do.

Farmers are also engaged in sending off their poultry, corn, grain, etc. to the Balto. markets. With their returns all the hands are paid off at Christmas, and enter upon their new engagements for the ensuing year at New Years.

Some changes are also being made. Families who intend to move are improving the good weather & good traveling by removing their stock & household goods to their new abodes now wherever they can do so, both among black & white. Christmas is the general moving time here all engagements contracts etc. are made at New Years & close with Christmas. This is a time honored custom throughout the South & the holidays are regarded by all and made the most of.

[. . .] I neglected to mention in my last, the consecration last Sun. of the white Methodist church here, which has been removed & repaired the present year. They has an "all day" meeting & raised a collection of $800.65 during the day, which clears the church from a debt of $500 upon it. It is said to be a very large collection for a little country place like this. There were many strangers present, & both the church & all around it was packed with people & carriages. They have now commenced a protracted meeting.

[. . .] Is little Doll up now every night as she used to be? Tell Bell I don't want anyone in my school that can not call the letters by their right names, at least, better than that. The little witch, I suppose she thinks herself somebody & very smart at that saying her letters & prayers. I would like to see her very much. I dream about her every week, and I often wonder whether she would recognize me now.

Yes indeed, I do enjoy my little sanctuary very much.

[. . .] These people will never change Josephine one iota. Leila is well fixed for winter. Has she the rings in her ears yet? If that clove cake of Bell's went so far it might have kept on to Royal Oak and then it would have found a door I'm sure. I have that which I brought from home yet & it's relished now and then very much. Mr. Thomas ate his long since bestowing much praise upon & expressing many wishes for the doner. Mr. & Mrs. Thos. are very generous always to me, & had me take my share of the nut cakes apart for my own special eating which I did.

[. . .] I have now penned all that's upon my mind & will therefore close with love to you all and to my friends, in which the family join me.

Rebecca

Chapter Ten

"And all nature is coming forth and clothing herself in beauty and fragrance."

1869

IN 1869 the Hartford Freedmen's Aid Society ceased operation and Rebecca was paid a final ninety dollars for her last three months of service. Ironically, Rebecca's letters from this year suggest that she had become a part of the Royal Oak community and the residents a part of her. She refers to Mr. and Mrs. Thomas as her family and, most important, she refers to her students as "my children." Clearly the residents of Royal Oak thought quite highly of her, for you will note that Rebecca writes not only from Royal Oak or Hopkins Neck but also for the first time from the Primus Institute, as the school was finally called in honor of her.

Nonetheless, although Rebecca finally seems a part of the community she devotes a great deal of her letters to Doll and Leila. Her longing for the two little girls illustrates her anticipation of returning home.

> Hopkins Neck, Talbot Co., Md
> Jan. 16, 1869
> Sat. 10 A.M.

My dear Parents & Sister,

This sheet is an evidence of the box's arrival which I know you'll be pleased to hear. I thought this delightful spring like morning I would take up my pen & tell you about it. It came safely by the boat

Tues. night, & I rec'd. it early the following morn'g. A few of the apples had begun to decay & the pies were somewhat mouldy upon the outside, but I put them in the stove & heat them through, & Mr. Thos. desires me to tell you he enjoyed his hugely. I also gave him his loaf with which he's also delighted, eating a portion every night to much evident satisfaction. I divided a portion of my eatables with the family & the occasion was an enjoyable one to us all. I am delighted with all my gifts, and I thank you over & again. My first thought was a wish to have made you all recipients of some gift from me, for your kind remembrance of the absent one. The two diaries puzzled me, but I've commenced Doll's, yet I expect I shall continue to use both, for 'twas very kind & good in Amorett to send me such a nice one. A less expensive one would have done as well.[1] I thank you many times Bell for the book, 'twas the very one I strove to procure last summer. Little Doll's alphabet is peculiar to her own dear little self, and what a queer little genius she must be. I shall be so glad to see her again & to listen to her little prattle. To see that little tongue roll over & to hear her <u>French</u>—for such it must be, seeing it is incomprehensible to you all, I think it will be real fun. I shall enclose a little note I wrote to her yesterday, & you must read it to her so that she may endeavor to understand it, & know that it came from her Auntie to whom she sent the diary.

[. . .] I am much pleased with the soles & have put them in my rubbers, for I'm obliged to wear them everyday now on acct. of the mud. The figs & gum drops I reserved exclusively to myself, & I shall hold on to the apples so long as they will last.

Shall you require the pan again? If not, I thought I'd give it to Mrs. Thomas. She's delighted with her tea & is much pleased with your piece of soap for which she thanks you much. Ned the boy that lives with us now, never tasted a piece of mince pie before & Mrs. Thos. told me he was in extasies over it—for I gave him a piece of mine, as Mr. Thos. ate all of him himself.

[. . .] Three or four couples among the gentry have been united in marriage in this community within the past two weeks, & another in contemplation among the col'd. people in our neighborhood.

Teachers arrived from Balto. this week for St. Michaels & Ferry Neck. The latter being a gentleman visited me at my school as he was en-route to his destination. He is so very fair & has such light hair I took him for a white man, yet I suspect he's what may be called a bright mullatto.

[. . .] We had for dinner, bacon, turkey, roast beef, boiled chicken, cabbage, sweet & Irish potatoes, turnips, bread & suet pudding; for dessert apple pie, sweet potatoe pudding or pie, with tomotoe and pear preserved. Just previous to our departure another table was spread with cake, small cakes, raisins & sweet cordial. We reached home soon after five o'clock. These people are determined to have a good time whenever they invite their f'ds.

Your very kind letter reached me yesterday P.M. & its interesting contents were very cheering. My toe is better since I've under taken to doctor it, but its bad enough now at times. It is not my big toe, but a new corn that has recently appeared upon the top of the second toe, & sometimes it carries me high as a kite, figuratively speaking. I think the people collected a nice sum of money for Mr. Dyson, & I'm glad too, to hear they think favorably of aiding Miss Smith, for she is deserving of their sympathy. I don't know how I should feel were I to be placed in her present condition, depending too, wholly upon myself for support as she is. And I hope although she's a stranger to all, each one will or may consider the cause in which she's laboring & then decide. Our people too, did well by Mr. John's, I presume they do not or <u>did</u> not understand about refreshments being participated in by the company. The people are doing well by him & his family, & I hope he'll manifest <u>his</u> appreciation of their regard for him, differently from what his predecessors have done. I think the weather with you last Sunday was just like that we had here.

We've eaten the opossum. It was nice but so very very fat. I only ate two of its little legs.

[. . .] I'm glad to hear the two little girls are again in possession of good health. How many teeth has Doll now, tell her I shall expect her to reserve some of thos big <u>smacks</u> for her Auntie Becca whose name she's learned to call. I don't think she ought to leave home for fear of taking cold & getting sick. I think today 'twill be better too for Leila for it did not benefit her any when she went on to Boston last winter. Tell Leila I don't believe Jim plagues her one bit, & that it's her who plagues him & I shall Doll to tell me all about it when I come. I understand now who all were that we're taken into church. Is Miss Linason still at Madame Tyler's establishment?

The new teacher at Ferry Neck was a guest at Mr. Turners today. He's a Virginian & is from Alexandria. His father preaches at one of the Zion churches in Balto. He is rather of a roving sort of a fellow I think, & will make a short stay in these parts. Now I've written all I can think of I'll close. Mr. & Mrs. Thos. send love to you all. Remember me to my friends & accept much love to yourselves.

From Rebecca.

Note the tone of the next letter. Rebecca speaks of herself as part of the "we" of the Thomas family. In fact, one might read this as a letter from the Royal Oak household to the Hartford branch of the family.

Royal Oak, April 11, 1869
Sun 3 P.M.

My dear Parents & Sister,

[. . .] I have held school same number of pupils for a wonder, with neither increase or decrease. Vesta Tilghman is getting better again. The tumor is now coming out on her neck & it looks badly enough but since it's been out she felt better. I presume 'tis the medicine she's taking that's sent it out. Her mother's had the tooth & face ache very badly all the week from a cold I presume.

The other children who have been ailing in our neighborhood are recovering. A white woman here has a cancer in her breast just as Mrs. Freeman had I should judge, & she's suffering very much from it. She's had it a long time & has tried many remedies for it but without success. She lies very low with it now.

Then there's a case of the "black measles" at the Oak. I'm told a young white man has them. It is this woman's son. A colored woman down ther is also very ill & under the Dr. It seems to be quite sickly all around us now.

We're as a family about the same as usual though we've our little ups & downs with the rest. Yet we're all able to keep at work and to eat our daily allowance.

We're glad to hear of the continued good health of you all, & trust it may ever remain the same. We thought you must have had snow last Sun. & were not surprised to hear that you were favored with a squall. 'Twas quite cold too with us & the wind was very

searching. There's no wind today. I rec'd. your welcome epistle Friday noon, & enjoyed a perusal of it soon after eating my dinner. In
regards to your being asleep Ma when writing, I do not think it's
constantly, but only now and then a <u>polite nod</u> or I may say a <u>gentle
inclination</u> of the head, & sometimes a more impulsive <u>jerk</u> I presume, many pages are written, & this accounts for the unfinished
sentences etc. that occasionally occur in your letters. I do not complain, but I'm let to smile & conjecture oftentimes, for I well know
how matters were at the time of writing. [. . .]

Old man Moore is quite feeble & it is thought will be sent to the
Poor House. He keeps about but is failing fast. The papers you spoke
of sending have not reached me yet. I presume they're along the
route somewhere. Mr. & Mrs. Thomas unite in sending love to you
all. Remember me to the friends and accept best love to yourselves.

From your absent Rebecca

Primus Institute, April 12, 1869
Mon. noon

My dear Sister [Bell],

I have just returned from dinner & favored with a ride, having
still a few moments to spare I take up my pen to write you a few
lines. Tis a lovely day though rather wet just the reverse of what
yesterday was. I have quite a full school today & the children are
now enjoying themselves upon the road in front of the schoolhouse.

The little package came safely to hand on last Wed. A.M. I was
pleased to rec. your letter & also very much pleased with the little
cloak & sacque. I like it far better than if it had been plain goods. I
think it really handsome. I have sent it to the little one for whom
'twas made, & it had given great pleasure & delight. Even the little
child is delighted with it & seems aware that it's for herself. The little
one is not as you thought a boy, but another cunning, bright & active
little girl just like little Dollie Dutton. And I am glad to hear that she
had the pleasure of Christening it. I wish you'd get her one for me,
as she felt so about taking off that I want her to have one of <u>her
own</u>, so you'll oblige me very much to get some more of the same
material & to make one for her. Tell her Auntie says she must have
one, get it for her to travel in. I am in every way satisfied with the
cloak & I am greatly obliged to you for making it etc. But I did not
intend you should make it gratis. I wanted you to take your pay for

trouble etc. I thank heartily for your kind offer to do anything for me. I do not doubt that in the least, for you've always done this & I do not hesitate to acknowledge it.

5 P.M. Home—I don't know what to think of Doll & all her little antics. She must be a real cunning little rogue. I should think sh'd need watching all the time. I was wanting to know whether she ever visited her absent Auntie's room—but what's the attraction there? I presume she has a dim recollection of what enjoyment herself & Auntie frequently took together there, & she probably tries to make you all know what it was & you fail to understand her, or to comprehend her meaning. She'd probably like you to feel that 'twas left in her <u>care</u>.

Jim must have had a real jubilee over that mouse. Tell him his mistress don't want him to get her counterpane so dirty still as he's lain on it so long I shall not object to his doing so now till I come. Ma neglected to tell me the message about the turkies. I regret to know he should have felt so very badly about them, but trust he shared a portion of one of not of those hanging in the cellar at that time.

I think you'll have favorable weather this month to enable you to make your long contemplated visit. I hope 'twill agree with Dolls health so as to fatten her up. I shall be delighted to get her picture for I long to see just how she looks. Leila's a hard case I suspect. Tell her I shall be compelled to give he Jesse unless she really does stop annoying Jim. I suppose she, Doll & Jim have a happy time together. The latter being the persecuted & most peaceable of the three. I thank you once again for getting & making the cloak & little sacque. All I now desire is to have little Doll to have one & this is the only favor I will ask of you for the present. Tell her the accepted kiss was splendid though Auntie failed to find it & in return sends a dozen. Tell her she must be a good girl till Auntie comes. Give love to both the little ones and accept the same to yourself. Mr. & Mrs. Thos. join me. The day has been fine. Yr. affect'te. Si.

Rebecca.

Hopkins Neck, Royal Oak, Monday Apr. 19, 1869
My dear Parents & Sister,

I've just finished my supper & have been from the schoolhouse only a half hour being partly detained by several of pupils who had

"And all nature is coming forth and clothing herself in beauty and fragrance."

unlearned lessons to commit to memory. It has been rather cloudy
and very windy today, still the air's been soft & warm & altogether
the day's been a pleasant one. For the first time today I had no fire at
school on acc't. of its being so warm. We sat without a fire here at
home yesterday for it was a real summer like day, it being warm and
delightful with not a cloud in the sky till night, [. . .] I rec'd. a letter
from Carrie with yours on Saturday. She's well, enjoying herself and
flying around as usual. She sends love to you all, & thanks you Ma
for your kind & good wishes in her behalf & says she needs all the
encouragement from friends that she can get. She had a festival
there just after the holidays but didn't do near so well as she
expected. She has 28 pupils. Miss Hoy has a large school averaging
60 pupils, her sister about 50 & Mr. Butler's son has had 91 this winter & now has 60. She's been told that she's in the darkest part of the
county, the measles & whooping have been among her pupils & her
school's been very much reduced thereby.

Prof. Day seems to be upon a preaching tour again, he having
preached twice recently in the town of Lewisburgh where her married sister lives, then again a Harrisburgh, Pa. I presume he's trying
to produce a sensation again now. Carrie & he are not such good
friends now as they have been for some reason known only to themselves. Her former suitor Richard Mason has charge of a school
under the Asson. She thinks him capable of filling the station but he
lacks <u>energy</u> & <u>inclination</u>. Miss Addie Green has declined teaching
any longer under the Asson. & I think he is placed over her school.
Carrie has no dealings with the Asson. This term she informs me.
She is under the Quakers of Penn. Also her sister is employed by the
same. Very unexpectedly yesterday P.M. we rec'd. a call from Miss
Snowden & her assist. They were going to pay a visit to Miss Laws at
St. M. & so called in. I was pleased to see them & the half hour they
spent with us was a very sociable & agreeable one. They came in a
covered carriage & in style. Miss Snowden is becoming more natu-
ralized & comes upon a level with the rest of her co-laborers, pro-
fessing much friendship for me. They're coming to spend a Sabbath
with us 'ere the term expires. Mrs. Thomas invited them.

[. . .] The earth's being prepared for corn now. Forward potatoes have already been planted. The wheat is coming on finely &
looks like a beautiful green carpet. The trees have begun to blossom,
& some of them such as peaches & cherries, are in full bloom. And

all nature is coming forth and clothing herself in beauty and fragrance. The little birds fill the air all around us every pleasant morn'g. with their sweetest and happiest songs. One can't but feel cheerful when all around is teeming with life and good cheer. I enjoy it all.

Mrs. Thos. has set one of her turkies upon twenty three eggs, & she's put the balance of their eggs under a hen. Both have stopped laying now. Her two muscovia ducks have commenced laying the past week. Most of the hens have about stopped laying & several are setting. She's asked me whether you'd any hens setting yet, & I tell her I don't think you've thought of so doing yet. Her little ducks are coming on finely now so that she anticipates having fried chickens Whit Sunday. One of her very largest & best hens has recently been stolen from her she thinks, & she's had a great time lamenting her loss.

[. . .] Josephine sent me one of her characteristic letters last week and is well. I expect she'll come walking in here some of these pleasant Saturdays, when if she'd let me know I'd. make arrangements to meet her.

[. . .] I'm glad to hear of the continued blessing of health bestowed upon you all, but poor little Doll I do wish her teeth could hurry & come through so as to cease from troubling her so much. Are those little pimples gone from off her arms & face yet? What ails Leila to make her so cross—a cold or is she still teething?

[. . .] Tell Doll her Auntie says she must stop climbing about so much or She'll get her little head cracked and that will be awful.

I don't know how Miss Porter's[2] going to get along so many of her help leaving her just now. The injured girl's fall must have been a very severe one. Poor girl 'tis too bad. I hope she'll be spared to reach her home. The last papers you sent have rec'd. and read throughout. I shall be very glad of those S.S. papers & when you see the lady thank her kindly for me. So I suppose Mr. Mitchells debt on the ch. is now canceled. Accept my love to yourselves & remember me to the fds. Mr. & Mrs. Thos. desire to be remembered to you all. Yr. absent Daughter.

Royal Oak, July 3, 1869
Mon. 7½ P.M.

My dear Parents,

This P.M. I returned from school with a dull headache, but as it seems to be wearing off I proceed to my very agreeable task of writing to the good "old folks at home."

Just at this time both my brain & hands are full in closing up our affairs & with our contemplated picnic & exhibition I find there is a great deal to do. Not withstanding two of our men were selected to take charge & they having appointed a committee of arrangements to aid them. Yet they're all looking up to me & at last pushed me forward so Sat. night I commenced begging for money to get our confectionery, cream etc. with & today I have $11.40 cash in hand & the eleven dolls. [. . .] is enroute to Balto. tonight for some of our things. Don't you think I've done well? There was Quarterly Meeting here yesterday so I went out A.M. & then again at night. At the close of each service I took aim & fired, scarcely one of my neighborhood people escaped me, & those who've not given money will donate refreshments—pies, chickens, fishes, cake, bread, etc. are promised, and I expect we'll have an abundance. This week I purpose devoting principally to drilling my children. I spent a half day at Easton Sat. Miss Snowden & Miss Ball have charge of th Union S.S. there & today they were to have a picnic and celebration for the Fourth. A speaker from Balto. was to address them. The whites here had an excursion today upon a sail boat. On Thurs. there's to be an excursion from Balto. The S.S. of the Sharp St. Ch. the one we attended Sun A.M. give it. They're coming to St. M. & will partake of refreshments in a grove just below the town. I think of going down to see how they manage their affairs.

My attendance at school was very small all last week but today I've been recruited. Had twenty-five present. Harvesting is all over & now some are preparing for maching out their wheat, an operation I've not yet seen, but hope to ere I leave.

[. . .] I'm sorry too that you did not know about the free entrance into the coliseum, so that you could have a glimpse of the inside. I presume little Doll thought 'twas splendid walking upon the Commons, & I'm glad she could enjoy it. I am truly glad she has the little rocking chair. Now she can take her satisfaction in rocking. But if she's not feeling well I think you'd better write for Bell to bring her home. 'Tis really too bad that she should have those gatherings upon her face. I hope something may be found to relieve her of them entirely.

[. . .] I hope that queer woman will be gone 'ere I come. Whose room does she occupy. Mrs. Saunders is so desirous of white society I don't why she could not have made arrangements to have accommodated her, instead of framing such an excuse and sending her to our house. [. . .]

The cherries, currants, & strawberries have certainly done well this season. I shall be glad to taste a good currant pie when I get home. I guess Nelson was delighted to get them.

I shall not take much more of that sulphur, shall only use the little I have already mixed. There was a good crowd went up to Springf'd. the occasion must have been quite a grand one. I suppose Gertrude & her brother were among the number. I'm glad to hear that Aunt Em is better and hope she'll continue to enjoy good health now. I suppose Sarah is progressing with her music & studies.

How does Jim enjoy the hot weather? I presume he desired you to tell his mistress that he is longing to see her etc. I look at little Doll's picture so much I imagine I can see her just as she is. I think Bell ought to bring her home before she gets sick. Give my love to them all. I hope they're still thriving.

I suspect Josephine has skedaddled again. I was expecting to have her prepare and read a composition at our picnic, but instead she sent a blank book containing some articles of her own production, & requests me to select from it whatever I choose while in the meantime she runs up to Balto, as she says. But she's not cheating me at all wherever she runs too. I imagine she's closed her school, Miss Snowden told me she was to have some kind of an entertainment on last Mon. night.

Miss Smith has closed her sch'l. & is coming up to our picnic on Sat. She gave up having an exhibition. The St. M. teacher is preparing for one, & she was to go to Easton today to attend Miss Snowden's.

Mrs. Thos. had company from Balto. to spend the Sabbath and tonight. He's returned, but him we've sent for our things and will rec. them Friday A.M. We think that girl a curiosity indeed. I would like to see her very much. Mr. & Mrs. Thomas were quite complaining all last week but are better this. I enclose my salary receipt for June & July which squares me up with the Socy. Love to you all & a kind remembrance to the friends. Mr. & Mrs. Thos. join me. Don't fail to send the money I wrote for. Yr. absent daughter.

Rebecca

Afterword

I ARRIVE in Easton, Maryland, at 1:30 a.m. The Greyhound from Baltimore lets me off at a Texaco station and an all-night convenience store. Since I knew that the town's taxis stopped running at five p.m., I had made arrangements in advance to have someone from Scottie's Taxi pick me up. "Call me at home when your bus gets in," said a pleasant voice on the other end of the phone.

At 1:40 Scottie, a handsome, fortyish black man in a shining black Oldsmobile pulls up and takes me to the lovely Tidewater Inn. On the way I explain the reason for my visit. "I am researching an African American woman who founded a school for black children in Royal Oak in the 1860s. Her name was Rebecca Primus, and the school was named for her, the Primus Institute." Scottie has not heard of the school, but does know Royal Oak. "Call when you are ready to go to Royal Oak tomorrow," he says. "I'll take you out there."

I spend the morning in the Talbot County Library. Ms. Scottie Oliver, librarian of the Maryland Room of the library, graciously pulls all the information on the history of schools in Talbot County and on the history of Royal Oak. A friendly older woman who works in the Maryland Room says, "Royal Oak—I live there—there was only one school in Royal Oak. There is nothing else." Then, "I shouldn't say that. There might have been another. If you find out, let me know."

Three hours later, I have found nothing on the Primus Institute or the school for black children in Royal Oak. I check the library's holdings on African American History. David White, a scholar who had done research on Primus's life, had informed me that the library used to have a "Journal on the Proceedings of the Board of School Commissioners" and that this document has information on Primus's school. I do not come across this publication during my trip.

In the Maryland Historical Trust State Historic Site Inventory there are nineteenth-century schoolhouses listed, but none seems to be Rebecca's school. I decide to check out one that was built around the same time. It is located across the road from the Pasadena Inn in Royal Oak.

267

At 12:30 p.m. Scottie and I drive out to Royal Oak. When we get to the Pasadena Inn, I ask the innkeeper, Dell St. Anna, a petite, pleasant woman, if that is the old school for black children. "Yes, I think that's it," she says.

She gives me a key and Scottie and I venture forth. It's a white-washed wood cottage. From the outside you can see that an addition has been built on. There are red shutters. Inside there are three rooms, one of which is a bathroom. This schoolhouse is listed in the inventory of historic sites, but the founder is not named and an exact date of its erection is not given. I say, "Maybe this is it."

I take pictures, walk around the property, and then Scottie and I return to his taxi-van. As we are pulling off he says, "I think you'd probably do better to talk to some of these older black folk down here. I want you to talk to the lady who lives in this house. She's real sharp, she might remember something about the school."

The very elegant, honey-toned Ms. Harriet Romero invites us in and offers lemonade. Her soft gray hair is pulled neatly back and reveals the face of a woman who is still very pretty. She wears a floral-print summer shift and her quick mind and able body belie her years. "I'm not going to admit my age, but I am in my eighties."

Scottie and I sit in the darkened living room. A charcoal toy poodle sniffs my feet.

"No, that wasn't no school for black children. I don't know what that was. The school for black children was up on Hopkins Neck."

"Yes, Rebecca writes some letters from Hopkins Neck, Royal Oak, Talbot County," I interrupt.

"I'm telling you that was the black school. I went there when I was a child. It used to be segregated, you know. My mother went there too. It's just past the old black church."

We talk a little more about her school days, about the years she spent in New York, about her return to Royal Oak to take care of her mother. And then she changes the subject: "Scottie, when are you going to start taking vans up to Atlantic City?" Scottie and I take our cue, thank her, and head toward Hopkins Neck.

Next to the Methodist Church there is a house and then there is what appears to be an overgrown graveyard—though there are some relatively recent headstones. About a third of them have the name Thomas on them. Across the street there is an older black man sitting next to a truck. He works with a radio, one of those popular after transistors but before boom boxes. His skin is a deep, dark brown—no wrinkles. He and Scottie exchange greetings. Scottie asks if he knows anything about an old schoolhouse for black children.

"That's it," he says, pointing to a rectangular structure with shingles of rotting, unpainted brown wood next to the graveyard. It is doorless; the front windows appear to be newer, more modern than those in the back.

I walk in. The floorboards are creaky. There is an old woodstove and a very big old table on three legs. Did Rebecca or some other teacher stand behind this table?

Outside, in back of the school, there is an outhouse and more graves, most unmarked. The ground holds water and I sink in before Scottie pulls me onto a log. "You are not in Philadelphia," he laughs. "Where are your sneakers?"

When Rebecca Primus arrived in Royal Oak she first taught in the church, then, at her insistence, communities in Hartford and Royal Oak raised funds to purchase lumber for a schoolhouse. A Quaker and his Confederate wife sold them the land; black men from the area built the school. Almost four generations of black children attended the school, which remained open until 1929.

I find Rebecca's school, not in the Inventory of Historic Sites or in the silence of the library, but through the insistence of a black entrepreneur and the memory of a gracious lady who offered me a cool drink on a hot July day.

Appendix

Royal Oak, Dec. 17, 1868

Mr. J.F. Morris, Dear Sir,

Yours of the 14th is just rec'd. & I acknowledge the receipt of your check without delay. I think I shall have no difficulty with it. However, in future I think I shall prefer to have my salary paid into my mother's hands per order of Miss W. & I will forward the receipt with my report in advance of the money as I've heretofore done to the Balto. Asson.

It will be more convient as the nearest bank is eight miles from me. From mother I can rec. what I require for present purposes in small amt. I report at the end of every month. This check should be for November instead of Dec.

Yrs. truly,

R. Primus[1]

The following letter, to Rebecca's sister Bell, is important for several reasons. First it is a good comparison with those of Rebecca, in that the writer was also a black teacher stationed in Maryland. Second, the writer mentions Addie in a not-too-favorable light. Is this indignation toward Addie the result of class differences? Third, the letter reveals information about the private life and desire of the writer for certain qualities in a potential mate. But most important, in its description of the trip to Washington the letter portrays the eagerness of black people to exercise their rights, to celebrate their liberation, and to commemorate the passage of the Equal Rights Amendment. It also reveals the hostility toward President Johnson that we have seen in both Rebecca's and Addie's letters.

Hopewell, Md., April 22

My Dear Belle:

I do not usually mean to pay my corrispondent in their own coin, but in your case, I most certainly have done so though it was unintentional. Procrastination is the thief of time, and he has stolen pretty well on mine, too I have been troubled with a toothache and rheumatisim, and even now the simply holding of my pen pains my hand and shoulder incredibly. Yet in spite of this I have not suffered any by loss of flesh but to the contrary I suffer from the increase of it. I weigh 15 lbs more than I when I came here, isn't that outlandish.

I am like yourself extremely sorry that you failed to get those pictures of Leila and yourself but if as you say she come back in the spring why spring is now here and you will still have an opportunity to secure them and to distribute them among your friends on which list I flatter myself I belong.

Your dress is perfectily magnificient and did it not savor so strong of money should myself like to have one like it.

The winter here has been much as you represent it, the most extreme cold vacillating to wrm balmy June like days and deceiving us in the belief that winter was over and gone when only last Monday we woke up to find the ground covered with 2 or 3 inches of snow, and though the people commenced gardening in March, they are not much further on than when they commenced.

Never mind Dear about the geography, I am much obliged to you for your trouble and wish further that you would send em the pattern for a hood of a waterproof and for a gored apron if it is not asking too much.

I am astonished at Addie Brown and do not know what to make of her, she has written me again, but i have not ans' tho she ask me to, and gave me her directions as changed to your street and I suppose to Mrs. Sands.

Gertie Plato writes me of her John's acceptance of your call and that he was to be on the first of April.

I have broken off with Richard. Now I tell you in confidence and <u>don't you tell Becca or any one else,</u> much as I regretted leaving you last fall as I did believe it was my salvation (that is the four weeks spent in his father house) handsome and preposessing as he is in company, he is a <u>perfect devil</u>, (to use a vulgar phrase) at home and then to he has no energy or ambition but is insolent, idle and nerveless, depending almost entirely upon his father, and that for a young man just expecting to get married I think was shameful and he is not by any means rich. You know he would never do for me for my husband must be able to gratify my every wish and never say a cross word in my hearing.

The Prof is splendid to entertain me still he is not what I want I prefer one who has not had the same experience that he has, Dear love, I wonder what he would say did he know what I am writing about him, I have a letter of his now awainting a reply. He was to see me two weeks ago.

As I had no holiday at Christmas I took one the past week and in company with the teacher from Darlington and the one from Havre de Grace and one or two of my Balto friends, went to pay a visit to our nation's capital we shopped in Balto and visited the conference which was sitting at the time and on Monday and Tuesday evenings went to hear Mr. J Meadison Bell the great colored poet, recite his own writings, or readings as he calls them. They were very fine I assure you and I was delighted I wish you could have heard him, perhaps he may visit Hartford as he is travelling through the country. His style is thoroughly dramatic. They are just enacting The Black Crook in Balto. Lucille Western is there.

Tell me please Belle if colored people do not have access to any part of the theatre in Boston, I have had a dispute about it but I forget. I was writing of my Washington trip well we had a delightful time called on Mr. Simpson, he has been very ill with typhoid fever, and is just getting so as to [. . .] a little on the 16th the colored people celebrated the Emancipation of the District. The Lincoln [. . .] were down from Balt and together with their own [. . .] made a fine appearance the procession had all the different trades represented, in it and was headed by a mounted guard of Police followed by a chariot bearing the Goddess of Liberty and her attending maids, inrobed in the flag of our country. The procession was a very long one and had it been a pleasant day would have been very fine, but you can imagine how whitre silk saddle cover and scarfs looked in a drenching rain and with such mud under their feet as no other city but Washington knows.

The whole procession passed the White House and old Johnson stood on the porch with his head uncovered but no one volunteered a simple cheer. I should have told you that the Lincoln Monument was dedicaed on the 16th and that old Johnson went up on the platform and unveiled the statue on the 17th. We visited the house of representatives and the dome of the capitol, took a lungch with Mr. George T. Downing of Newport, attended the impeachement trial heard several reportes and Sec. Wells testify, and "Beast Brother" make a speech, and at seven o'clock took the cars for home, and as we only had the $1.50 per day for board we only regretted we had not longer to stay.

I heard from Becca while in Balto through Miss Booth and Mis Breiggs who were up there but she has been owing me a letter for a long time and I am [. . .] looking for it and daily disappointed. Mis Usher writes me she expects to accompany Becca home for the vacation.

My new school house is progressing finely they promise me I shall go in to it the first of May. but I think not before the middle, haven't you got a donation to give me for it? such will be thankfully received but it is school time and I guess I have wearied you with my nonsense. The kiss you sent me is accepted and I send one in return and believe me as ever your loving friend
Carrie
write soone please Miss Belle Primus

Royal Oak, July 8, 1868

Mrs. H. Primus,

As you have not yet received an expression of thanks from any of the denizens of our little village, I deem it but my duty to express my heartfelt thanks for the action you have taken in prospering the cause of education with us. I refer to your donation of funds for assistance in erecting our model school-house. This benevolent act, my dear madam, is, and will be cherished by the many who are now deriving the benefits of the same.

The lady-like deportment, sterling ability, and real personal worth of your highly esteemed daughter, late in charge of our flourishing school, has been highly commended by all classes, and has been particularly spoken of by our white friends, and she has left us with many deep regrets.

Wishing you much and continued success in your future life, and many years yet to live,

I beg leave to subscribe myself
Your humble sevant,

Charles Thomas.

This letter is from Rebecca's eccentric friend and colleague Josephine Booth.

Oxford Sept. 31, 1866

Kind Friend:

I wish to tell you how I arrived here. After you left it soon begun to rain and after the boat arrived at Easton it poured down in torrents, but I found a covered conveyance to take me to Oxford twelve miles and reached Nathan Mills' house about six o'clock. They were good and attntive on the boat and the driver was very good and polite. Mrs. Mills is a pleasant agreeable person and made me a nice soft bed in a good room. They believe in haveing somthing to eat too. There was a nice blazzing fire which was bery acceptable after the day's journey. I think something can be done here, but Sunday being so stormy there was no service at the Church. Mr. Mills will notify the people and says there are many who will send to this church children to be taught. I thought you would like to have [. . .] how I arrived and where I Stopped.

I have found the people friendly and hospitable so far, and any coming among them with plain manners and a desire to benefit them I think will meet with success.

And above all I shall endeavor to impress upon them their moral and religious obligations. Let us Rebecca who have had the advantages of knowledge and Christian culture lift up the standard of truth and peace. That in the pursuit of wisdom they may not forget nor undervalue that wisdom which comes from above. For I am persuaded that if the people knew where their highest privilege lay, they would rise before the world as light out of darkness. If with our mind and heart they shall serve the Lord, their enemies would be put to flight and condemed. if you should write to Mr. Cook tell him how I arrived and I will also write to him as soon as I shall get located. I thank you for all your kindness to me since I left Hartford and shall remember it in a more substantial manner. My respects to Mr. and Mrs. Thomas although strangers. and hope you are well and enjoying yourself. It was quite rainy and cloudy Saturday and Sunday, still it is cheerful to me.

I think it a good rule not to let outside influences control our feelings, but we can be happy without reference to them. I shall write again soon.

Yours Truly,
Josephine

This is the only letter to Addie that we have. Neither the writer nor the date is noted. It seems to be from her husband, Joseph Tines, as he mentions missing her and the children, which means it must have been written between 1868 and 1870, prior to her death. The towns Howardsville and Silverton are in Colorado. Since this letter was preserved it lends some hope that Rebecca's letters to Addie might also exist.

Dear Addie. How I would like to see you and the children. When I get home again I will stay if I have to stal to get a living. The place where I am is four miles from Howardsville, The mountains are on all sides of me. I do not see the sun untill 9 am and at 3 pm it is behind the range on the West. The mine is 10,000 feet above sea level and the mountains rise 3000 ft above us on all sides. It is the grandest sight I ever saw or dreamed of there its lots of snow on the mountains. But not any at the mine. The weather is beautiful. There has not been a snow since I came here. I got into Silverton Sunday night. Monday I went on the train to Howardsville and from there rode a Bronch [. . .]. If you and the babies was here or near enough I could come home once a week I should think I was the lucky man. The work is all right. The board is fine. But you and the children are so far away. As Burd said there is a hell of a loth of land west of Danbury and some of the finest that ever lay out doors. On my trip out here I passed through York State, Penns, Ill, Neb, New Mexico before I reached Denver. I passed three or four colonys [. . .] dogs. Saw one jack rabbit. I also saw the little owl that lives with them standing on the burrow within 200 miles of Silverton I saw lots of hogs, horses and cattle all fat but what they got on I don't know for the land looks as bare as could be except the sagebrush, wind mills are to be seen everywhere also wells that flow a great many all day.

From Howardsville to our camp I saw lots of mines, the ore is what the call [. . .]. It consist of lead silver copper gold and (bed Brig) (NB they do not find the BB in the mind but on the boarding [. . .]) The gold bug mine Willie Mitchell is going under if they [. . .] raise some more money and a lot of it, that is what those that know say. I will not give the names of any but one is related to [. . .] This company has spend over one million $ and not a cent to show for it as yet but there are lots of mines that are paying big. [. . .] is nothing [letter ends]

Rebecca Primus in Later Life

DAVID O. WHITE

IBELIEVE that one of the joys that can be experienced in performing historical research is to take a little-known but relevant story of the past and make it available for others to read and study. When the American Revolution Bicentennial Commission of Connecticut produced a series of booklets on a variety of topics on the Revolution it was my good fortune in 1973 to be able to write one entitled "Connecticut's Black Soldiers in the American Revolution."

In researching materials for the black soldiers study it was gratifying to be able to locate the names of so many African Americans who had served in the American Revolution. One of the men who intrigued me more than the others was Gad Asher of Guilford, Connecticut. This was mostly because his grandson, Jeremiah Asher, wrote an autobiography in 1850 that included a few details about the elder Asher and his life in Africa, in slavery, in the war, and in freedom.[1]

However, a continued interest in other areas of African American history led me to discover at the same time the Primus papers at the Connecticut Historical Society. A quick reading of some of the letters in this collection made me realize that they provided a greater opportunity than the soldiers had to study the lives of local African Americans in our history. As a result, I put Gad Asher on hold.

There were six members of the Primus family, and the Primus papers consisted of letters written by a son in Boston, a daughter in Maryland, and a family friend living in Hartford. This unique correspondence was a rich source of information about a family's identity and the personalities of its members, but was virtually unknown to the public because few had ever worked with the collection before. I began to search for additional information on the Primus family and looked through a variety of historical sources in and around Hartford. One of these sources was an obituary on Holdridge Primus, father of the family, which indicated he had moved to Hartford from Guilford.[2]

My devotion to the Primus papers had made it impossible for me to find time to work on Gad Asher's background, but now that I had two topics to research in Guilford a trip to the town's archives was in order.[3] I went there with a dual purpose. First, I wanted to find as much information as I could about the ancestors of Holdridge Primus, particularly the names of his parents. Second, I wanted to locate the names of any descendants of Gad Asher in an effort to learn more about his family. To my amazement, what appeared to be two separate quests was actually one. Holdridge Primus turned out to be a grandson of Gad Asher.

Linking Gad Asher and Holdridge Primus was one of a number of interesting and important discoveries connected with my research on the Primus family, and I was certain that if I traveled to Royal Oak, Maryland, where Rebecca wrote nearly all of her letters, I would find more. This seemed particularly promising since her correspondence was more descriptive than that her brother Nelson wrote from Boston, but also because a rural town like Royal Oak would seem less likely to have changed than a city the size of Boston. Once in Royal Oak I learned that the schoolhouse built under Rebecca's direction in the late 1860s was still standing in the 1970s and was being used as a private residence. However, it had continued to be a school for the black population of Royal Oak until 1929, which was sixty years after Rebecca left the area. For most of that time it was operated under the jurisdiction of the state of Maryland and consisted of one room serving primary through the seventh grade.[4] Evelyn Ross and Helen Murray, two lifelong residents of Royal Oak, attended this school when they were children. In fact, Mrs. Ross's father, Joseph Thomas, and her grandfather, Henry Thomas, had been students there as well. Henry was the younger brother of Charles Thomas, and because he was born in 1855 may well have been a student there when Rebecca was its teacher. Although it was later known as the Royal Oak School, the children who attended its classes jokingly told others that they had "graduated from Primus Institute."[5]

When Rebecca left Maryland in 1869 and returned to Hartford she again entered the world of historical obscurity, in the sense that the informative letters that revealed so much about her activities and of those around her no longer needed to be written; therefore, little can be found about her subsequent life. Any correspondence that she did write, which would have likely been mailed to people outside of Hartford, has not survived to anyone's knowledge. Documents in the Primus papers and information from other sources reveal a little about Rebecca

and her family, but not much. Holdridge continued to be employed at
the Seyms grocery store, and his house on Wadsworth Street in Hartford
was valued at five thousand dollars. Hettie was still a dressmaker. Nelson remained in Boston with his young family and would eventually
move to California. There is no indication that the Hartford school
Rebecca conducted before she went to Maryland was continued in the
1870s. The 1870 census simply listed her as "at home." Whether she
held jobs of any kind is not indicated in the Hartford city directories or
census records. Rebecca's interest in her church never faded and she
was the assistant superintendent of its Sunday school in 1871. However, she gave up this position for the next ten years, and this may have
been connected to the appearance in the city of her close friend and former landlord, Charles Thomas of Royal Oak.

In Hartford, Charles Thomas boarded with the Primus family in
1872 and worked first as a janitor and later as a gardener. Sometime
between 1872 and 1874 Thomas and Rebecca were married, and by
1874 they had moved to a house on Wolcott Street, which was not far
from her parents' home on Wadsworth Street. The relocation of Charles
Thomas from Maryland to Hartford and his immediate association with
Rebecca indicates that they had made a greater impression on each
other than her letters reveal. However, it also poses an interesting question, since my research in Maryland never turned up a date of death for
Sarah Thomas, his wife in Royal Oak. On October 12, 1871, Sarah
deeded her portion of their Royal Oak property to her husband, and two
months later he entrusted this property to William Tilgham to pay off
any debts and collect any rents "which the said Charles H. Thomas
could do if personally present." When he sold this property in 1875
Rebecca signed the deed as his wife.[6] When I mentioned this situation
to Evelyn Ross and Helen Murray they informed me that family lore
had always been that Sarah Thomas "died of a broken heart" when her
husband left her for the New England schoolteacher. My personal journey in the study of Rebecca and her values makes me believe that
somewhere in the records of Maryland is a different explanation. I only
wish I had found it.

Like Holdridge Primus, his father-in-law, Charles Thomas became
well known among Hartford's black community. In 1876 he obtained
work in Philadelphia on the grounds of the Centennial Exposition that
celebrated the hundredth anniversary of the signing of the Declaration
of Independence. An August 19, 1876, letter from a relative in

Philadelphia informed Rebecca that her husband "is looking fine now he has got fix up nicely again he says he is doing a good business."[7] On a hunch that Rebecca might have traveled to Philadelphia and visited the Connecticut building on the exposition grounds I examined the register that had been kept there for visitors to that building to sign their names, and found that Rebecca and Mehitable had added their signatures on November 2, 1876.[8] Ten years later Thomas was hired as a doorman by the Connecticut General Assembly at the State Capitol building during the legislative session of 1885–86. Because he was the means through which messages from the governor's office reached the lieutenant governor he was later referred to as "Senator Thomas."[9] Employment as a doorman by the state Senate was probably an honor for anyone at that time, but for an African American it would likely have enhanced Thomas's status in Hartford more than it would have had he been white. A letter written to him in 1887 by an old friend in Royal Oak not only indicates that Thomas had maintained ties to his former world, but the writer also concluded that Thomas had shown courage in moving north to live with strangers and in doing so developed "a reputation that any one of our class should be proud."[10]

Deaths impacted the Primus family beginning in 1884 when Holdridge died of a paralytic stroke. He was buried at a family plot in Zion's Hill Cemetery in Hartford. Hettie inherited the house at 20 Wadsworth Street along with property in Branford that had been given to Holdridge's father by Gad Asher. The wording in the obituary for Holdridge Primus indicates that whoever read it would have been acquainted with his existence. He had worked for Seyms and Company for over forty years, and earned additional money as a waiter at private parties in the city. Apparently, he was so well known among white families that his advice was sought in locating women to be servants in their homes. When Augustus Washington, a Hartford educator and early photographer, moved to Liberia in the 1850s to escape racism in the United States he wrote of the hardships he found in his new country, but that Holdridge Primus would be a success there. With nearly fifty years of service to the Talcott Street Congregational Church—service that began before the popular minister James Pennington arrived—the church passed resolutions on his behalf in losing what was likely one of its major supporters.[11]

The death of Charles Thomas in 1891 had a greater impact on Rebecca. He apparently had been hit on the head by a stone while watching a street fight and subsequently was unable to work regularly, which left him and Rebecca somewhat destitute.[12] With his death she moved in with her mother at 20 Wadsworth Street. In 1899 Hettie Primus died and the Talcott Street Congregational Church held an elaborate service in honor of her more than sixty years of service to the congregation. She was buried next to her husband. The family's homestead on Wadsworth Street was sold and Rebecca, her sister Bell, and Bell's husband, William Edwards, moved to a house on Adelaide Street in the southern part of Hartford.

Not many African American families lived in south Hartford in the early 1900s but there were several individuals still active in the city in the 1970s who remembered Rebecca Primus during this period of her life. From them I was able to obtain a limited amount of material, which was basically recollections about an elderly woman by those who were then in their youth.[13] Rebecca's neighbor on Adelaide Street was Warner Lawson, who had sung with his wife in the Fisk Jubilee Singers, and in the early part of the twentieth century had taught music in Hartford. Their son became a professor of music at Howard University and their daughter became a professor at the University of Hartford. Nearby was the family of Louis Peterson, whose son wrote the 1953 play *Take a Giant Step*.

During her years on Adelaide Street Rebecca Thomas was known as Aunty Thomas, or Aunt Becky. One acquaintance had been told that Rebecca once taught in South Carolina and another was under the impression that she and Charles Thomas had been missionaries in Africa.[14] None of this was true, but it appears that those who did remember her were not aware of her work with the freedmen's schools at the end of the Civil War. Yet in old age she was still an inspiration. She continued to be part of the Talcott Street Church's Sunday school, where her favorite role was that of teacher to a class of young men she referred to as her "boys," but others dubbed "Aunt Becky's boys." It was said of her at that time that she was the "nearest thing to being a saint" that anyone knew. She attended church every Sunday and read the Bible every day. Aware of her interest in the worship service and that she was hard of hearing, the minister gave her typed copies of his sermons.

Warner Lawson was the organist for the Talcott Street Congregation and on many Sundays took Rebecca to church. In return, Rebecca provided baby-sitting services for the Lawsons, and sometimes washed their dishes because she believed that Mrs. Lawson dropped too many of them. She also did light cleaning at Mr. Lawson's downtown studio, but this was more to please her than due to any real need for her services. In addition to being sufficiently hard of hearing that people had to shout, Rebecca had poor eyesight and used a magnifying glass to read. She is remembered as being short, thin, and quite dark in complexion. The only known picture of her is a 1922 photograph of the members of her church standing on the sidewalk of Talcott Street.[15] More than one person interviewed about Rebecca recalled that she was well liked and several used the term "a wonderful person."

One of the interesting sidelights of my conversations with two individuals who remembered Rebecca was their belief that she and Charles Thomas had had a child. While I was unable to find a record of such a birth, one said that she saw a picture in Rebecca's room of a son who had died many years earlier.[16]

Rebecca Primus Thomas died on February 21, 1932, at the age of ninety-five. She had suffered a long illness and spent her last days at Hartford's Municipal Hospital. She was survived by two daughters of Bell and a daughter of her adopted sister, Phrone. Her funeral was held at the Talcott Street Church where she worshiped all her life, taught for many years, and eventually became a deaconess.[17] Rebecca was buried next to her parents, but without a headstone. She was the last of Hartford's Primus family. The collection of family letters and documents she had kept for so many years found its way to the Hobby Shop in Hartford, and in 1934 this collection was acquired by the Connecticut Historical Society.

Bibliography

Asher, Jeremiah. *Incidents in the Life of the Rev. J. Asher Pastor of the Shiloh (Coloured) Baptist Church, Philadelphia, U.S.* London: Charles Gilpin, 1850.

Baecking, Barbara. "Finding Rebecca Primus." *Northeast Magazine,* Feb. 25 (1996): 10–22.

———. "The Primus Papers: An Introduction to Hartford's 19th Century African American Community." Trinity College, Master's thesis, 1995.

Boyd, Melba Joyce. *Discarded Legacy: Politics and Poetics in the Life of Frances E.W. Harper.* Detroit: Wayne State University Press, 1994.

Carby, Hazel. *Reconstructing Womanhood: The Emergence of the Black Woman Novelist.* New York: Oxford University Press, 1987.

Cott, Nancy. "Passionlessness: An Interpretation of Victorian Sexual Ideology." *Signs* 4 (1978): 219–36.

Collins, Patricia Hill. *Black Feminist Thought: Knowledge, Consciousness, and the Politics of Empowerment.* New York: Routledge, 1991.

Curry, Leonard. *The Free Black in Urban America, 1800–1850: The Shadow of the Dream.* Chicago: University of Chicago Press, 1981.

DuBois, W. E. B. *Black Reconstruction in America.* New York: Atheneum, 1969.

Faderman, Lillian. *Surpassing the Love of Men: Romantic Friendship and Love Between Women From the Renaissance to the Present.* New York: William Morrow, 1981.

Fields, Barbara. *Slavery and Freedom on the Middle Ground: Maryland During the Nineteenth Century.* New Haven: Yale University Press, 1985.

Foner, Eric. *A Short History of Reconstruction, 1863–1877.* New York: Harper & Row, 1990.

———. *Reconstruction: America's Unfinished Revolution 1863–1877.* New York: Harper & Row, 1988.

Forten, Charlotte. *The Journal of Charlotte L. Forten.* Edited, with an introduction and notes by Brenda Stevenson. New York: Oxford University Press, 1988.

Foster, Frances Smith. *Written By Herself: Literary Production by African American Women, 1746–1892.* Bloomington: Indiana University Press, 1993.

———, ed. *A Brighter Coming Day: A Frances Ellen Watkins Harper Reader.* New York: The Feminist Press, 1990.

Hansen, Karen. *A Very Social Time: Crafting Community in Antebellum New England.* Berkeley: University of California Press, 1984.

Higginbotham, Evelyn Brooks. *Righteous Discontent: The Women's Movement in the Black Baptist Church 1880–1920.* Cambridge: Harvard University Press, 1993.

———. "Beyond the Sound of Silence: Afro-American Women in History." *Gender and History* 1 (1): 50–67 (1989).

Bibliography

Hine, Darlene Clark. "Rape and the Inner Lives of Black Women in the Middle West: Preliminary Thoughts on the Culture of Dissemblance." *Signs* 14, no. 4 (1989):912–20.

———. "Lifting the Veil of Silence." In *The State of Afro-American History: Past, Present, and Future.* Ed. Darlene Clark Hine. Baton Rouge: Louisiana State University Press, 1986.

Horton, James Oliver and Lois Horton. *Black Bostonians: Family Life and Community Struggle in the Antebellum North.* New York: Holmes and Meier, 1979.

Jacobs, Harriet. *Incidents in the Life of a Slave Girl.* Edited, with an introduction and notes by Jean Fagan Yellin. Cambridge: Harvard University Press, 1987.

Jones, Jacqueline. *Soldiers of Light and Love: Northern Teachers and Georgia Blacks 1865–1873.* Chapel Hill: University of North Carolina Press, 1980.

Litwack, Leon F. *North of Slavery: The Negro in the Free States 1790–1860.* Chicago: University of Chicago Press, 1961.

New York State, Census for 1855. Albany: C. Van Benthuyin, 1857.

Ockenga, Starr. *On Women and Friendship: A Collection of Victorian Keepsakes and Traditions.* New York: Stewart, Tabori and Chang, 1990.

Perkins, Linda M. "The Black Female American Missionary Association Teacher in the South, 1861–1870." In *Black Women in United States History: From Colonial Times Through the Nineteenth Century.* Ed. Darlene Clark Hine. Vol. 3, 1049–1064. Brooklyn: Carlson Publishing Co., 1990.

Peterson, Carla L. *"Doers of the Word": African-American Women Speakers and Writers in the North (1830–1880).* New York: Oxford University Press, 1995.

Piersen, William Dillon. *Black Yankees: The Development of an Afro-American Subculture in 18th Century New England.* Amherst: University of Massachusetts Press, 1988.

Smith-Rosenberg, Carroll. "The Female World of Love and Ritual." *Signs* 1 (1975): 1–29.

Sterling, Dorothy. *The Trouble They Seen: The Story of Reconstruction in the Words of African Americans.* New York: DaCapo Press, 1976.

———, ed. *We Are Your Sisters: Black Women in the Nineteenth Century.* New York: W. W. Norton, 1984.

Tate, Claudia. *Domestic Allegories of Political Desire: The Black Heroine's Text at the Turn of the Century.* New York: Oxford University Press, 1993.

United States Census Office, The Seventh Census of the United States, 1850. Washington, D.C., 1853.

———, The Eighth Census of the United States, 1860 Population. Washington, D.C., 1864.

White, David O. "Addie Brown's Hartford." *Connecticut Historical Society Bulletin.* 41, no. 2 (April 1976): 56–64.

Notes

Introduction: "Beyond the Silence"

1. My title invokes that of Evelyn Brooks Higginbotham's 1989 article "Beyond the Sound of Silence: Afro-American Women in History," *Gender and History* 1, no. 1 (1989): 50–67.

2. Evelyn Brooks Higginbotham, "Beyond the Sound of Silence: Afro-American Women in History." Darlene Clark Hine, "Rape and the Inner Lives of Black Women in the Middle West: Preliminary Thoughts on the Culture of Dissemblance," *Signs* 14, no. 4 (1989): 912–20. Valerie Smith, "Loopholes of Retreat: Architecture and Ideology in Harriet Jacobs' *Incidents in the Life of a Slave Girl*," in *Reading Black, Reading Feminist: A Critical Anthology*, ed. Henry Louis Gates, Jr. (New York: Meridian Books, 1990). Hortense Spillers, "Interstices," in *Pleasure and Danger: Exploring Female Sexuality*, ed. Carole S. Vance (Boston: Routledge, 1984). Claudia Tate, *Domestic Allegories of Political Desire: The Black Heroine's Text at the Turn of the Century* (New York: Oxford University Press, 1993).

3. Scholars such as Darlene Clark Hine and Deborah Gray White have insisted that the documents were available but we might have to search in uncommon places for them. Noting that few black women donated their papers to manuscript repositories, White said this is "in part a manifestation of the black woman's perennial concern with image, a justifiable concern born of centuries of vilification. Black women's reluctance to donate personal papers also stems from the adversarial nature of the relationship that countless black women have had with many public institutions and the resultant suspicion of anyone seeking private information." See Deborah Gray White, "Mining the Forgotten: Manuscript Sources for Black Women's History," *Journal of American History* 74 (June 1987): 237–42.

4. For information on how the letters arrived at the Historical Society, see David O. White's essay in this volume. During the past sixty years, only three scholars have explored the contents of this rich and invaluable archive: David White, former director of the Connecticut Historical Society; Barbara Beeching, former graduate student at Trinity College, Hartford; and Karen Hansen, historical sociologist at Brandeis University.

5. Delmore Schwartz, "In Dreams Begin Responsibilities," in *In Dreams Begin Responsibilities and Other Stories* (New York: New Directions, 1978).

6. Patricia Hill Collins, *Black Feminist Thought: Knowledge, Consciousness, and the Politics of Empowerment* (New York: Routledge, 1991), p. 96.

7. Lillian Faderman, *Surpassing the Love of Men: Romantic Friendship and Love Between Women from the Renaissance to the Present* (New York: William Morrow, 1981).

Carroll Smith-Rosenberg, "The Female World of Love and Ritual," *Signs* 1 (1975): 1–29.

8. Frances Smith Foster, *Written by Herself: Literary Production by African American Women, 1746–1892* (Bloomington: Indiana University Press, 1993). Carla L. Peterson, *"Doers of the Word": African-American Women Speakers and Writers in the North (1830–1888)* (New York: Oxford University Press, 1995).

PART ONE: *The Early Years*

1. Charles Thomas served as doorman of the Connecticut General Assembly at the State Capitol. In this capacity, he held a modicum of status within Hartford's African American community. He was affectionately known as Senator Thomas.

2. The journals of Charlotte Forten Grimké and the letters of Frances Harper were among the only known primary sources relating to the experience of black northern women teachers of the freedmen.

3. Dorothy Sterling, ed., *We Are Your Sisters: Black Women in the Nineteenth Century* (New York: W. W. Norton, 1984).

4. Ibid.

5. Henrietta was born in 1839, Nelson in 1842, and Isabella in 1843.

6. See David O. White's essay in this volume for more information on Gad Asher, Holdridge Primus's grandfather.

7. Information about nineteenth-century black Hartford has been culled from the following sources: Elihu Geer, *Hartford City Directory.* 1860 U.S. Census, Hartford. "The Colored People Who Live in Hartford," *Hartford Courant,* Oct. 24, 1915. David O. White, "Augustus Washington, Black Daguerreotypes of Hartford," *Connecticut Historical Society Bulletin* 39, no. 1 (Jan. 1974): 14–19. David O. White, "Hartford's African Schools," *Connecticut Historical Society Bulletin* 39, no. 1 (April 1974): 47–53. White, "Addie Brown's Hartford," *Connecticut Historical Society Bulletin* 41, no. 2 (April 1976) 56–64. White, "The Fugitive Blacksmith of Hartford: James W. C. Pennington," *Connecticut Historical Society Bulletin* 49, no. 1 (Jan. 1984): 5–29.

8. Addie Brown to Rebecca Primus, Dec. 1861.

9. See Barbara Beeching, "The Primus Papers: An Introduction to Hartford's 19th Century African-American Community," unpublished master's thesis. Trinity College, 1995.

Chapter 2 "If you was a man . . ."

1. I am grateful to Stephanie Shaw for drawing my attention to this connection.

2. Addie Brown to Rebecca Primus, 1859; Addie Brown to Rebecca Primus, Sept. 30, 1867.

3. Date surmised from Rebecca Primus's letter, Dec. 1865 [n.d.]; the year from Addie Brown's letter, June 30, 1865.

4. John Hope Franklin, *From Slavery to Freedom: A History of Negro Americans* (1947; 6th ed., New York: Alfred A. Knopf, 1988).

5. Jacquelyn Grant, *White Women's Christ and Black Women's Jesus: Feminist Christology and Womanist Response* (Atlanta: Scholars Press, 1989).

PART TWO: *The Civil War Years*

1. James Weldon Johnson, *Black Manhattan* (New York: Knopf, 1930), p. 58.

2. Leonard Curry, *The Free Black in Urban America, 1800–1850: The Shadow of the Dream* (Chicago: University of Chicago Press, 1981), pp. 23–24.

3. George Walker, *The Afro-American in New York City, 1827–1860* (New York: Garland, 1993) pp. 12–13.

Chapter 3 "Like meat to a hungre wolfe"

1. For excellent explorations of women at sea as "part of the blue water work force," see the essays in *Iron Men, Wooden Women: Gender and Seafaring in the Atlantic World 1700–1920*, ed. Margaret Creighton and Lisa Norling (Baltimore: Johns Hopkins University Press, 1996). For a history of African American sailors in the eighteenth and nineteenth centuries, see W. Jeffrey Bolster, *Black Jacks: African American Seamen in the Age of Sail* (Cambridge: Harvard University Press, 1997).

2. Addie is referring to Shiloh and St. Phillips, two prominent black churches in nineteenth-century New York.

Chapter 4 "Call you my sister"

1. See Philip B. Kunhardt, Jr., Philip B. Kunhardt III, and Peter W. Kunhardt. *P.T. Barnum: America's Greatest Showman* (New York: Knopf, 1995).

PART THREE: *The Reconstruction Years*

1. According to Barbara Beeching, the average marital age among Hartford's black population in 1860 was 24.6, so Rebecca was older than most of the single men in her community when she left Hartford.

2. The society, founded in 1865 by prominent Hartford whites, sponsored three schools. Its first president was Reverend Calvin Stowe, husband of Harriet Beecher Stowe. It was dissolved in 1869.

3. David O. White, unpublished manuscript.

Chapter 5 "There is great excitement about putting money in the bank"

1. Barbara Fields, *Slavery and Freedom on the Middle Ground: Maryland During the Nineteenth Century* (New Haven: Yale University Press, 1983), p. 11.

2. In this respect my interpretation differs from that of Karen Hansen, who argues that the community knew of the nature of Addie and Rebecca's relationship and supported it, but nonetheless encouraged both women to eventually turn their affection to men.

3. See David O. White, "Addie Brown's Hartford," *Connecticut Historical Society Bulletin,* 41, no. 2 (April 1976), p. 64.

4. This tells us that Rebecca is writing Addie on a weekly basis, as she did her family.

5. See White, "Addie Brown's Hartford," p. 60.

6. When Addie shares gossip with Rebecca, she often attributes it to Madam Rumor.

7. Rebecca's aunts Emily and Bathsheba.

8. Her sister Bell might have taken over Rebecca's school. This is further suggested in later letters.

9. Nelson Primus, Rebecca's brother.

10. Addie will eventually live with and work for a white family, the Crowells.

Chapter 6 "Justice, impartial justice . . ."

1. For a discussion of racial uplift ideology see Kevin Gaines, *Uplifting the Race: Black Leadership, Politics, and Culture in the Twentieth Century* (Chapel Hill: University of North Carolina Press, 1996).

2. Eric Foner, *A Short History of Reconstruction, 1863–1877* (New York: Harper & Row, 1990), p. 110.

3. John W. Alvord, *First Semi-Annual Report on Schools and Finances of Freedmen,* January 1, 1866 (Washington: Government Printing Office, 1868), p. 8.

4. Wormwood is recommended for heartburn as well. John Lust, *The Herb Book* (New York: Bantam, 1974).

5. David O. White writes: "The move to 153 Market Street by Gertrude (Plato) was first noted in the 1866–67 City Directory of Hartford. . . . Letter was probably written in 1866."

6. President Andrew Johnson.

7. Peter Schullin and Donel Soyor, "Fraternal Orders," in *Encyclopedia of African American Culture and History,* ed. Jack Salzman, David Lionel Smith, and Cornel West (New York: Simon & Schuster, 1996).

8. James A. Miller, "Connecticut," in *Encyclopedia of African American Culture and History* (New York: Simon & Schuster, 1996), p. 643.

9. Mr. Tines.

10. New York.

11. Addie is probably referring to the *Weekly Anglo African*, the most influential African American journal of the period. Published by Thomas Hamilton and edited by his brother Robert, the journal published the work of Martin Delaney, Frances Harper, Charles Mercer Langston, and Daniel Payne.

12. The term used for those who supported the Confederacy.

13. Reverend F. Israel, the secretary of the Maryland District of the American Freedman's and Union Commission, was based in Baltimore.

14. Addie is referring to the *Narrative of the Life of Frederick Douglass*, since *The Life and Times of Frederick Douglass* was not published until 1888.

Chapter 7 "I am pleased to hear of the success of those freedmen"

1. Henry Howard Starkweather (1826–76), a Connecticut state legislator elected in 1856, was also a delegate to the National Republican conventions that nominated Lincoln in 1860 and Grant in 1868. Lincoln appointed him postmaster of Norwich in 1861. He served in the Republican Congress from 1867 until his death. It is not clear why Rebecca feels this way about him.

2. See Tera Hunter, *To Joy My Freedom* (Cambridge: Harvard University Press, 1997).

3. Friendship albums were books exchanged among friends in the nineteenth century.

4. Eliza eludes the slave catchers when she crosses the frozen Ohio River.

5. Emily was a young housekeeper who lived with and worked for the Thomases.

6. Carroll Smith-Rosenberg, *Disorderly Conduct* (New York: Knopf, 1985), p. 59.

7. See pages 192–93.

8. Rebecca never tells who sends her roses.

9. Richard Lane, the postmaster at Royal Oak.

10. It is most likely that these were political meetings. In December 1866, the Republicans began pushing through the Fourteenth Amendment. There were three Reconstruction Amendments: the thirteenth freed slaves, the fourteenth made African Americans citizens, and the fifteenth gave them the right to vote.

11. Reverend N. J. Burton served as one of the directors of the Hartford Freedmen's Aid Society in 1867.

Chapter 8 "We must have a school house"

1. Eric Foner, *Reconstruction: America's Unfinished Revolution, 1863–1877* (New York: Harper & Row, 1988), p. 282.

2. Barbara Fields, *Slavery and Freedom on the Middle Ground: Maryland During the Nineteenth Century* (New Haven: Yale University Press, 1985), p. 144.

3. Actuary of the Baltimore Association for the Moral and Educational Improvement of the Colored People.

4. Rebecca's cousin, daughter of Aunt Bashy.

5. Children born with a caul were thought to be gifted with second sight, prophesy, and psychic powers.

6. Hartford-based author and poet Lydia H. Sigourney, secretary of the Hartford Female African Society. The society was made up of white women who supported the American Colonization Society. Sigourney is perhaps best known for her books *Letters to Young Ladies* and the autobiographical *Letters of Life*, published in 1866, one year after her death. It is not clear which of her many books Primus refers to here.

7. A prominent Hartford property owner who collected funds for Rebecca's school.

8. Name originally given to northern Democrats who opposed Lincoln.

9. Lydia Maria Child, abolitionist, author, and editor.

10. Harryette Mullen, *Muse and Drudge* (Philadelphia: Singing Horse Press, 1995).

11. Use of the term *image weavers* is inspired by a collective of Philadelphia-based black women filmmakers called Image Weavers.

12. See Richard Fuke, "Hugh Lennox Bond and Radical Republican Ideology," *The Journal of Southern History*, vol. XLV, no. 4 (November 1979).

13. One of the young women boarding with the Primuses. Rebecca is comparing her to Emily, the young woman who lived with the Thomases, but left when she became pregnant without being married and asked to return when the baby died.

14. Former president of the Confederacy; spent two years in federal prison following the defeat.

15. See Frederick Douglass's *Narrative* of 1845.

16. Mr. Tines.

17. For more information see also Michael Fitzgerald, *The Union League Movement in the Deep South* (Baton Rouge: Louisiana State University Press, 1989).

18. Mr. Seyms was Holdridge Primus's employer.

Chapter 9 "The people are quite cheered up & hopeful once more."

1. Addie might be referring to the practice of conjuring.

2. Thomas Saunders was the son of William Saunders, a free black tailor from Hartford who was Connecticut's first agent for William Lloyd Garrison's *Liberator*. Thomas and his brother Prince were also tailors. (See Barbara Beeching, "The Primus Papers: An Introduction to Hartford's 19th Century African American Community," unpublished master's thesis, Trinity College, 1995.)

Chapter 10 "And all nature is coming forth and clothing herself in beauty and fragrance."

1. Primus's diaries are not in the collection at the Connecticut Historical Society. Given her penchant for writing it is not at all surprising that she kept a journal, and hopefully the diaries, too, are awaiting discovery.

2. Rebecca is referring to the founder and director of Miss Porter's School in Farmington, Connecticut, where Addie Brown and Rebecca's aunt Emily and her husband were employed.

Appendix

1. Hartford Freedmen's Aid Society Collection at the Connecticut Historical Society.

Rebecca Primus in Later Life

1. Jeremiah Asher, *Incidents in the Life of the Rev. J. Asher, Pastor of the Shiloh (Coloured) Baptist Church, Philadelphia, U.S.* (London: Charles Gilpin, 1850). This book was reprinted in 1971 by Books for Libraries Press, Freeport, New York. See pp. 15–20.

2. The obituary of Holdridge Primus is in Obituary Scrapbook, vol. 3, p. 53, Connecticut Historical Society, Hartford.

3. Among the records consulted on Gad Asher and the Primus name were the Guilford Probate Records, vol. 25, 1834–37, pp. 307, 319, 415–16, 434, and 444, and North Branford Deeds, vol. 1, pp. 103, 170, 239, and 240. Thomas Fitch's book *Guilford Private Records, 1784–1815,* at the Connecticut State Library, helped to connect Gad Asher to the Primus family. See pp. 1 and 34.

4. Information on the school Rebecca Primus established at Royal Oak and maintained after her departure can be found in the *Journal of Proceedings of the Board of School Commissioners* at the Talbot County Free Library, Easton, Maryland.

5. Interviews were held with Mrs. Evelyn Thomas Ross (born 1914) and Mrs. Helen Murray (born 1904) on October 15, 1973, at their home in Royal Oak.

6. Talbot County Deeds, County Court House, Easton, Maryland, Folios 75, #304 and #305.

7. Emma to Cousin Rebecca, August 19, 1876, Primus Papers, Connecticut Historical Society.

8. The ledger kept at the Connecticut building in 1876 is owned by the Connecticut Historical Society, but the names of the visitors to the building are printed in *Souvenir of the Centennial Exhibition, or Connecticut's Representation at Philadelphia, 1876* (1877). Rebecca and her mother are listed on pages 251 and 253.

9. Annual Legislative Statistics of State Officers, Connecticut, January Session, 1884, by Palmer Bill, vol. IV, no. 5 (1884), p. 3, and Charles Thomas Obituary.

10. Horace Turner to Charles Thomas, April 18, 1887, Primus Papers, Connecticut Historical Society.

11. "A Letter from Liberia" in *Hartford Daily Courant,* September 27, 1858, Obituary Scrapbook, vol. 3, p. 53, at Connecticut Historical Society.

12. Charles Thomas obituary.

13. Interviewed about Rebecca Primus Thomas in 1973 were Mrs. Elizabeth Andrews of Boston, Mr. and Mrs. George W. Evans, Jr., of Bloomfield, and, in

Hartford, Mrs. C. G. Mitchell, Mrs. Louis Peterson, Mrs. Rocelyn Putnam, and Mr. Louis H. Taylor.

14. Mrs. Mitchell mentioned South Carolina and Mrs. Peterson noted Africa.

15. Louis Taylor was suffering from a mild stroke when I met with him and he was unable to recall much about Rebecca. His cousin, Miss Arnita Taylor, was present and indicated that Mr. Taylor had a 1922 picture of the church members that included Rebecca. Mr. Taylor donated this picture to the Prudence Crandall Museum, which was being organized by the Connecticut Historical Commission.

16. Mrs. Mitchell and Mrs. Putnam.

17. Rebecca Thomas obituary in the *Hartford Courant,* February 22 and 24, 1932.

Index

Page numbers in *italics* refer to illustrations.

Index

A NOTE ON THE TYPE

THE EDITOR'S text was set in Bodoni, a typeface named after
Giambattista Bodoni (1740–1813), the celebrated printer and type
designer of Parma. The Bodoni types of today were designed not
as faithful reproductions of any one of the Bodoni fonts but
rather as a composite, modern version of the Bodoni manner.
Bodoni's innovations in type style included a greater degree of
contrast in the thick and thin elements of the letters and a sharper
and more angular finish of details.

The letters were set in a type called Baskerville. The face itself
is a facsimile reproduction of types cast from the molds made for
John Baskerville (1706–1775) from his designs. Baskerville's original face was one of the forerunners of the type style known to
printers as "modern face"—a "modern" of the period A.D. 1800.

Composed by North Market Street Graphics,
Lancaster, Pennsylvania
Printed and bound by Quebecor Printing,
Fairfield, Pennsylvania
Designed by Virginia Tan